MAMBU

KENELM BURRIDGE

MAMBU

A MELANESIAN MILLENNIUM

PRINCETON UNIVERSITY PRESS
PRINCETON, NEW JERSEY

Published by Princeton University Press,
41 William Street, Princeton, New Jersey 08540
In the United Kingdom by Princeton University Press,
Chichester, West Sussex
Copyright © 1960 by Kenelm Burridge;
copyright © renewed 1988
Preface to the Mythos edition is copyright © 1995 by
Princeton University Press

This book was originally published in 1960
by Methuen & Co., London,
and is reprinted now, with a new preface,
by arrangement with the author

Library of Congress Cataloging-in-Publication Data

Burridge, Kenelm.
    Mambu : a Melanesian millennium /
Kenelm Burridge.
        p.   cm. — (Mythos)
    Originally published: London : Methuen, 1960.
    With new preface.
    Includes bibliographical references and index.
    ISBN 0-691-04388-4 — ISBN 0-691-00166-9 (pbk.)
    1. Cargo cults—Papua New Guinea.
    2. Acculturation—Papua New Guinea.
    I. Title. II. Series: Mythos (Princeton, N.J.)
GN671.N5   1995
299′.92--dc20   94-42499

Princeton University Press books are printed on
acid-free paper and meet the guidelines for permanence
and durability of the Committee on Production
Guidelines for Book Longevity of the Council on
Library Resources

First Princeton Paperback printing, for the
Mythos series, 1995

Printed in the United States of America

1   3   5   7   9   10   8   6   4   2

To my Father's Memory

Acknowledgements

The field research on which this book is based was carried out as a Scholar of The Australian National University under the supervision of the late Professor S. F. Nadel. For permission to use materials which have already been published I have to thank the Editors of *Oceania, Man, South Pacific, The Southwestern Journal of Anthropology, American Anthropologist,* and *Annali Lateranensi.* I thank Dr R. G. Lienhardt for his constant encouragement, Dr Rodney Needham for reading the first draft, Mrs C. R. Barber for help with German texts, Drs F. G. Bailey and D. F. Pocock for suggestions and comments, Mr J. Jardine for many pungent criticisms, Madame Berthe Oudinot for many kindnesses whilst writing under rather difficult circumstances in Baghdad, my son for his forbearances and Mr A. Ewing and Father Cornelius Van Baar for their generous hospitality and company.

My friends in Tangu and in other parts of New Guinea—villagers, labourers, missionaries, planters, traders, and administrative officers—were always kind, patient, helpful, and understanding. I should like them to know that I value their friendship, and that though in writing about anyone some measure of criticism is implicit, I have written this book mainly for them in the hope that they will find the notion of the myth-dream helpful and useful in their work.

Contents

Illustrations

PLATES

MAPS AND DIAGRAMS

Author's Note

Vernacular words and Pidgin English words are italicized. It will be obvious which words are Pidgin and which vernacular. Because there is no generally accepted way of spelling Pidgin words, and because Pidgin plurals are inelegant in an English text I have anglicized certain spellings and given them English plurals.

Preface to the 1995 Edition

The phone call from Princeton came as a surprise: "May we have your permission to consider *Mambu* for our mythology reprint series?" First published by Methuen in 1960, republished as a Harper Torchbook in 1970, here it is again, neither edited nor rewritten, a response to varieties of demand.

A lot of water has flowed under the bridge since those days in the fifties when cargo cults, often described as bizarre or weird, attracted the keen interest of missionaries and administrators as well as laypersons and anthropologists. The idiom —ecstatic or, sometimes, more sober magico-religious activities directed toward obtaining cargo, manufactured goods— seemed to fascinate Euro-American materialist society, which had perhaps forgotten not only much of its own history and origins but also that if you really want to win a lottery against long odds you had better pray or find a potent magic. And although over the last forty years or so the sharper edges of interest have been blunted by hundreds of accounts, cargo cults are still being written about (see, for example, Barr and Trompf 1983) under a variety of other names. No longer regarded simply as rather odd events, an administrative rather than a sociological problem, cargo activities and their analysis came to be seen as challenges to social theory.

In those days, however, despite the work of Haddon (1917), considered passé as an anthropologist, Fülöp-Muller (1935), not recognized as a professional, and Knox (1950), as a cleric almost a missionary (sociocultural anthropologists have long been familiar with their own changing parochial political correctness; for an amusing satire see Lawrence 1967), most analyses, hung up on the meanings of "cult" and "movement," shunning history as unscientific, and belying the generally social tenor of their description of events and activities, tended to be cast in naive psychological or functional terms. The implications of aberration requiring therapy (usually education) and a return to an appropriate subservience to a given socioadministrative order were clear.

In 1957 Peter Worsley went to the literature and to history and, going behind the idiom of cargo, revealed the activities as based in real social, political, and religious discontents and aspirations. In the same year, an irony often missed, Norman Cohn published a more general work on millenarian movements that seated them in a psychological trauma: paranoia. And even though analyses based in psychologies of various kinds, as in Wallace (1956), continue usefully to appear today, a much larger number of essays and major works (e.g., Fuchs 1965, Guiart 1962, Lanternari 1960, 1965, Lawrence 1964, Schwartz 1962, Steinbauer 1971, 1979, Wilson 1973, 1975; see La Barre 1971 and Barr 1983 for extensive bibliographies) have chosen to go to the socioreligious and political contexts within whose terms the instructions of the "prophet" or leader (sometimes different persons) directing or organizing the activities seem to gather meaning and relevance.

What's in a name? Through the years, attempting to find a more inclusive term but rejecting *millenarian* and *messianic* as too loaded, cargo activities have been subsumed under a variety of terms. And these, going to interpretive framework and apparent main emphases, are certainly not mutually exclusive. Thus there are *accommodative, acculturative, adaptive,* and *adjustive* that, also used in their noun forms, assume one culture attempting to harmonize its ways with another more powerful and intrusive one; *crisis* and *disaster* assume a prior natural or culturally traumatic event; *nativistic, militant,* and *denunciatory* indicate forceful renewals of traditional ways in response to foreign rule. *Dynamic* or *dynamistic, vitalization* and *revitalization* evoke self-motivated cultural renewals in the face of what is seen as moral decay; and *Holy Spirit, charismatic, prophet,* and *salvation* emphasize Christian missionary influences; *cult, movement,* and *activity,* though formally indicating ranges of inclusiveness, tend to break down and become interchangeable in the face of what actually happens.

So many names. The reader may choose. I think *millenarian* smells sweetest because the activities envisage or imply a new belief system combined with a new social order, showing cargo activities as comparable with, say, medieval millenarisms or eighteenth- and nineteenth-century enthusiasms as well as many other reform and socioreligious renewal movements around the world on the one hand, and events such as those at Waco or Jonestown on the other. Whatever the name, however, cargo activities remain the expression in a particular cultural idiom within a historical bracket of what seems to be a universal human proclivity. The accidents and processes of history, particularly Christian influences, surely have played their significant parts, but if there is any other basic condition required to bring that proclivity to action I would today place less emphasis on the *presence* of features of history and the social ambience and pay more attention to *absences* or gaps in the social structure, particularly the absence of agreed loci of trusted and relevant authority (Burridge 1993). We need constant reassurance regarding the truth of things, and for most of us external structures have to provide it.

WORKS MENTIONED

Barr, John. 1983. A Survey of Ecstatic Phenomena and 'Holy Spirit Movements' in Melanesia. *Oceania* 54: 109–32.

Barr, John, and Garry Trompf. 1983. Independent Churches and Recent Ecstatic Phenomena in Melanesia: A Survey of Materials. *Oceania* 54: 51–72.

Burridge, Kenelm. 1993. Melanesian Cargo Cults in *Contemporary Pacific Societies*. Englewood Cliffs, New Jersey: Prentice Hall, 275–88.

Cohn, Norman. 1957. *The Pursuit of the Millennium*. London: Secker & Warburg.

Fuchs, Stephen. 1965. *Rebellious Prophets: A Study of Messianic Movements*. New York: Asia Publishing House.

Fülöp-Muller, Rene. 1935. *Leaders, Dreamers and Rebels*. London: Harrap.

Guiart, Jean. 1962. *Les Religions l'Oceanie*. Paris: Presses Universitaires de France.

Haddon, A. C., and E.W.P. Chinnery. 1917. Five New Religious Cults in British New Guinea. *The Hibbert Journal* 15: 448–53.

Knox, R. A. 1950. *Enthusiasm.* Oxford: Clarendon Press.

La Barre, Weston. 1971. Materials for a History of Studies of Crisis Cults: A Bibliographic Essay. *Current Anthropology* 12: 3–44.

Lanternari, V. 1965 [1960]. *The Religions of the Oppressed.* New York: Mentor.

Lawrence, Peter. 1964. *Road Belong Cargo.* London: Manchester University Press.

———. 1967. *Don Juan in Melanesia.* Brisbane: University of Queensland Press.

Schwartz, T. 1962. The Paliau Movement in the Admiralty Islands 1946–1954. *Anthropological Papers of the American Museum of Natural History,* vol. 49, part 2.

Steinbauer, Friedrich. 1979. *Melanesian Cargo Cults.* Trans. Max Urohlwill. London: George Prior Publishers.

Wallace, Anthony F. C. 1956. Revitalization Movements. *American Anthropologist* 58: 264–81.

Wilson, Bryan. 1973. *Magic and the Millennium.* New York: Harper and Row.

———. 1975. *The Noble Savages.* Berkeley and Los Angeles: University of California Press.

Worsley, Peter. 1957 [1968]. *The Trumpet Shall Sound.* London: MacGibbon & Kee.

Preface

Mambu is the name of a native of New Guinea, a Kanaka who in the late 'thirties of this century led what has come to be known as a 'Cargo' movement. Most of his activities took place in the Bogia region of the Madang District in the Australian Trust Territory of New Guinea. Mambu was a rebel, a radical, a man sufficiently able to free himself from the circumstances of his time to grasp what he thought to be valuable in tradition and weld it to his perception of what he would have liked the future to be. Because he could, in a sense, transcend himself and become the new man he saw as well as persuade others of the truth of his vision, he symbolizes the main theme of this book.

Cargo movements, often described as millenarian, messianic, or nativistic movements, and also called Cargo cults, are serious enterprises of the *genre* of popular revolutionary activities. Mystical, combining politico-economic problems with expressions of racial tension, Cargo cults compare most directly with the Ghost-dance cults of North America,[1] and the 'prophetist' movements among African peoples.[2] Typically, participants in a Cargo cult engage in a number of strange and exotic rites and ceremonies the purpose of which is, apparently, to gain possession of European manufactured goods such as axes, knives, aspirins, china plate, razor blades, coloured beads, guns, bolts of cloth, hydrogen peroxide, rice, tinned foods, and other goods to be found in a general department store. These goods are known as 'cargo', or, in the Pidgin

[1] See for example: James Mooney, The Ghost-Dance Religion and the Sioux outbreak of 1890, 14th Report, *Bureau of American Ethnology*, pp. 653–947; Leslie Spier, *The Prophet Dance of the Northwest and its Derivatives: the source of the Ghost Dance*, General Series in Anthropology, No. 1, Menasha, Wisconsin, 1935.

[2] See for example: Bengt G. M. Sundkler, *Bantu Prophets in South Africa*, Missionary Research Series, No. 14, Lutterworth Press, London, 1948.

English rendering, *kago*. Large decorated houses, or 'aero-
planes' or 'ships' made of wood, bark, and palm thatch bound
together with vines, may be built to receive the goods, and
participants may whirl, shake, chant, dance, foam at the
mouth, or couple promiscuously in agitated attempts to
obtain the cargo they want, not from a shop or trade store,
but directly from the mystical source supposedly responsible
for manufacture and distribution. Men of European descent
have been threatened and even attacked because, though it is
obvious that they know how to gain possession of the articles
in question, how to tap the source, it would seem to many
participants that they have not cared to reveal their 'secret'
to their less fortunate black-skinned brothers. As a corollary,
too, participants often assert that all manufactured goods
were originally meant to be distributed to everyone, but that
white men, being greedy, have in various ways intercepted the
cargo *en route*, holding it for their own use.

Though comparatively tiny in scale—which, however, makes
them more easily appreciated as a total phenomenon—Cargo
cults are movements of positive protest and dynamic aspiration whose study can provide insights of value into such
convulsions as the French and Russian revolutions, and the
more gradually emergent African and Asian nationalisms.
The questions they ask are to be encountered in studies of
millenarian, revivalist, and enthusiastic movements everywhere, whether they have occurred within the Christian tradition or outside it. And the villager or peasant, robust and
secure in his tradition, self-reliant wherever he may be living,
has much the same problems as the Melanesian when the
panoply of the modern industrialized State, with its officials,
services, laws, clichés, slogans, and immense material wealth,
begins to intrude upon the simple dignities of his native
country fastness. Not merely concerned with adjusting to new
and unfamiliar circumstances, Cargo cults pose the problem of
the individual in relation to society at large. They ask,
bluntly, whether a man is a vote, a unit of labour, or endowed
with a divine spark—worthy of playing an honourable part in
association with other unique individuals. By attempting a

passage through an adjustment[1] to existing circumstances to a state of society which may be utopian—but which is, nevertheless, a creation in its own right—they show how new men may be made. Participants in a Cargo cult want to create for themselves a new way of life,[2] a new order of living. And momentarily, in the action of a cult, they do so. For minutes, days, or weeks they shape a new way of life for themselves, creating new customs, new ways of behaving towards one another.

This almost numinous translation from one order of being into another lies at the core of all Cargo cults. Sporadic, usually of short duration and involving relatively small numbers of men and women, they are known to have been taking place in the Melanesian archipelago from New Guinea eastwards to the New Hebrides and Fiji and in other islands of the south seas since the late nineteenth century. Gradually increasing in numbers and effect through the earlier decades of this century, since the second World War they have been recorded more and more frequently—though it may be that similar kinds of movements had been taking place regularly before Europeans first took cognizance of them and committed their thoughts and observations to writing. The hallmarks of a millenarian movement are there. Those who take part in the cults look forward to the future, envisaging days of bliss and plenty when no one will want for anything. There are prophecies, revelatory messages, psycho-physiological states such as hysteria, trances, paroxisms, and rites and ceremonies that, to a European, often seem extremely bizarre. Since the participants possess no recorded history, nor a testament of truth, they cannot easily cast back into the past to the ancient, regarded as purer, more primitive forms from which to take inspiration: instead, they have to look into themselves as they are, and into the past as they think it might or ought to have been. Many Cargo cults have

[1] Piddington calls them 'adjustment cults': *vide*: Ralph Piddington, *An Introduction to Social Anthropology*, Oliver and Boyd, London, 1957, Vol. II, pp. 735–44.

[2] cf. Anthony F. C. Wallace, who calls them revitalization movements in Revitalization Movements, *American Anthropologist*, Vol. 58, No. 2, pp. 264–79.

approaches uniquely their own, and a survey of all the recorded instances would show a wide variety of ceremonial and ritual. But there are also general similarities of context. Such factors as a restless discontent with things as they are, being under-privileged politically, poverty in European terms, and conse-quently a very restricted access to manufactured goods, play a large part in the genesis of any Cargo cult. On the other hand, equally if not more important is the positive moral content: the spark in the tinder which generates the flame. Almost always, in the van of a Cargo movement, urging the participants on, there is an individual who assumes the role of a leader, deliverer, or hero; who, as might a messiah, parenetically tells of the wonderful days to come. Mambu was just such a man, a charismatic figure.

So far as an outsider is competent to judge, those involved in a Cargo cult are acting in accordance with the dictates of their emotions rather than their intellects, from what they feel rather than from what they have thought out. It is true that, *post hoc*, participants may express themselves as being dis-contented with things as they are—but the gusto with which they live out their day-to-day lives hardly bears out the oral expression. Rationalization afterwards there may be, but there seems to be little or no prior intellectualization of what are, basically, intuitive perceptions. Of course they would like more money—who would not? Of course they would like the means to have freer access to the goods of this world, and of course, too, they want to have an authoritative voice in the administration of their own affairs. What makes the difference between an all too familiar political unrest combined with the economic disabilities of a multi-racial society, and the occur-rence of a Cargo cult, is a sudden onset of moral and emotional passion concentrated to the point of action by and in the sort of man Mambu was. And the kinds of things a charismatic leader says, does, and encourages others to do, clearly reveal that the participants in a cult are striving after moral renova-tion. They want to put on the new man. Out of the crucible of moral regeneration they want to mould and shape for them-selves and their children a new, more satisfying world. Not so much tired of the conditions in which they live they are, rather, both weary of being what they think themselves to be, and eager to grasp the opportunity to become what they think they might be. They tend to evoke the supposed glories of the days before the European came to Melanesia, the days when men were men and each man knew precisely what to do to gain the approbation and respect of his fellows. And since Kanakas, natives of New Guinea, generally see their downfall from this state as a direct result of European penetration, in all Cargo cults there are elements of anti-Europeanism. In itself the latter combination had led to Cargo cults being described as nativistic.

Very much the same conditions obtain throughout Melanesia where the European has penetrated. But Cargo cults have not occurred everywhere. That is, there is not a simple relation between conditions obtaining and the occurrence of a cult. We can only say that under certain conditions a Cargo cult might occur. The catalytic spark which explodes into a cult cannot be pinned to a where or a when. Nevertheless, the general conditions, the moral problems to which a Cargo cult could be seen as a response, have grown out of a series of events and circumstances which may be reasonably well defined. Many of the old customs, institutions, and modes of behaviour which together constituted viable frameworks of traditional and trusted ways of life are either fast disappearing or have already died out. Those that remain seem not to be adequate to the environment in which the people concerned now find themselves, and fresh institutions must take the places of those that have gone. To an individual trapped in his own narrow scale of time the process is neither swift nor definite. The elders who once controlled the destinies of their peoples are impotent in the face of the new found wealth of their sons who work on European owned plantations. New fashions, new habits of thought learned from other native peoples as well as from white men have wrecked the old certainties. At any chosen moment some institutions may be obsolescent, others in genesis. And since institutions contain and express series of moral notions there can be little certainty that *this* institution expressing *these* sentiments will not soon be replaced by *that* institution expressing other ideas. The result is a general perplexity as to which doctrines should guide in particular circumstances, a many cornered fight between a variety of conservatisms on the one hand, and different kinds and orders of radicalism on the other.

To those who participate in a Cargo cult the current situation appears wholly confused—altogether too much to comprehend in a sweep of imaginative thought. By concentrating on the necessity for gaining a living from the soil, from the sea, from the jungle, or from work as a domestic or as a labourer in a plantation, Kanakas succeed for a while in pushing the number and variety of moral choices into the background. Nevertheless, there comes a time when these choices insist on being confronted and resolved, when a man— together with other men—must decide in more or less permanent terms what is to be good and what is to be bad. Then an attempt must be made to make the new man. Many would prefer to evade such a 'moment of truth'. Others, more courageous or more rash, turn their faces to the dilemma and attempt to persuade their fellows to do the same. Slowly, the bulk of the population in Melanesia is beginning to grasp something of the general nature of the problem. The imposed peace of the white man facilitates travel and communication. News and gossip about other peoples' activities fall on many ears, exciting enthusiasm, criticism, and wonder. For the most part discontent, anxiety, desire, and the agonies of choice are buried in feelings, in the stomach, searching for a fit and proper articulation from the intellect. They express themselves in turbulent, locally co-ordinated activities of very small scale. And as the problems and associated feelings become more and more generalized so are they narrowed, more accurately defined, and partially articulated by men such as Mambu.

Those who take part in Cargo movements feel their problems rather than know them, and they feel rather than know that these problems have to be faced and resolved by themselves if they are to command self-respect and a future for themselves. A relatively new European world is swallowing them up. But it can be pressed into distinctive Melanesian patterns. In general, the evidence reveals that Kanakas do not want these new patterns devised for them by others. And since it is impracticable at the present time for Kanakas to make their future entirely by themselves, a crucial problem is what kind of help, whether material or in the shape of ideas, may be accepted in what circumstances. For of this we may be sure. Kanakas want to so fashion their future that it accords with their own conception of it. To think of themselves as simply the charges of white men, going in the way the white man has mapped out for them, is not to be suffered. They want to be men in much the same way as white men seem to them to be men: competent, independent individuals capable, through conflicts of choice, of ordering their own lives in their own way within a framework of accepted institutions and conventions. Presently, however, their circumstances are in flux. The atmosphere spawns—almost demands—demagogues: cheats and other riff-raff are provided with their opportunities in a world made temporarily disnomic. Nevertheless, for all the hubris evident in Cargo cults there is an underlying dignity, a bedrock of honest endeavour revealing the moral in man.

It is one thing to say that a study of Cargo cults provides insights into movements that have occurred within our own cultural and historical tradition, quite another to go beyond and assert that they are sociologically comparable. But if there are obvious, surface differences the range of similarity in principle is seductive. Again and again, quarrying into the huge *corpus* of writing on revolutionary, millenarian, enthusiastic, nativistic, and messianic movements which have taken place in many parts of the world at different times in man's recorded history, the same features come to light and recur. So, too, with the considerable literature on Cargo cults. Long ago Haddon pointed out that, 'An awakening of religious activity is a frequent characteristic of periods of social unrest. The weakening or disruption of the old social order may stimulate new and often bizarre ideals, and these may give rise to religious movements that strive to sanction social or political aspirations. Communities that feel themselves oppressed anticipate the emergence of a hero who will restore their prosperity and prestige. And when the people are imbued with religious fervour the expected hero will be regarded as a Messiah.'[1] And since Haddon wrote, numerous anthropologists, administrative officers, and missionaries have made their valuable contributions to the subject. New facts have been brought to light, old facts have had their more shaded facets burnished, and Haddon's acute if relatively simply phrased observations have been adumbrated, developed, and pushed closer to the growing mass of emerging detail. All students of the subject, not least the present writer, stand in their debt: the names of Allan, Belshaw, Berndt, de Bruijn, Elkin, Firth, Guiart, Hogbin, Hölkter, Inselmann, Keesing, Lawrence, Mair, Mead, Piddington, Stanner, and Williams come to mind at once.[2] In particular, Belshaw, Hogbin, Keesing, Mair, and Stanner have provided us with standard works on the Melanesian scene. Most notably and recently Peter Worsley, with his *The Trumpet shall Sound*[3] has not only given us a comprehensive and comparative review of the material available and the problems involved in Cargo movements: he has made excellent sense of it, forcibly demonstrating historical and evolutionary links within terms of a coherent and intelligible schema.

There is no need, I think, to go over the same ground and repeat what Worsley, Hogbin, Mair, and Stanner and others have said so well. Nor is there much to be gained by continually referring the reader to comparative material. All of us who have worked on the same problems in the same field have had very similar experiences though the interpretative models may differ. This book is intended to be in the nature of a

[1] E. W. P. Chinnery and A. C. Haddon, 'Five New Religious Cults in British New Guinea', *The Hibbert Journal*, Vol. XV, No. 3, 1916, p. 455.

[2] For the works of these authors the reader is asked to refer to Appendix A which contains a select bibliography.

[3] Peter Worsley, *The Trumpet shall Sound*, MacGibbon and Kee, London, 1957.

modified field monograph: comparison is implicit, not explicit. Though it is presented as a supplement to the more general and comprehensive standard works on the area and its problems it is addressed not so much to my colleagues as to those whose work takes them to faraway places, and whose knowledge of Social Anthropology and what anthropologists do and experience may be limited. My concern is with certain people only, with men and women who were known to me at first hand and who happen to have been involved in a Cargo situation. Although an interpretative model must emerge, far from presuming to account for Cargo cults in general the matter presented attempts, rather, to penetrate an atmosphere created by both white men and black, charged with emotions and fluid ideas, yet existing side by side with, and at the same time as, the humdrum tasks of a workaday world. Interest is centred on the activities, thoughts, and feelings of Tangu, a people living in a knot of hills about fifteen miles inland from Bogia Bay in the Madang District in northern New Guinea, and on the people of Manam island, an impressive volcano lying a dozen miles to the north and seaward of Bogia. In drawing the limits of relevance I have kept close to the themes that seem to arise from the fieldwork experience, and I have cut out that ethnographic detail which seems to be only of secondary importance in the context. Within this framework I have tried, first, to 'explain' or make intelligible the events narrated in the *Prologue*, and secondly, because the atmosphere of Cargo cult is not only one of anomy, of 'disorder, doubt and incertaintie over all . . .'[1] I have tried to show how and in what senses Cargo cults reveal moral notions in genesis. This seems to me to lay the basis for, and to be the proper approach to, the quite different problem of the connexions between Christian dogmatics on the one hand, and the indigenous religious beliefs on the other.

[1] Lambarde, *Archeion* (1653).

MAMBU

Prologue

When in the field anthropologists frequently have experiences which they tend to reserve for dinner parties or as a relaxation after seminars. Only rarely do such anecdotes find their way into serious discourse. And in many ways it is a shame that this should be so.

During the first few weeks of my stay with Tangu I was impressed and puzzled by an atmosphere of suspicion, reticence, and even expectancy. But it was not until after some months had passed, after the difficulties of language had been hurdled and we had come to know each other quite well, that Tangu gave me the clue to what I had begun to think was a normal reaction to having a stranger living among them.

A few months before I arrived, they said, they had received news of a dream which had been dreamed by a youth of the village of Pariakenam, fairly close by but not a Tangu village. If Tangu would perform the rites and ceremonials which had been revealed in the dream then all sorts of good things such as rice, tinned meat, cloth, knives, axes, beads, soap, hydrogen peroxide, and razor blades would appear in quantities for the common use. There would be plenty for everyone.

Accordingly, some people in Tangu, men as well as women but by no means the whole of any one community in Tangu, went ahead and performed the rites that had been revealed in the dream.

These rites were comparatively simple. The participants provided themselves with a large communal meal at which everyone present ate. After the feast, they formed circle round a single individual. Then they started to dance, moving and stamping their feet, and chanting rhythmically. Neither dance nor chant was taken from their own familiar dances and chants.

With the cadence gradually quickening the person in the centre of the circle excitedly urged the others to '*Otim!*' (Hot it up!)

After some minutes the man (or woman) in the centre of the circle was expected to fall flat on his (or her) back in a trance. Thereupon an aide, one of the dancers, would step into the circle to massage the mouth of the prone man whilst the others chanted slowly, as in a dirge, '*Yu-ker-ap, Yu-ker-ap!*' (Like *Otim*, not Pidgin English, but an attempt at the English 'You get up, You get up!')

The prostrate man was then lifted to his feet. He was expected to talk, shout, or cry out. The participants hoped that the utterances would communicate something to them, but in fact they do not seem to have been intelligible.

The cycle ended when the man in the centre of the circle had regained his senses. It started again when any other who wished to do so took his turn in the centre. Not all who attempted the feat were able either to fall into a trance, or communicate.

These activities, in spite of attempts at secrecy, came to the knowledge of the missionary resident in Tangu, and they were suppressed by administrative action.

At about the same time as Tangu were busying themselves with the news from Pariakenam, another series of rites were revealed in a dream to a man of Jumpitzir, a group of settlements bordering Tangu. Tangu participated.

The dreamer announced that if the villagers would build a large shed near the cemetery, and then followed his instructions, the shed would be filled with tinned meat, axes, knives, beads, soap, aspirins, cloth—and so on. Forthwith the villagers turned to and built the shed. The rites commenced with the adults of both sexes drawing water from the stream in bamboo barrels, heating the water, and then washing themselves. This done, the participants gathered at the cemetery in complete silence, neither dancing, nor singing, nor talking. Quite still. At a given signal the women loosed their grass skirts, the men threw off their breech-clouts, and all engaged in promiscuous sexual intercourse.

Precisely how promiscuous it was difficult to tell. No one who admitted to taking part in the rites would, or could be expected—if indeed they knew—to reveal the names of those

2

with whom they had copulated. Nevertheless, one may presume a form of *coitus interruptus* since the men's semen and the women's sexual secretions had to be collected, bottled, mixed together with water, and poured over the burial place.

These rites, too, came to the ears of the administration and they were suppressed. The shed was destroyed, and, as a sharp lesson, the participants were made to carry the timbers some seventeen miles to the sea.

When Tangu had finished telling me about these rites, their Cargo cult activities, a number of what had seemed to be discordant features of their culture began to fall into place. It was vexing not to have been informed about them beforehand, but it was also instructive.

In explaining why they had performed the ceremonies Tangu first recounted a myth, a myth which appears in this book as the Primal Myth.[1] Pressing them further they went on to tell me about Mambu, a man who had once lived in the Bogia region, and who, in 1937, had been the leader of a Cargo movement which had caused the authorities no little trouble.[2] They told me, too, of their impressions of Yali, a Kanaka from the Rai coast who in the years following the Japanese war had been the leader of a movement rather more mature than that initiated by Mambu, but otherwise rather similar.[3] Bit by bit a pattern began to take shape.

Months later, when the time came for me to leave Tangu, I packed my bags and went down to the coast. There, having some spare time, and hearing that there had been troubles on Manam island, I decided to go and see for myself.

I visited Manam island for a fortnight. My host was the Catholic missionary, a priest of the Society of the Divine word. I stayed at the mission station, a tourist, on holiday.

I was particularly interested in meeting Irakau, a Kanaka businessman who had organized his kinsmen and co-villagers into a copra producing concern, and whose home was at Baliau, the largest and most important of the Manam villages.

[1] Discussed *infra* p. 147.   [2] *Infra* p. 177.   [3] *Infra* p. 196.

When first I went along to Baliau village the villagers received me with cold indifference. It was strange not to be offered the milk of a green coconut in welcome, more disconcerting to be plainly ignored. Nobody showed the slightest interest.

I walked into the middle of the village, sat on a log, and made play with lighting my pipe. I waited.

A few of the villagers, I thought, seemed to be showing some curiosity at such modest behaviour. As a European I ought to be bustling about, demanding attention, getting things done. Still, no one was sufficiently inquisitive to ask what I wanted. It was obvious that my presence was repugnant.

Finally weakening, I took the initiative. I asked a passer-by for the Luluai, the government appointed headman. Curtly, he was pointed out.

I crossed over to where the Luluai was working and sat down on a tree trunk a few feet away from him, watching him carpentering. He was making a stool. He ignored me studiously. I smoked.

After some minutes he looked up from his work and said, pointedly, in Pidgin, that if I cared to wait until the evening meal was cooking—three hours away—I might have some refreshment.

Having spent nearly a year with Tangu, and being accustomed to the ways of Kanakas, especially their hospitality, the behaviour of this Luluai seemed to me exceedingly rude.

Remarking, therefore, that tobacco blunted hunger, I offered some from my pouch.

Confused, rather doubtfully, he accepted. I knocked out my pipe and rose to go.

At once he protested. I said I had work to do—another time perhaps. He protested again, shouting to the other villagers. I offered my hand. We shook hands. I walked off.

A small crowd followed, asking me to be sure and come back. A couple of boys, I noticed, had climbed a coconut palm and were slashing at the green nuts. . . .

My second visit to Baliau elicited a very different kind of

response. Though, to my disappointment, Irakau had left on a trading voyage, his relations took me into his house. I was entertained and handsomely fed. I was given matches, tobacco, cigarettes of English make, fruit, and a cup of tea as well as many kinds of native food. Table and chair were placed at my disposal, and I was invited to stay for the dance to be held that evening. So generous was the welcome that I was ashamed of—and never offered—the gift I had prepared myself with: a dozen sticks of cheap 'twist' tobacco.

In the course of conversation one of my hosts pointed to my notebook and remarked that they of Baliau had such a book in which all the lore of the ancestors was written. If I cared to see it I could. Only the nobility of Manam, only those holding the rank of *Tanepoa*, might see it. Others, especially administrative officers and missionaries, might not.

I asked if the book was exactly like mine. They said no, it was of another kind. They added that there were other things they would like to show me. I would be delighted, I said.

In a few minutes I was taken to a small shed built on stilts behind Irakau's magnificent *Tanepoa* house. The shed was painted in lurid washes, but very dilapidated. The floor boards were rotten and in a state of collapse. Carefully, a young man crept inside the shed to fetch the objects that were going to be shown me. The rest of us waited outside chatting in the sun.

The young man brought out for my inspection, first, a wand of hardwood, about seven feet long with a spray of very dirty, dusty, and tattered cassowary plumes bound on one end; second, a stone axe-blade, well made and polished; third, a carved wooden statuette of the human form about five inches high, rudely executed, unfinished, dusty, with smears of red and white chalk on it; fourth, a broad circlet of decorated turtleshell, battered, and apparently very old. This was the 'book'.

It seemed to me as I handled these things, examining them, that they were the common objects of a former age when the people of Manam were renowned in the region as sailors, traders, and fierce fighters. No longer made as they used to be,

5

as a matter of course, they were quite literally the 'things' or 'lore of the ancestors'. Apart from their age they had little merit.

I had just finished looking at these objects when one of Irakau's sisters—a cousin as we would say—pressed forward and begged me to shake hands with her. I did so. She burst into tears.

The others around me, men and women, also started to weep. Not the conventional wailing on a death or a parting, but deep, uncontrollable sobs with tears coursing down their faces.

Later, when we had had some more tea and were comfortable with our pipes, they explained to me why they had wept. 'We sympathize and feel for you,' they said. 'We like you. You have just seen something to do with *Tanepoa*, things to do with our nobility, things belonging to our ancestors. Your home is far away. You do not come from Australia quite close by, you come from England—ever so far away. And you have come all that way to see us, we, black-skinned men of New Guinea. That is why we like you. That is why we like you to be with us.'

One impetuous young man broke in with, 'You see, this, the things you have seen, belong to us. They are ours, our own, and all we have. We think that white men have deceived us. So we are turning back to our ancestors. How is it that white men have so much and we have so little? We don't know. But we are trying to find out.'

There was little for me to say, little I could say. And as the sun settled to the horizon the people of Baliau gathered in the village, dressed in all their finery. They were going to dance.

The Luluai who was sitting next to me remarked that in Baliau they were very progressive. The dance would last a couple of hours.

I expressed some surprise because in Tangu it was usual for dances to go on all night. 'We do not dance all the night through,' said the Luluai. 'We are not bush-Kanakas! (uncouth, uncivilized jungle folk).'

In an orderly way, precisely and without fuss, the dance proceeded. I was impressed. Unlike Tangu, who were wont to dance with abandon, these Manam islanders were dancing coolly, with quiet dignity, each step carefully disciplined. Thrumming hand-drums kept perfect time, the crescendos faultlessly executed to the rhythm of limbs moving in unison.

When the dance was over, food was distributed. Again, quietly and without fuss. Then the villagers lined up in front of Irakau's house for night prayers. I was surprised, for the missionary had told me that Baliau villagers avoided the mission; that though most of the islanders had been baptized, not a man and only a very few married women came to Mass on Sundays.

The prayers, as I heard them, were the standard night prayers taken from the Catholic prayer book, without alterations or additions. A renegade catechist, a mission teacher who refused to have anything more to do with the mission, led them.

'You see,' the Luluai remarked, 'we are not bad people. We are all good Catholics. Only this—we want to say our prayers for ourselves.'

Prayers over, ending with each one making the Sign of the Cross, I was asked if I would shake hands with the assembled villagers.

As we came down the steps from Irakau's house the villagers, men and women, sorted themselves into a single straight line stretching to the end of the village. In company with the Luluai and two or three others, I started across the open space to the head of the line. One by one, hand by hand, we went down the line in the gathering dusk. Nobody said anything. It was perfectly quiet.

About half-way down the line the air seemed to have become perceptibly charged—with I know not what. A little further and someone started to sob. First he, then another, then everyone—all started to weep.

Next day, a little disturbed, I went to the village of Aberia, beyond Baliau. As I reached the houses a youth approached me. 'Ah!' he exclaimed. 'You have arrived. I think you have got something for us. I think you have a message for us—

something you will tell us which would straighten things out for us.'

'No,' I replied. 'I have no message for you.'

Mambu, I remembered, had gone round the villages of Bogia giving the people a message, telling them what they should do to get cargo—the good things of life. And then again, there was that other one, Yali, who had gone from village to village exhorting the populace to mend their ways. Had Mambu and Yali been greeted like this in the villages they visited? Were they awaited as anxiously? Both Mambu and Yali had had a message. And they had both been imprisoned.

'No,' I repeated. 'I have no message . . .'

'I think that you have got a message for us,' insisted the youth. 'And I think you will tell us your message when you are ready.'

It must have been difficult for Yali not to respond, not to wipe away the tears and give them the message they wanted. 'You are mistaken, my friend,' I said. 'What kind of message are you waiting for?'

'I think you have a message which will straighten things out for us,' said the youth.

Whilst working in Tangu I used sometimes to explore into the hinterland and environs. On one such journey I chanced on a missionary priest. After mutual introductions and greetings he asked me how long I intended to stay in Tangu. I told him I would be there another four months.

'Ah!' he exclaimed. Then, 'Have you any family?' he asked.

'Yes.'

'Well,' he advised. 'You had better write to them soon. Perhaps you will not see them again.'

He had seen fiery signs in the sky, he told me, and from these he had learned that the end of the world was at hand. Early in October.

He had lived on his station for month upon month, in country thick with expectations of marvels to come, among people such as I was now meeting in Manam. In some scarcely

definable way he had become—as I was by way of becoming—
a part of the atmosphere of Cargo.

Down on the coast, on the mainland opposite Manam, I had
encountered a European planter. He was certain, he told me,
that he was being watched by a Russian submarine. He had
seen the periscope out at sea, and he had heard it charging its
batteries by night on the surface.

'But why should a Russian submarine come here?' I asked
him.

'To make a chart, of course!' he snapped. 'Or to land agents.
Stirring up trouble. Something ought to be done!'

If the people of Manam were waiting for a message, why
should they think that I, a European, should bring it?

One evening in Manam while I was strolling through the
bush after a walk, a Kanaka came down through the shrubs,
following a few paces behind. 'Hummm . . .' he murmured.
'Hummm . . . Ha.'

Back in the throat, like our own idea of a punctilious civil
servant, and in the English. 'Hummm . . . Yes! Hummm . . .
Okeydoke!'

It was impossible to ignore him, equally unsatisfactory to
turn and confront him. So I sat on a rock, and, as he drew
level, offered him my pouch.

'Thank you, brother!' he said.

Masta (Master) was the correct Pidgin term of address from
Kanaka to European. Why *barata*, brother? Perhaps he was
trying to draw me closer, curry favour, by using the more
intimate term—or was he assuming a moral relationship, the
kind of relationship between moral equals which had already
been established at Baliau?

At any rate, he was friendly even though he might have
been presuming a little.

We smoked contentedly, remarking the weather and where
either was bound. Then he nodded sagely, eyeing me askance.
'*Mi save!*' he announced. 'I understand!'

'Oh yes? What is it that you understand?' I asked.

9

'Ah! I understand well—see!' My companion slipped off the rock to his knees. He skimmed the palm of his hand over a dry patch of sand, flattening it smooth. Then he started to draw. (Figure 1.)

'This here,' he said pointing to the dot in the middle of the drawing, 'is where *bigpela bolong ol gat ap*, where the greatest imaginable being (usually God) created himself or was born.'

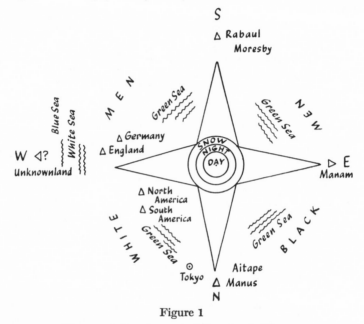

Figure 1

Diagram taken from sand drawing in Manam

'All round him,' continued the Manam islander, 'was snow in the upper layers, night, and day.' (Represented by the concentric circles of the diagram.) 'There was water. He (God) said the word and the lands came up.'

Drawing in the four cardinal points he labelled them—wrongly if we take them to refer to the points of the compass. Rabaul (in New Britain), Moresby (in Papua), Manam, Aitape, Manus (the last two in the vicinity), North America, South America, England, Tokyo, and Germany were identified and charted in. All these places were in the Green Sea around the cardinals. Then a triangle was drawn, set off from the cardinal labelled 'west'. From 'England' a voyager would have to cross the White Sea and then the Blue Sea to get there.

'What is the name of this place?' I asked, pointing to the triangle.

He looked at me craftily. 'That is the place *you* know all about,' he replied.

Did I? 'I do not know the name of this place,' I said. 'You tell me where it is.'

'Aha!' he exclaimed. 'You know very well what it is called. And,' he added confidently, 'I know too!'

'Very well,' I said. 'You tell me the name of the place and I will tell you whether you are right.'

'But,' he objected, 'what is the point of telling you what you know already?'

So we settled to a classical charade, giving nothing away. Of what use was it to ask what grew there, whether it was hilly or flat, if the people had white skins or black? But I asked all the same. Since I knew all about it, he said, and he knew all about it, and he knew that I knew, and I knew that he knew—well then, what was the point in telling each other what both already knew?

It was annoying. In Tangu a somewhat mysterious place, where all good things were, had been doubtfully identified as *Sewende*, the Pidgin rendering of Seventh Day Adventist. And while not wanting to put the word into my present companion's mouth it would have been nice had he said it. But he didn't. Instead, as the sun was sinking into the sea, he made a decision. 'No one,' he said suddenly, 'no one in the world has seen this place or knows its name.'

I visited Yasa one day. It was a small village, but the people were talkative. The headman said—'The Germans told us to do things—plant coconuts, for instance. So that we could get money by selling copra. In those days money could buy something. Now it is not so. Everything costs too much. When the "English" came we were just rubbish—poor. We had to stay like that. We have only the things we have always had—and we have lost most of those. If the Germans had stayed I think we would have had everything. . . .'

Another man said—'You see, we do not understand. We are just in the middle [of nowhere]. First the Germans came—and the Australians pushed them out. Then the Japanese pushed out the Australians. Later, the Australians and the Americans forced the Japanese to go. It is beyond us. We can do nothing. When a *kiap* (administrative officer) tells us to carry his baggage we have to do it. When a German told us to carry his baggage we had to obey. When a Japanese told us to carry his baggage we had to do it. If we did not we might be killed. All right, there it is. Take it or leave it. *Nogat tok*. I didn't say anything, that's just how it is, that's life.'

Not a day of my short visit to Manam passed without an incident of the kind I have mentioned. I stayed in the mission station, and awoke to the clatter of stones being hurled on to the tin roofs of the mission houses by youths who were trying to annoy the missionary and make him lose his temper. With the missionary I shared in the stares of men and youths who were trying to put him out of countenance. But when I left the mission buildings—then things were different. Then, apart from, and after the opening incident in Báliau, Manam islanders were friendly. However, conversations which started on yams, or harvests, or the role of *Tanepoa*—the nobility of Manam—quickly came to rest on Irakau, the mission, the administration, and the kind of message I might have for them. There were some, it is true, who curled the lip and would not speak. Others, encountered on the paths in the bush, satisfied themselves with the (unrequited) request for money. Whatever happened one could not but be aware of tension, and a ferment of unrest and expectancy.

It would be impracticable if not impossible to answer the many questions these anecdotes could bring to mind. But it is possible to go a part of the way. We can glance briefly at what lies behind the incidents. We can examine the ways of life of Tangu and Manam islanders and pick out some of the dominant springs of action. We can see what they live by, what they like doing, what they do not like doing, and what they have to do whether they like it or not. We can see, too, what Europeans are doing and trying to do in New Guinea, and so appreciate why they also are involved in the atmosphere of Cargo cult. We can try to isolate some of the conflicts and search for the principles which express and contain particular kinds of behaviour. Mambu, Yali, and the youth of Pariakenam evidently meant something to Tangu removed from the ordinary run. What was their meaning? Something of more than anecdotal relevance, surely, can be culled from the rites, from the diagram in the sand, from the behaviour of Manam islanders when shaking hands, from their attitude to Irakau. If, in short, we can make the incidents intelligible, we shall not be answering the final question, Why do Cargo cults occur?—but we may be providing the groundwork of a basis for doing so.[1]

[1] Some but not all of the events described in this *Prologue* were reported in another context in: Cargo Cult Activity in Tangu, *Oceania*, Vol. XXIV, No. 4, 1954; Racial Tension in Manam, *South Pacific*, Vol. 7, No. 15, 1954.

CHAPTER I

The New Guinea Scene

Because men of European descent are involved in Cargo movements, events such as those which have been described in the *Prologue* belong to a complex far greater than might be implied simply by 'Tangu' or 'Manam island'. In both localities the situation is to a large extent determined by political and economic decisions taken in Port Moresby, the administrative capital of Australian New Guinea, which itself looks for directives from Canberra. In turn, Canberra must react to what is happening at Lake Success or in other world capitals. The decisions taken inevitably guide or limit to a greater or lesser degree the activities of individuals— especially of Europeans—in Tangu or Manam island. The Europeans responsible for executing the policies thought out in faraway capitals are at the bottom of a long chain of delegated responsibility. They have little say in forming the policies they are expected to implement, and the New Guinea situation itself not only imposes restraints of its own, but it often provides individuals with considerable scope for personal initiative. Nevertheless, if Europeans are forced to put themselves into an equation balancing general directives against particular circumstances the native peoples concerned have little choice but to try to manipulate the situation as they find it. That is, there exists a basic situation of conflict. And its principal elements may be appreciated through a short historical survey.

The island of New Guinea lies a few degrees south of the equator off the northern shores of Australia. The western half, a tangle of swamp, jungle, and mountains, is a Dutch possession. The south-eastern quarter, Papua, more accessible country, was annexed by Queensland in 1883 and later became, and today remains, an Australian Commonwealth

14

responsibility. The third portion, the Australian Trust Territory of New Guinea—which also includes New Britain, New Ireland, Bougainville, and some smaller islands—was a German colony until Allied forces took possession during the first World War. Thereafter it became an Australian Mandated Territory as from the League of Nations. Then, temporarily occupied by Japanese military forces during the second World War, it became a Trust Territory of the United Nations under Australian administration.

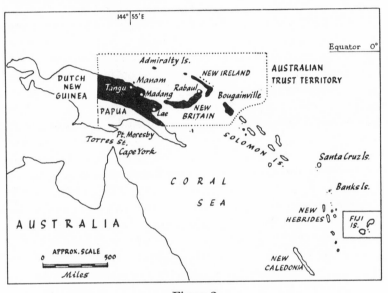

Figure 2

Australian Trust Territory (black) and Melanesian Islands

Strategically valuable, and a natural bridge between Asia and the Indonesian islands to the west, and Australia and the Pacific islands south and south-eastwards, New Guinea is a hard and savage country which is still only partially explored. Running down the centre of the island from west to east, like a backbone, are high mountains enfolding grassy plateaux drained by four main rivers: the Sepik and Ramu flowing generally north, and the Markham and Fly flowing east and south respectively. Hills rise abruptly from the seaboard in

15

serried rows of steep-flanked, thickly forested ridges; a heavy rainfall ensures a lush vegetation picked with vividly coloured blossoms. The air is humid, and the sun burns out of a tropical sky on to generally fertile soils. During the dry days the many mountain streams cut their valleys as musical brooks; in the rains, or after a heavy shower they rush headlong in muddy, boiling spate, flowing into larger rivers, bog, and swamp. Earth tremors are frequent.

The native peoples of the island, generally dark or copper skinned with thick curly or frizzy hair, are to be found living in fairly large organized groups on the highland plateaux, and in much smaller and more exclusive communities in the bays and inlets along the coast, or on the crests of the ridges further inland. Highland peoples speaking the same mutually intelligible language may number several thousands. Within twenty or thirty miles of the tide marks villages or groups of hamlets of no more than two hundred souls may enjoy quite distinctive languages or dialects as well as possess exclusive customs and institutions. Yet, everywhere kin and economic relationships reach across linguistic, cultural, and organizational boundaries. And, over the last half-century Pidgin English, a language with its own vocabulary and syntax, has made great strides as a *lingua franca*. Indeed, it is mainly through the use of Pidgin that natives of the Trust Territory have come to identify themselves as Kanakas, black skinned folk, distinct from men and women of European descent.

In most places in the Territory a simple village life continues. Yams, taros, sweet-potatoes, bananas, beans, and other vegetables are cultivated in garden plots. Pig rearing, sows mating with wild boars, is general. Coconut, sago, and areca nut palms are grown where possible. Some of the indigenous social institutions have fallen into decay, and other kinds of activity have been introduced. Local warfare and feuding have, for practical purposes, ceased. Clubhouse organization and rituals, foci of the traditional ways, are falling into disuse under the impact of mission teaching and administrative influence. The belief in sorcerers and sorcery, in the existence of men who kill, or induce illness, mainly by mystical means,

16

has, on the other hand, continued to be strong and general; and dancing and feasting, hinges of prestige, political life, and the distributive systems, remain popular, favoured activities. More and more young men from the coastal villages leave their homes to go to work for Europeans for cash as labourers, policemen, seamen, porters, or domestics on plantations or in such centres as Port Moresby, Lae, Rabaul, and Madang: European tools, knick-knacks, and gew-gaws bought for the cash thus earned are gradually replacing native made equipment, decorative furnishings, and art forms. Steadily, European civilization is extending its blessing.

General administration of the Territory—which consists of keeping the peace, maintaining law and order, regulating the flow of migrant labour and supervising the treatment of native workmen, and establishing schools, technical training centres, co-operative enterprises, hospitals, post offices, and banks—is effected from Port Moresby in Papua. From thence authority devolves to territorial Districts—themselves divided into sub-Districts and Patrol posts—down through a hierarchically organized chain of European (Australian) officers to locally appointed Kanaka officials who, unpaid, are responsible to the District Officer through Patrol Officers and sub-District Officer for a village or collection of hamlets. They are, first, the Luluai with general supervisory duties; second, the Tultul, under the Luluai and nominally the village constable; third, the Doctor boy who is held responsible for general hygiene, the upkeep of a medicine hut, and the care of the sick. Each of these officials has a blue, peaked, bus conductor's cap as the badge of his office.

Realizing an administrative ideal in such country as the Territory presents cannot be other than difficult. Roads, their foundations undermined by tremors and rain, slip off the hillsides or are washed away by floods. Communications by sea tend to be intermittent at best, and when away from the coastal centres officers must rely on couriers, or the battery or treadle wireless. More and more frequent use of light aircraft and airstrips have made things much easier, but, for the most part, administrative officers still have to make their rounds—

patrols as they are known locally—laboriously on foot, accompanied by a few police boys and a train of bearers to carry supplies and equipment. The Europeanized seaport towns and townships remain the chief logistic supports for administrative, educational, and commercial enterprises along the coast, inland, and even in the relatively recently discovered highland plateaux.

Generally almost as important, and in specific instances perhaps a more influential factor in New Guinea affairs than the administration itself, is Christian religious missionary activity. Few of the larger denominations are not represented: in 1952 there were some forty differently named mission bodies[1] operating in Papua and the Trust Territory, each typically regarding itself as in some way competing with the others. Only three are of interest here: the Roman Catholic Society of the Divine Word (S.V.D. mission); the Seventh Day Adventist Mission (S.D.A. mission); and the Protestant Lutheran Mission, generally referred to as 'Lutherans'.

Early in the German period, during the 'eighties, the Lutherans established themselves in Madang, and in Bogadjim not far from Madang. From thence they fanned out south and east. Rather later, the S.V.D. mission set up their main base at Alexishaven, some miles north of Madang, and worked westwards towards Bogia and Manam. Both missions carried their traditional rivalry from Germany and the Low Countries into New Guinea. They survived the first World War and throughout the period of the Mandate both organizations continued to recruit from their Houses in Europe. They established mission stations on the off-shore islands, along the coast, and even a little way inland; European clergy were in charge, and each station was logistically dependent on the main bases. Both missions recruited and trained native teachers, catechists as they are called in New Guinea, built and ran schools, staked out plantations, and set up trade stores of rice, cloth, razor blades, beads, hydrogen peroxide—to bleach the hair of young bucks—knives, axes, and sundry other articles. To connect their scattered stations

[1] A list of missions in New Guinea is given in Appendix B.

private shipping services were started, and by 1952 the S.V.D. mission was using a couple of light aircraft.

Lutheran and S.V.D. missionaries in New Guinea have always been explorers, men who were interested in the country, its peoples, and their customs and languages. Articles in the learned journals attest their ability and scholarship. They are also practical men who skipper small ships, teach, build, run commercial enterprises, and walk long distances over rough country to minister to the needs of pagans as well as converts. Formerly financially dependent on their own resources, and on donations from the faithful in Europe, the Japanese war hit both missions hard. They had to accept financial grants in aid from the administration. Nevertheless, they still have a moral and economic interest in New Guinea which is also at least quasi-political; and because they learn native dialects as a matter of course, and live among their charges for long periods, they know their own areas in a way that few administrative officers can. The European elements of the Seventh Day Adventist Mission, on the other hand, much later arrivals on the scene, have tended to remain in residence round a hospital, school, and chapel in the more metropolitan atmosphere of the coastal towns. From thence Kanaka teachers are despatched to outlying areas where conversions are deemed to be likely, and after a few months they return again to the main school. Financial support is almost wholly from outside New Guinea. Sincere, exclusive, and taking their departure from what might be criticized as a rather too narrow and oblivious viewpoint, S.D.A. missionaries work quietly, with and among themselves rather than with others. Their own stake in the country might be almost irrelevant: they are not tied to its traditions and atmosphere in the same way, or to the same extent as are Lutheran and S.V.D. missionaries. If, for the latter, the administrative machine is often a rival, to be influenced and steered, for the S.D.A. it simply exists, a protective and ordered framework within which others may work.

In 1850, if we may take a round date, Kanakas of the Territory were living their own lives in their own ways: there were no missions, no administration. Their cultures were rich in rituals, myths, and art forms. From childhood until death their lives were ordered by a relatively narrow, but complex ambience of kin obligations. Their tools were of stone and shell. They enjoyed, for the most part, what we call subsistence economies. They produced huge surpluses of foodstuffs which were consumed in feasts to yield prestige and political influence: they engaged in barter, trade, and food exchanges. For particular purposes, such as in the arrangements for a marriage, industry and productive capacity could be translated into 'valuables' such as rare shells, pigs' tusks, or dogs' teeth. Feuding, based largely upon beliefs in sorcery, and organized within terms of small local and kin groups, was endemic. Generally, individuals were proud, self-centred, and quick to recognize a slight: warrior values went hand in hand with hard work in the gardens, business acumen, and a fiercely independent and ethnocentric spirit. By the 'nineties these same Kanakas were being drawn into the peripheries of European modes of thought, values, techniques, and relationships: and their channels of understanding were explorers, adventurers, traders, missionaries, and administrative officers. A generation later Kanakas of the Territory had become a factor in world politics; and their own comprehension of the world outside was being concentrated into the triangle of relationships formed by themselves, missionaries, and administrative officers. Relationships with traders, planters, and other white men, though significant, were relatively simple and direct: a passage of cash in exchange for services, and a minimum necessary moral component.

During the decade preceding the first World War the triangle began to develop. After the war, with the change in administration, it took a fresh, more complicated direction. Through the triangle, for the whole of the Mandate period, the separate economies and ways of life of many Kanaka communities could be affected by financial and political crises in Europe, the United States, and Australia. With limited means, and with confidence sapped by those who actively advocated the return of the Territory into German hands, development could not be other than slow. Capital, the will to sink it, and the means to use it, seem to have been lacking. The world wide economic depression hit Australia as hard as anywhere else, and could not but have its effect on the New Guinea scene. Individual adventurers and prospectors searched the hinterland areas for minerals; and eventually they found gold in workable quantities. Coconut plantations, most of which had been established during the German days, were maintained but not greatly extended. Labour recruitment from the native villages was general. The missions gradually extended their ranges of influence, bringing to Kanakas schools and Christianity. The administration explored, opened up new country, and, with a thinly spread corps of officers, kept and regulated the peace.

The second World War passed over the Territory as might a series of summer cyclones. The triangle was broken. Few preparations had been made, and the Japanese came in overwhelming force. Those Europeans who did not escape were captured and imprisoned. Missionary work came to a standstill. Despite the fact that a large number of them were German nationals, allies of the Japanese, Lutheran and S.V.D. missionaries bore the brunt of insults and maltreatment in front of those who had been their parishioners. Some died of privation early: later, many more were to lose their lives.[1] Existing Kanaka officials were dismissed, and others were appointed in their places. Labour gangs were recruited for work on military installations, and villagers had to fend for themselves. Administration, such as it was, was put into the hands of Japanese political officers.

For Kanakas a period of relative quiescence but increasing dearth and finally famine was brought to an end by the departure of the Japanese and the arrival of Australian and American troops. Huge quantities of canteen goods and war material began to pour in. The labour gangs which had melted into the bush as the Japanese retreated were re-recruited

---

[1] A Japanese ship carrying missionary priests and nuns to prison camps in Indonesia was bombed and sunk off Manam island by Allied aircraft.

and reorganized into pioneer detachments on a scale of rations and wages which had hardly been dreamt of in the Mandate, and which were, indeed, quite impracticable then. General administration of the Territory was the responsibility of a military body known as the Australian New Guinea Administrative Unit (A.N.G.A.U.). After a while, as military considerations began to shrink in importance, a few surviving missionaries were allowed to return and pick up again the threads of their work.

The years following the war were a period of general unrest; and though the triangle began to reform the relationships within it altered appreciably. The war had brought ruin and devastation in its train, and the losses to be made good were not only of a material kind. Combined with a vision of splendid possibilities there was also a certain disenchantment in the air. During the war Kanakas had seen a wealth of material goods hitherto beyond their imaginations: and they wanted some of it. Administrative officers, old guard and new, were imbued with a fresh but secular missionary zeal. The work of Kanaka stretcher-bearers during the fighting had made 'niggers' into 'angels with black faces'. Education, technical training, animal husbandry, agricultural schools, forestry institutes, village co-operatives, cash crops, compulsory minimum ration scales for Kanaka employees of Europeans—the schemes multiplied. In the meanwhile, latter day carpet baggers were quick to take their profit from Kanakas who had been receiving (for them) fantastic wages whilst working for military units. There were enormous dumps of unwanted war materials which Europeans with initiative converted into small fortunes, and which many Kanakas also turned to good account. Finally, generous distributions of cash compensation for war damages boosted general inflationary pressures. Prices soared and cash in Kanaka hands bought less and less.

During this period missionaries were particularly hard pressed. Between the wars Lutheran and S.V.D. missionaries especially had wielded an influence which might be described justly as excessive. Almost alone they had borne the burden of education and technical training. Self-sufficient, strongly fibred, well organized, and on the whole more highly educated than the administrative officers to whom they owed many of their opportunities, they had always been difficult to control. But the war caused them grievous losses in personnel which could not be made good for many years to come. Their schools and equipment were rubble and dust; their plantations had been ravaged, or were overgrown and uncared for. Administrative schemes competed with them directly, and administrative officers themselves, filled with a typically competitive missionary spirit, had most of the financial backing they wanted for their task of rebuilding and moulding the characters of their charges. Kanakas, too, were reluctant to seek the aid of missionaries and to abide by what seemed to them at the time to be an old fashioned way. Missionaries might suffice for 'bush-Kanakas', but they and their teaching were not adequate for the newly experienced. The idea that God and religion were simply a hoax to be fed to the simple minded gained some currency.

Nevertheless, missionaries set themselves to their task. Accepting financial grants in aid from the administration—and so bowing the head to administrative control in a number of matters including *curricula*—logistic reorganization was combined with more schools, more teachers, and bigger classes. Recruitment of personnel shifted from Europe to the United States. And, whereas before the war it had only rarely been possible to train Kanakas to the point when they might be ordained, now the policy of so doing became more purposeful and organized, showing results.

The tremendous acceleration of activity within the interrelationships of administrative officers, missionaries, and Kanakas during the years following the war had moral as well as other significances. Though many planters and traders would say that they wanted more out of Kanakas—and were prepared to put more in—than a direct, commercial relationship which would yield a satisfactory margin of profit, whatever else is demanded the symbols of the relationship remain largely concrete and measurable in terms of goods, cash, and labour exchanged. Administrative officers and missionaries, on the other hand, dedicated and competent men, have been

23

and are competing for the loyalty, trust, attention, and confidence of Kanakas. The symbols of their relationships tend to be many and diffuse, measurable largely in moral criteria which themselves are not entirely firm, stable, or well defined. Together, with explicit purpose, they have been bringing, severally as individuals as well as representatives of organized bodies, selected parts of the whole *corpus* of European secular and religious traditions and forms into the Kanaka environment. In doing so they take on themselves a great responsibility, a responsibility which implies a readiness to cope with the consequences of their initiative. But because, in present circumstances, they cannot but compete with each other, each is often blind to the consequences of his own activities and only too well aware of the difficulties occasioned by the activities of the other.

In spite of the idealism and ability of administrative officers and missionaries, however, Kanakas themselves have never been wholly acquiescent to the ambitions of either. They have strong beliefs and traditions of their own. They know well how to bargain, and they understand the commercial relationship. But they are apt, sometimes, to view the attentions of the zealous with distaste and resentment. Often, their integrity as men, culturally enjoined, lies in the ability to repulse the persuasiveness of another. They would like to learn, but they demand that they will choose for themselves what to do with the knowledge. As adults they do not mind being taught, but they resent being treated as children. They do not want to accept from white men what no white man would accept from another. This, the attempt by Kanakas to establish their integrity as men in relation to administrative officers and missionaries, forms a large part of the story of a Cargo cult.[1]

[1] Standard works on the area are: Cyril Belshaw, *Island Administration in the South West Pacific*, Royal Institute of International Affairs, London 1950a; *Changing Melanesia*, Oxford University Press, Melbourne 1954; H. Ian Hogbin, *Experiments in Civilization*, Routledge, London 1939; *Transformation Scene*, Routledge and Kegan Paul, London 1951; *Social Change*, Watts, London 1958; L. P. Mair, *Australia in New Guinea*, Christophers, London 1948; W. E. H. Stanner, *The South Seas in Transition*, Australasian Publishing Co., London 1953.

Bak'n in taros

A household prepares to wash sago

A hunter apportions his kill—a cassowary

CARGO CULT:
APPROACH TO THE PROBLEM

All the reports about Cargo movements show them to be directly related to the presence of men of European descent, or their ideas, actions, and products. Yet one should not be too hasty in assuming that Cargo cults are wholly derived from the colonial situation. They may be a cultural inheritance. Cargo cults may be a particular kind of expression of a similar type of cult with which the peoples concerned were already well acquainted.[1] For if Cargo cults are symptomatic of social and cultural change, unless we assume a completely static historical situation it is not unreasonable to suggest that movements rather like Cargo movements were occurring in Melanesia before the white man came there. The suspicion, at any rate, is legitimate.[2] The numerous, culturally diverse, and generally small communities traded with each other, fought, and often intermarried. In spite of linguistic difficulties individuals and whole communities were probably used to the knowledge of strangers, to different ways of life, and indeed to the adoption of customs and activities which might be learned from encounters with foreigners. Such changes as did take place, or were contemplated, must have had their champions and opponents, and that major issues were not accompanied by strong emotions and opposed interests is barely conceivable. If the presence of Europeans and domination of the native populations by them have made the problem of Cargo cult an urgent moral and practical issue for our generation, one still cannot help feeling that the activities of administrative officers, missionaries, and Kanakas are but particular expressions of principles with a deeper and wider import. Awareness of their motives, interests, roles, and

[1] There are indications that this might have been so in, for example, the Taro cult, F. E. Williams, *Orokaiva Magic*, Oxford University Press, London 1928, pp. 23–30.

[2] For an example of how the sight of an aircraft gave rise to a typical Cargo movement before the people concerned had seen white men see: R. M. Berndt, A Cargo Movement in New Guinea, *Oceania*, Vol. XXIII, 1953, Nos. 1 and 2, pp. 40–65, 137–158, 202–33.

purposes is but one entry into understanding the events of the *Prologue*. A generalized picture of what happens, or is thought to be happening in a Cargo cult is another.

First some preliminaries. The Pidgin[1] term *kago* is derived from our own English 'cargo', and it normally refers to imported European equipment and manufactured goods. But in the context of a cult it may be dressed with quite other and more significant connotations. To save confusion, therefore, 'cargo' is used here to refer to manufactured goods, and Cargo, with a capital C, when what is meant is the whole complex of meanings, symbols, and activities to be found in a Cargo cult. Then there is the word 'value'. In this book it is used in a more generalized sense than is sometimes conventional. It covers activity, notion, ideal, and motive: it does not refer exclusively to what a majority may deem to be good or beneficial.[2] Finally, though what is here called a 'myth-dream' has clear associations with the work of Freud, Jung, and Fülöp-Miller,[3] it is not used in quite the same sense

[1] Pidgin is really a vocabulary of words for use in the European environment. Though missionaries teach Pidgin with a regular syntax, spelling, and grammar, in general Pidgin spellings tend to be optional in fact, and Kanakas who are not 'Melanesian' language speakers normally use the Pidgin vocabulary with their own native syntaxes. Thus though Tangu and Manam islanders, for example, use the same words when talking Pidgin, they use them in different ways. Understanding and intelligibility only come with practice.

[2] If A is gardening the activity, gardening, is a value. What A thinks about his gardening while he is engaged in it, what he thinks about gardening in general, what others think about gardening, his own motives for gardening, and what others in the community think his motives are or ought to be are also values. Gardening has obvious economic value, and for most Kanakas it has political, ritual, and mystical values. So long as the reader rids himself of the prejudice that 'value' has exclusive connotations of 'good', 'preferred' and the like, the context will make it plain what meaning should be attached to 'value'.

[3] C. J. Jung, *Psychology of the Unconscious*, trans by B. M. Hinkle, Moffat, Yard and Company, New York 1917, esp. Chapter 1; C. J. Jung and C. Kerényi, *Introduction to a Science of Mythology*, Routledge and Kegan Paul, London 1951 esp. pp. 227–8; Sigmund Freud, *On Dreams*, trans. by M. D. Eder, William Heinemann, London 1914; René Fülöp-Miller, *Leaders, Dreamers, and Rebels*, trans. by E. and C. Paul, George Harrap & Co., London 1935.

or context as any one of these writers has used it. Generally, though the full implications will become clearer as the argument proceeds, a myth-dream is a body of notions derived from a variety of sources such as rumours, personal experiences, desires, conflicts, and ideas about the total environment which find expression in myths, dreams, popular stories, and anecdotes. If those involved in a myth-dream were capable of fully comprehending and intellectualizing its content and meaning then 'aspiration' might have been a better word. As it is myth-dream, because of its previous associations, better meets the case.

The use of myth-dream makes possible generalization of a particular kind: and the fact that a myth-dream may not have been reported as such does not mean that it did not exist. Consistent with the wide cultural diversity of Melanesia the responses to the new techniques, ways of thought, and forms of social organization being imposed upon them vary considerably. Some movements are syncretic, others appear reversionary, excluding anything to do with Christianity and Europeans.[1] Either expression, however, may relate to the same deeper cause which may have to be recognized by some rather more abstract proposition. Other distinctions may refer to the politico-revolutionary content,[2] whether they are purely religious or politico-religious, or whether they reveal simply an opposition to Christianity and Christian missions.[3] Then again many cults lead one to dwell on the economic and politico-economic aspects expressed.[4] And the kinds and numbers of contacts with Europeans that the native people concerned have had may also be used to distinguish one sort of Cargo movement from another.[5] The truth is that it is impossible

[1] cf. particularly J. V. de Bruijn, The Mansren Cult of Biak, *South Pacific*, Vol. 5, No. 1, March 1951, p. 1.

[2] cf. particularly Jean Guiart, Cargo Cult and Political Evolution in Melanesia, *Mankind*, Vol. 4, No. 6, May 1951, p. 227.

[3] cf. Georg Höltker, How Cargo Cult is Born, *Pacific Islands Monthly*, Vol. XVII, No. 4, November 1946, p. 16; Rudolf Inselmann, Cargo Cult not caused by Missions, *Pacific Islands Monthly*, Vol. XVI, No. 11, June 1946, p. 44.

[4] cf. Belshaw 1954 at p. 83.

[5] cf. Belshaw, The Significance of Modern Cults in Melanesian Development, *The Australian Outlook*, June 1950b, Vol. IV, p. 116.

to generalize over the mass of cultural detail that is available. At the same time it is not necessary for a generalization to cover all or even most instances of Cargo movements in their cultural particulars. For there are other kinds of uniformity. If generalization can provide a logical model in which the cultural detail might be appreciated to better advantage— then it is worth making the attempt to abstract and generalize.

With these provisos in mind, then, we may speak of a Cargo movement as occurring in three phases. The first is the creation of the myth-dream. Over a period of time which may be days, weeks, months, years, or a generation parts of the myth-dream sift themselves into a relatively few demands or precepts which gain doctrinal, compulsive force as tension mounts. Then comes the second phase. Essentially an attempt to realize the myth-dream, to translate or externalize its content into direct and effective activity, to transcend in fact —physically as well as mentally and emotionally—the difficulties presently being encountered, it commences with the emergence of an individual, the charismatic figure,[1] who may combine in his person all or merely some of the attributes of a hero, a prophet, a teacher, or a seer. In whatever way he may be described, however, this man concentrates attention to himself. He has something exciting and pertinent to say. And what he says is not the summary of his personal opinions and knowledge, but is claimed or presumed to have been revealed to him in a dream or some other, similar mystical experience. In the main his declarations tend to echo important features of the myth-dream. It may be that only a few will accept his message at once, but though, at first, there may be opposition, general acceptance accelerates later. Often the revelation is given a concrete referent or symbol such as a book, or a piece of sculpture; otherwise it is contained in a less tangible symbol, in a myth or a dream.[2] Promises of material

[1] The word taken from Max Weber, *The Theory and Economic Organisation*, trans by A. R. Henderson and Talcott Parsons (Wirtschaft und Gesellschaft, Pt. I), William Hodge and Company Limited, London 1947.

[2] This symbol may take an almost infinite number of forms, and is part of a much more complex symbol. See Cargo Cult Activity in Tangu, p. 243n; *supra*, p. 5, 'The things of the ancestors'.

prosperity, spiritual salvation, and political independence are made conditional on the observance of a series of commands, rites, and ceremonials; and, on the other side, there are threats of disaster if the content of the revelation is not accepted in its entirety. Destruction of crops, livestock, and other symbols of the old way of life are not only enjoined as an expression of faith in the future, but also to indicate the rejection of the old and of the present in the past. Finally, an oracular, physical sign is postulated. An earthquake, a resurrection, a consuming holocaust, or merely the appearance of a ship or aircraft, will herald the end of the old and the beginning of the new.[1]

The third phase is both aftermath and possibly a recommencement of the cycle. Usually because they are suppressed by the governing authority, or because the promises are not made good, but also because the dramatic fervour of a cult cannot long be sustained, the then current and particular activities are abandoned. Nevertheless, many if not all of the basic notions contained in the myth-dream remain viable. The first of the three phases again becomes evident. The myth-dream undergoes revision, refinement, and qualification until it is revealed to a new hero how to pass through the impasse.

The succession of phases seems inescapable. But the ordering of particular events within them in a chronological sequence is not only variable, but may even be irrelevant. Much more important are the interrelations of the notions and activities, in symbolic form or otherwise. Moral regeneration and political independence which are subsumed in the new man and the new society, and a desire for material wealth together with a latent opposition between governors and governed, combine and meet in the advent of a hero through whom the conflicts implied in these factors will be eclipsed. Though the focus of a Cargo cult is on cargo, material wealth, what is distinctive in the logic of Cargo cults is that though the participants have never gained any form of material wealth without pragmatic as well as mystical

[1] cf. Hogbin 1958, pp. 207–33.

techniques, in the cult situation mystical means may be relied on to gain pragmatic ends. It is this that forces us to ask whether the explicit ends and means are not symbolic representations of other ends and means which may be discovered by inspection.

Even within the relatively narrow context of Tangu, or Manam island, it cannot be assumed that there is any necessary homogeneity of the quality of thought. Some minds are more aware of themselves and external problems than others, and many, especially at the emotional and unintellectualized level of the myth-dream, can contain with facility what appear to be quite contradictory ideas and sentiments. Differences in intellectual comprehension and awareness are typical. Most Kanakas of the Bogia region when thinking of cargo would associate access to it with certainly specialized, and also with what we would call mystical techniques. Others, more acute perhaps, have seen that if mystical techniques cannot obtain the cargo then other means may have to be used. In 1952 rumours about a Cargo cult that would take place in Pariak-enam began to circulate in the Bogia region. In Tangu expectations were roused, men talked secretly in whispers and hurried off to tell others the news. Then there was a burglary in the sub-District Headquarters settlement of Bogia itself. Quite large quantities of goods and cash were stolen from the mission store, and the thieves left the police with no clues.

Rumours of a Cargo cult that *this* time was surely going to succeed grew markedly stronger.

Some time after the burglary a Kanaka came into the administrative Post Office in Bogia with a high denomination note for which he wanted small change. In the circumstances the incident could not be passed over, and the man was asked to wait while the change was procured. The number of the note was checked, and, accordingly, when he had finished his business, the man was trailed. He led the police to Pariak-enam, to the cache where the goods stolen from the mission store had been hidden, and to his comrades in theft.

Rumours of the cult died.

If the thieves had been completely successful they might have shared the loot between themselves, they might have spent the money in small amounts, they might have gone away and spent it elsewhere, or they might have hoarded both goods and cash using them as opportunity offered. In fact they had decided to make it appear in a Cargo cult. Had they tried to make use of their spoils themselves they could never have kept the theft a secret. Village life is too close and intimate. As a theft some envious man would soon bear a tale to the authorities; and mystical access would demand publication at once. Thievery and gangsterism have their own conventions of access and redistribution. The only way in which these thieves could have profited from their theft within the ambience of their village community relationships was to have the money and the goods come in a Cargo cult. Thereby they would gain wealth, prestige, and political power. In the Kanaka environment simple possession of quantities of cash and manufactured goods is pointless unless it is linked to community moral, political, and economic values. Further, sudden access to quantities of manufactured goods is inevitably linked to a cult. Any man with a shilling in his pocket can go to a trade store and buy some razor blades. What he cannot do is buy unlimited quantities—Who can? But then, why should a Kanaka appear to think that unlimited access is possible without any money at all?

If it can be said, as a working hypothesis, that the rites and activities of a Cargo cult satisfy the yearnings both of single individuals and the community concerned, there is still the fact that all Cargo cults are, apparently, failures. The cargo does not arrive. Either, therefore, the activities themselves satisfy community and individual ends and are independent of a success in terms of actually obtaining cargo, or the participants are being faced with repeated frustrations. On going to the evidence we find something of both. When their Cargo activities were over, Tangu said, 'It was no good. We were silly to listen (to those who advocated the rites).' They were disappointed—because the cult had not worked. Yet, independent of obtaining cargo, the activities of the cult and the expression of its symbols appear as ends in themselves. The myth-dream continued in potency after the failure of the cult, and if portions of it have altered a little the implication is surely that the experience of the cult is subtly changing the meaning and relevance of the symbols contained in the myth-dream.

The point may be enlarged by putting it another way. Let us say that the participants of a Cargo movement are attempting to find particular and relevant symbols which will express certain conflicts and the ideal solutions of them; and let us also say that they are trying to externalize and relate these symbols together into some durable form which will have validity for succeeding generations. We shall see when we come to consider the people of Tangu and Manam island in detail that they are indeed searching for a theory or philosophy of life which will bear out their own experiences, their feelings, and their conclusions about both. History is wanting. Common consent to a minimum number of moral axioms valid for the total environment is lacking. The faraway days of the ancestors, when truth was, must somehow be morally linked with the coming of the white man, his techniques, and ideas; with two world wars, cash, plantation labour, manufactured goods, Christianity, and the teaching of Europeans—sometimes accepted, at other times rejected, but always powerfully insistent—that in the days of the ancestors truth was not. For Kanakas the present appears as an isolated time span of some three generations—How may they make it and the future intelligible in terms of the traditions handed down from the ancestors? How may they work towards a common consent in the selection of a bewildering array of alternatives? For, until the connexions between past and present become clear, and permit of significant generalizations, Kanakas do not feel it is possible to hand on a future to their children.

For a European, with history, the present may always be explained in terms of the past. Verifiable events and relationships form fixed points in an imaginative but disciplined pattern: beginnings are either authentic, or presumed to be so.

Kanaka beginnings are shrouded in doubt. A Kanaka is faced with understanding himself and his new, Europeanized world with intellectual tools and categories of understanding derived from quite another environment. His problem is threefold. He has to understand one set of relationships through one mould of thought; a different set of categories has to make do for another;[1] and finally, in his transference from one environment to another some synthesis is necessary. Unwilling to forgo all that the ancestors have given him, unwilling to accept all that Europeans have brought, and unwilling to divide himself morally in two, a Kanaka can only find himself whole and entire within terms of a synthesis that contains both worlds and is, therefore, larger than either. He must make a new man. And to do so he must resort to his learning and truths as he finds them.

Most if not all truths, and much of the learning and lore of Kanakas such as Tangu and Manam islanders goes into a myth or a story. There each piece of knowledge is remembered, correlated, and threaded into a meaningful pattern. The traditional myths, overtly telling of the past but also accounting for the present and linking present with past, have been undermined by missionary teaching, by conversations and experiences with administrative officers, traders, planters, and other white men. Yet few Kanakas are willing to abandon the form of a myth as a means of expressing their truths. And while there is a conservative reluctance to alter the detail contained in a particular myth, over the years myths do undergo changes in content and meaning. Some parts drop out, other items are added. The chief criterion of placement is consent. Though an imaginative storyteller may make additions of his own they will not endure into the versions of others if they lack the consent of the community. Thus, if myths contain truths, and if truth is dressed in a myth, truth itself is dependent upon what most people think it to be. It

[1] If the use of Pidgin widens the range of idea implicit in the use of a language, it does not necessarily increase an appreciation of the new ideas or alter the mould of thought implied by the native language or dialect—see note on p. 26.

follows that truth will remain stable only so long as the society remains stable.

One of the prime questions which Tangu and Manam islanders are trying to answer is, 'What are the criteria of truth?' Their starting points are their myths: and these they have to place against their latter day experiences. For the time being they cannot do otherwise than ask themselves which parts of which stories are true; and each decision must rest with the community as a whole—acting not through a committee or any other organizational form but piecemeal, implicitly, through community *rapport*. About some of their myths Tangu, for example, are definite. They say of them, in Pidgin, that they are '*sitori nating*, just a story'. As certainly do others contain truths, and truth. The remainder are in issue. And when its myths are in issue all that a community lives by, holds dear, and regards as 'self-evidently' valid or true, is also in issue. Kanakas can only use their emotions to feel their way towards truth because they have no other instruments: no written language, no formal logic, no scientific tools. Their 'objective' criterion, checking the whim of an individual, is community consent.

Because Europeans have provided Kanakas with so many alternative choices, few single articles can possibly obtain the necessary consent—until, momentarily, man and woman are caught in a Cargo cult. While some missionaries have been teaching one doctrine others have been preaching rather different versions as well as explictly decrying the efforts of their rivals. Many Europeans, outside the mission bodies but as strongly prejudiced in their own favour, have expressed open contempt for this or that mission, or all missions, whilst —curiously enough—striving to demonstrate the superiority of their own codes of maxims. Village Kanakas going away on contract labour have learned not only the bits and pieces of many formal or ideal codes of behaviour: they have had their own experiences with individual Europeans, the stories of fellow workers, and the experiences of others to collate and pattern. A Catholic from Tangu might have much in common with a Catholic from Manam, but as a Christian he would be a near stranger to a Lutheran, and understandably bewildered by the Seventh Day Adventist who told him that Sunday was on Saturday, and that he should not eat pork, chew betel, dance, feast, or smoke—all of which the Catholic missionaries allowed him to do quite freely—if he was seriously thinking of Paradise. Finally, the trader from whom he bought razor blades, or the plantation manager—neither of whom would be human if they could resist a receptive audience—might tell him, rather sharply, that money was '*samting tru*', that God might be, but that religion was '*samting nating*'.[1]

Both Tangu and Manam islanders provide a clue to a part of their general dilemma when they point to the German period as a kind of Golden Age. For an Englishman brought up under certain convictions as to the nature of German colonial rule such an attitude might seem almost unintelligible. Yet, investigation adequately clears up the matter. During the German period Kanakas seem to have been on a wave of optimism: a new life filled with all kinds of possibilities had dawned. Then, too, the Germans provided Kanakas with a minimum of choice. Their requirements were clear and direct, of the 'Do as I say! Get in or get out and take the consequences' kind. The bosses themselves gave common consent to a relevant set of values, and once these were known Kanakas knew where they stood. Life held few unmanageable 'incertainties'. By contrast, their successors have remained unpredictable: a set of unique individuals who fall loosely into the categories of *Kiap* (administrative officer), *Kampanimasta* (trader, planter, recruiter, prospector), and *Pater* or *Misin* (missionary or mission). Recruited from English Public Schools, the Australian Outback, European and American seminaries, Nazi concentration camps, farms, ranches, small towns, cities, the moneyed and the poor, white men in New Guinea provide a bewildering diversity of creeds, traditions, and social upbringing. Kanakas themselves reduce this medley to a main uniformity: *waitsikin*, white men. Their problem is to find other uniformities within the main classification.

[1] *Samting tru*, something valid, true, or good. *Samting nating*, of little consequence, worthless, nonsense.

The 'nature of the white man' is an important and complex problem not only *per se* but also because certain attributes of the European must enter the amalgam that will be the new man. The few categories available reflect either much common ground in the attitudes of white men, or simply a lack of perception on the part of Kanakas. In fact, of course, besides there being a good deal of both, the situation as it exists guides Europeans into the adoption of certain well defined responses and tends to mould the viewpoint of Kanakas. A European who is unwilling to be placed in the available categories is forced to make a fight of it.[1] With precisely the same conceptual tools as have served to order his village life, the yearly visit of an administrative officer, the missionary over the hill, and the trader exploring new markets, on entering the European environment the village Kanaka has to understand an ambience which is not only much wider than that to which he has been accustomed, but is one in which his largest and most important set of categories—those of kinship which imply moral obligation—is almost useless. But he manages. And he does so largely by ignoring the implications of his new environment. The categories he already has themselves predicate particular attitudes and relationships, and by doing so tend to preclude the recognition of others. He creates for himself 'brothers', 'sisters', and 'friends' firmly based on the expectations of such categories in his village. Similarly, all Europeans tend to be understood in terms of the relationships he is already familiar with.

But if a Kanaka tends to recreate his village in the town, and if there are, in fact, too many different kinds of individuals and too few ways of distinguishing them, it is a further step yet from understanding what white men are and do to appreciating why they do what they do. Particular experiences tend to contradict the teaching of Europeans and bear out the advice given by other Kanakas. Manam islanders, for example,

[1] When first I arrived in Tangu I was placed, first, as an administrative officer; then as somebody belonging to the mission; then as a trader. The expectations in relation to each category were clearly defined. Tangu tested each category in turn and, as it became evident that they would not fit, resorted to proper names and kinship appellations.

feel that white men are habitual liars and hypocrites. White men say much the same of Manam islanders. And, in their own lights, both sides are quite right. Both white men and Manam islanders would agree that without hypocrisy, without the 'white lie' and conventional courtesy where dislike is felt, social life would become impossible. The difficulty is that the situations which call for a conventional hypocrisy among Manam islanders are not those which call for precisely the same technique in any one kind of European. What might be obnoxious to a white man might be culturally enjoined for a Manam islander and *vice versa*. On the whole Kanakas are anxious to know about white men because they cannot do otherwise than deal in European ideas and ideals when thinking about their own future. So often, however, white men—particularly administrative officers and missionaries— are excluded from the dreams of Utopia. These are the men whom Kanakas encounter most, who teach an ideal and do not always appear to Kanakas to act it out, who so often seem to say one thing and do another. Why?

It seems pedantic to try to explain to Kanakas that all men do this; that they have not enough words to understand Europeans; that the misunderstandings are mutual. But if misunderstandings are recognizably part of the educative struggle towards a mutual accord, or decisive rupture, they are certainly not the sum.

Given what we know today, many Kanakas would say, and being free from interfering Europeans—who keep adding new knowledge and new uncertainties to life—some kinds of moral unity might be achieved. Yet, in a Cargo movement the new dispensation, in which is involved the creation of the new man, is contingent upon repentance and atonement. And the middle term separating repentance from atonement—which in its literal sense directly implies the fusion into a unity—is guilt. If atonement is to be attained by a full and complete repentance, both are conditional on removing guilt. Guilt is the barrier. To make a true repentance a knowledge of all transgressions is necessary, and if a full atonement is not

37

achieved it is clear, within the logic, that a full and complete repentance has not been made: there is a residue of transgression which composes the guilt. It follows that if repentance is to be made—and made not only by an individual but by a community acting together—then the residue of transgression must be discovered. The guilt must be laid.

In the aftermath of a Cargo cult guilt continues to find expression both in myths and in explicit statement. Tangu, for example, said they were 'dirty' and 'unworthy'. There is also a typical ambivalence. In general Tangu dislike white men, but they wish they resembled them. Tangu know that white men are more competent in the new environment than they are themselves, but when they admit it, with bowed head, seated, the initial submissiveness burgeons into passionate denial, upright, body tensed and balanced on toes, adze lifted to strike. Just as a successful Cargo cult would signal a complete atonement, that complete transcendence of the present situation, so a failure demonstrates at most only a partial atonement, a partial repentance, and the presence of a residue of wrongdoing. The cult has failed in its explicit object because of guilt, or, the failure of the cult is evidence of the existence of guilt. And because the unities being sought through a Cargo cult are not actually achieved it seems sensible, and logical, to tackle the guilt and make another attempt.

The guilts Tangu carry around with them in the traditional spheres of their life are known, accepted, and lived with. The presence of evil in men is accounted for in several myths and stories, and in daily life the evil man is thought of as a sorcerer and a sorcerer is thought of as an evil man. They cause sickness in others, kill them, steal, commit adultery, and generally cause trouble in the community. But sorcerers are not considered to act at random or capriciously. There is purpose behind what they do, a purpose intimately related to what the victim has been doing or has done; and Tangu, like other Kanakas, have conventional procedures for dealing with sorcerers and their victims. Tangu first resort to confession. Confession of one's misdeeds should satisfy a sorcerer who is not wholly intent on a killing, and it certainly should satisfy a man who is hiring a sorcerer to make another sick. Then they have divinatory and identification techniques which will give them the name of the sorcerer and enable them to kill him or force him to stop his wicked ways; they may resort to feud; and both victim and sorcerer may be satisfied by an exchange of valuables. But if, in the large majority of instances, Tangu are able to regulate the activities of sorcerers, it does not stop them from remarking how wonderful life would be if there were no sorcerers. They know full well that such thoughts are whimsy, and that ever since the gods became men mankind has been devilled with sorcerers. Nevertheless, even though the activities of sorcerers are ultimately beyond their control, Tangu are able to live with them because, knowing what sorcerers do and why they do those things they have developed conventional procedures for dealing with them.

Tangu also remark, in much the same mood, how much better things would be if there were no white men to harass them. The difference is that while Tangu know about sorcerers, how they came to exist, what their methods are, and how to deal with them, they cannot account for the quality of their relationships with white men—who might, as indeed they did during the Japanese war, disappear as suddenly as they came.

Like sorcerers, white men beget trouble. But neither Tangu nor Manam islanders have yet found a completely satisfactory way of heading off the troubles that white men make. In Tangu recalcitrant sorcerers who act outside the conventions which control them are beaten up, exiled, or killed. White men, on the other hand, so it would seem to Tangu, make their own laws which Tangu have to obey, give their own orders, pay what wages they choose, and imprison when they feel like it. Not only do white men appear to be all-powerful and immune, they are scarcely impressed by what Tangu have to offer. They cannot be pleased, importuned, or even corrupted directly. Both in Tangu and in Manam accepting the gift is to accept the man; and repayment of the gift is of paramount importance. Tangu and Manam islanders accept

European goods and ideas but they are unable to accept the men who have brought them because these same men will not allow themselves to be accepted except exclusively on their own terms. When Kanakas try to repay the gifts of goods and ideas they are either patronized or laughed at. In general white men are neither accessible to, nor appreciative of, native ideas. Kanakas and white men live in different social environments; and white men find it difficult to come down from the pedestal on which their forefathers have placed them. Who shall blame them for not being saints? When an administrative officer, or trader, so forgets himself as to join in a native dance, Kanakas are tremendously pleased. Each is participating in the same activity, and therefore, in that situation, equal beings, parts each of the other. When, on the other hand, Tangu say that white men ought to be thrown into the sea, they are generalizing on typical behaviour and giving white men, in their minds, the same kind of treatment they mete out to their refractory sorcerers.

If Tangu could account for the more typical Europeanized sectors of their lives by an intellectual comprehension they will have made a start in dealing with it. But they cannot yet do so. There are, on the whole, insufficient numbers of mutually accepted conventions in which either group can have relations with each other, or by which their interrelationships might be ordered. 'What is wrong?' Tangu ask. 'Why are we as we are—black, dirty, without learning, without cargo, without power?' Sometime in the past, they say, something went wrong. What went wrong? Who did wrong? If only the transgression could be identified it and its effects might be controlled. If Tangu and Manam islanders are to look forward to the future in confidence they feel they must know what is wrong with the present, and who or what is responsible. They feel themselves held in contumely. And even white men like to find out who or what is to blame when the group with which they identify themselves comes into obloquy.

If Europeans were eliminated from the situation repentance and atonement might be more possible because either might

An ageing manager with his second
wife's family

Confirmed bachelor of Riekitzir
stitching roof thatch

An 'informal' feast in the garden

An ambitious young manager with his first-born

be achieved within conventions having common consent. Presently, while white men are there, co-operation to consent is impracticable. And it seems an easy short cut to exclude them formally from the new dispensation. But in fact the reality is otherwise. Cargo, a complex notion, is inevitably bound up with Europeans and the things they stand for. In bald and oversimplified terms the problem of Cargo is, first, how to live in an environment which is neither European nor Kanaka, but something *sui generis* compounded of both; and second, how to transcend the division and make the environment an intelligible unity. Despite the efforts of some charismatic figures the part played by cargo in Cargo movements hammers home the moral that the objectives of Cargo cannot be achieved by excluding white men. Further, as we shall see in a later chapter, the myth-dream makes it quite clear that the objectives of Cargo can only be achieved with the help of white men. For Kanakas on the ground the problem is to find ways of co-operating with white men, and to persuade white men to co-operate with them. But a prerequisite is laying the guilt. For if all men are guilty Kanakas feel that the present situation demonstrates that they carry more guilt than do white men. Atonement, the passage through conflict to unity, needs the co-operation of both white men and black.

Guilt, and the ambivalent attitudes which derive from it, is never forgotten by the charismatic figure in the van of a Cargo movement. As a practical politician he must play upon the reservoirs of passion that the situation engenders. But in doing so, in excluding and inveighing against white men, he disqualifies himself from succeeding in what is supposed to be his ultimate object. Though he may be able to see quite clearly the mistakes of the past, and though he may look forward from the present and discern a future invisible to his fellows, he must continue to excite the energies begotten by the dilemmas he is setting out to solve. Nevertheless, he remains the man who can articulate parts of the myth-dream, reducing them to a series of precepts which have the advantage of clarity even though they may be difficult to execute. He and

41

his disciples, who can help with the realities of social organization and elaboration of precepts, have it in their hands to channel the zeal of their followers—providing that what they say and do accords with certain conventions and meets community expectations. In Tangu the internal political values preclude the exercise of authority, or outright leadership, by a single individual Tangu. But they are willing to accept outsiders in such roles. Thus, in Tangu, no hero emerged from within: he came from outside. In Manam, on the other hand, where the political system allocates power and authority to specific ranking persons, the living hero conforms to type and is the child of his people. That is, though the hero must necessarily be out of the run of ordinary men, both in himself and what he says he is not untrammelled by community prejudices.

If the desire for direct access to European goods reflects an economic situation it is only a part of the meaning of Cargo. The greater portion lies in the connotations. Some Kanakas would seem to believe that cargo can be made to appear out of thin air by a mystical ordinance, and the most sceptical are sure that the ability to make cargo requires a *nous* which can only be divinely inspired. Just how far do such beliefs go? What would happen if, by some strange chance, the cargo arrived while the rites were in train? All Kanaka communities have very carefully particularized ways in which wealth should be redistributed: kin and political relationships are intimately associated. Yet nowhere in the available literature is there any indication of how the cargo would be distributed were it to arrive. The usual answer is that since there would be plenty for all the need for distributive arrangements lapses. But is this really so? Would not a people who really believed that the cargo was coming make arrangements for its distribution? After all, Kanakas are expert business men: they spend their lives trading, exchanging, bargaining, and redistributing their wealth. Supposing by some oversight there were plenty of razor blades but only two axes—who would take the axes? Supposing the first consignment was a small one—what then?

Would a first consignment be considered sacred? Would such a symbol of outright success be consumed or enshrined? What would, or could a people such as Tangu do with their cargo when they got it?

The fact that so many questions which can trip off the tongue do not find answers in the evidence available suggests that they may be wrong questions. Or that the assumptions about Cargo which imply that clear answers exist are mistaken. In the context of a cult cargo cannot be discussed as though it were a superior order of yams: that is just what cargo is not. Cargo movements are not like stones in a jeweller's shop, hard, clear, each facet sharply defined; nor are they regular institutions such as marriage, or a council of elders, within terms of which conflicts may develop and resolve themselves. They involve just those antitheses which have no institutional channels; and their range of effectiveness depends on the variety of energies living individuals breathe into them. Their vigour derives from roughness of thought, not clarity; from convictions which, though downright at times, are born of uncertainty and cannot be permanent or fixed; from notions that have not been submitted by the participants to analysis and test; from myth-dreams which no individual could shape by himself, and to which all have added their mite. Items of belief are temporary articles of faith, passionately grasped, held firmly for a while, and loosed as impulsively. For most of the time there is little common consent. Individuals seek where they will in a ferment of experience for kernels of truth, the myth-dream their guide. Mutually contradictory propositions, separately derived from and valid for the different social environments and symbolic systems, may be held in the same moment and situation—producing acute strain and perplexity. Then, quite suddenly, from the stomach and out of a myriad confusions, consent and a hero merge into an instant of time. Almost as swiftly the moment is lost in its history. A function of anomy,[1] the essence of Cargo cults is that they cannot wholly be reduced to a logic derived from stability and order: they have a logic

---

[1] But see *infra*, p. 274.

of their own. Themselves creative of new forms the old law cannot contain them.

Tangu and Manam islanders are as hard-headed, rational, and emotionally tough as any that live. If they thought Cargo cults were mere folly they would not keep the notion of Cargo alive in a myth-dream. To base analysis on a distinction between the rational and irrational or non-rational is to take up an extreme ethnocentric if not egocentric position, and to ignore what is fundamental. As we have seen, access to quantities of manufactured goods as such outside the context of a cult is pointless. Though 'cargo' refers to manufactured goods, it means something quite different.

CHAPTER II

The People

[i]

To appreciate the Kanaka point of view, and to be aware of the kind of responsibility that is put on the shoulders of administrative officers and missionaries—who must, if they are to initiate changes and a new way of life, first select what they consider to be wrong or mistaken, and then set about persuading their charges that they are wrong or mistaken, and finally accept the consequences of what they do—the problem of synthesis, of grasping new ideas, mastering new techniques, and working out organizational means, must be seen through the interpretative lens formed by their habits of daily life, and their own notions of leadership and social organization which are inevitably coloured by their relations with Europeans.

We may make a start with Tangu.[1]

Tangu are hunters, gardeners, and gatherers. Generally non-literate, though a few who are Christians can write a little Pidgin English, the total population of some two thousand souls is distributed through approximately thirty settlements of various sizes situated on the spurs and crests of a relatively high, closely bunched, jumble of ridges.[2] Some settlements are composed of one homestead only, others of three or four, and yet others of between twenty and thirty homesteads. In each, houses built of forest woods, on stilts, walled with strips of

[1] Because we ourselves cannot but appreciate our own history except in the light of our present circumstances, this brief outline of Tangu life as it is today precedes their history which is taken up in Chapter IV. If the reader wishes he may skip this and the following chapter and come back to them later.

[2] In approximately 4° 25′ South, 144° 55′ East.

bark stitched together and thatched with palm fronds, are sited on either side of an open space used for dancing and feasting. Coconut palms and areca nut or betel palms fringe

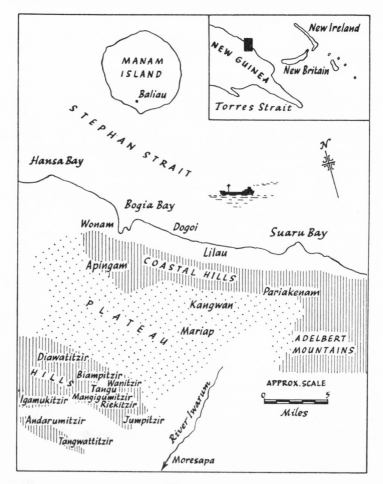

Figure 3
Tangu and Manam Island

the perimeter. Beyond lies the bush, jungle or secondary forest.

Tangu are divided into four named neighbourhoods,

46

Wanitzir, Biampitzir, Mangigumitzir, and Riekitzir.[1] Each of them contains one or more major settlements and also several of much smaller size. Wanitzir, nearest to the coast, on the east side, is composed of five medium sized and compact settlements which are sited on a high escarpment looking out over grassy downs rolling to the sea. Some smaller hamlets are sited on the lower slopes. Biampitzir, west along the curve of the ridge from Wanitzir, consists of rather smaller and more dispersed clusters of homesteads disposed around the highest feature of the region. A little further south-west along the Biampitzir ridge is Mangigumitzir, a long straggle of contiguous hamlets. Finally, Riekitzir, a collection of three large and many smaller settlements tucked into a maze of ridges, lies south across the ravine from Biampitzir and generally south-west of Wanitzir.

Tangu neighbourhoods are not organized entities: they are territorial aggregations, parts of a whole, the members of which enjoy certain minor distinctive cultural features. But, for administrative purposes, a large settlement together with a number of smaller ones is organized into a local unit and placed under a Luluai, a Tultul, and a Doctor boy, each of whom is responsible to sub-District headquarters at Bogia. Wanitzir is divided into three such administrative communities, Riekitzir into two, and Biampitzir and Mangigumitzir each constitute one. Mission influence is exerted through a missionary priest (S.V.D.), who lives in his station centrally situated on the borders of Wanitzir and Biampitzir, and through catechists, responsible to the priest, resident in each of the neighbourhoods. Communications within Tangu, or from Tangu to the coast or into the hinterland, are by bush-path, on foot. And though the going is rough many settlements are within a few minutes of another, most are within fairly easy walking distance of several others, and the distance between those furthest apart may be spanned within three hours.[2]

[1] The suffixes -itzir, or -tzir, may be translated as 'neighbourhood', 'the people of', or 'those who live in the vicinity of'.

The populations of the four neighbourhoods are, respectively, 650, 350, 340, and 660.

[2] If we take the areas including Tangu, Diawatitzir, Igamukitzir,

Culturally, Tangu belong to an enclave of peoples settled in the hills of the Bogia region, inland from the coastal ranges and succeeding plateaux, and between the Ramu, flowing north-west, and the Iwarum, flowing south. Superficially, Tangu dress much as their outside neighbours do: the men in a beaten bark breech-clout held in a cane-work belt, the women in pandanus fibre skirts. Only the practised eye will note the differences that are peculiar to Tangu and the further niceties that pertain to a neighbourhood or settlement within Tangu. In each neighbourhood there are dances which the members of the neighbourhood regard as peculiarly their own, but the popular dances are common to all Tangu who are, anyway, always eager to import from abroad other dances that may take their fancy. Some myths are told more often, or are better known, in one neighbourhood rather than another, but again, much of their content has common ground with the myths told among neighbouring peoples. The slit-gong, a hollowed out section of tree trunk which is struck sharply with the end of a wooden wand to make sound signals, is common to all the peoples of the region. Some of the signals made in a neighbourhood are intelligible to outsiders, but the majority are mutually intelligible only to those who live in the four neighbourhoods.

Though there are differences of tone and accent from neighbourhood to neighbourhood, all Tangu speak the same language. Westwards into the hinterland, in Tangwattitzir, Igamukitzir, Andarumitzir, and a little further afield, live peoples who speak variants of the Tangu language. But they do not regard themselves, nor are they regarded by others, as Tangu. North of Tangu, in Diawatitzir, or Dimuk, the people speak a language structurally similar to Tangu but equipped with a quite different vocabulary. South to Jumpitzir, and towards the coast, the languages are entirely dissimilar. Many Tangu can speak Pidgin English, and in each neighbourhood there are one or two experts who can *tonim tok*,

Andarumitzir, Tangwattitzir, and Jumpitzir, Tangu themselves account for some 27 per cent. of the total population in an area which is but 9 per cent. of the whole on a plan projection.

speak and understand the neighbouring 'foreign' tongue.

Ascendant genealogies proliferate from Tangu as the spokes of a wheel from the hub. They may be followed through on the ground from one Tangu community to another and beyond into adjoining territory. Marriages tend to be mostly between members of the same neighbourhood within Tangu, rather less between members of different neighbourhoods, and much less between Tangu and outsiders. Nevertheless, actual and putative kin ties reach out far beyond the territorial boundaries of Tangu. Within Tangu itself one may distinguish relatively small groups with characteristic patrilineal, matrilineal, double unilineal, and ambi- and bi-lineal forms of organization. Yet, if such differences affect the way in which claims to land are phrased in various parts of Tangu, the group that works the land, the means they use, and the ends to which their labour is directed are common values. Rules of incest have lapsed to an equal extent all over Tangu, and though the norms of inheritance and tracing ancestries may differ, everywhere in Tangu the brother-sister relationship emerges as the most significant.

Tangu families, composing households, make new gardens each year, either from the forest on the west side, or from the grasslands eastward. They cultivate yams, a sub-species called *mami*, bananas, sugar-cane, pit-pit cane, tobacco, shrubs whose leaves are valued as relishes, and sweet potatoes, maize, beans, tomatoes, pumpkins, cucumbers, and other vegetables whose seeds were originally introduced by missionaries or returned labourers. Out in the forest, or across the downs, Tangu hunt pigs, cassowaries, lizards, and bush rats: there also they gather wild leaves, nuts, and fruits and plant breadfruit trees, sago palms, and areca nut groves in favoured places. Close to each of the major settlements in a neighbourhood is a plot of land given over to the cultivation of rice, a cash crop which was introduced by the administration and which is worked under the direction of Luluai and Tultul by the members of the community for whom these officials are responsible. Many of the young men go away to the coast to work as contract labourers for cash.

Day by day families go out into their gardens or into the bush to hunt. Dressed in a breech-clout and armed with a spear, or adze, and axe, the husband leads the way. His wife, or wives, and their children follow behind. Arrived, the husband sits down for a quiet smoke while wife and daughters bend to their work. Sons take it easily, pretending to be men. Often, for gardens are widely scattered, and some are at a fair distance from the settlements, a family will elect to stay one or several nights in the garden shelter or hunting lodge rather than set out on the long walk home. Otherwise, families return to their settlements late in the afternoon, burdened with food, to cook the evening meal, eat, smoke, chew betel, and gossip. Generally, only at dusk, or on festive occasions, or at weekends when members of the community are supposed to be at the disposal of the Luluai, Tultul, and Doctor boy to work in the rice field, dig latrines, or clean the paths approaching the settlement, is any substantial proportion of a large settlement present.

For most of the year Tangu have plenty of food. The shift from old garden site to the new takes some months to complete, and crops are planted—and therefore harvested—in an ordered succession. By the time the last yams have been pulled out of the old garden, taros are beginning to ripen in the new. When the taros are finished, bananas—of which there are numerous varieties, some requiring to be cooked— are ready; then *mami* begins to ripen, and after *mami* the more highly prized yams are ready for eating. Sago flour, pit-pit cane, and breadfruit are also fitted to the cycle. Thus, although they overlap, it is possible to divide the Tangu year —as they do themselves—into the pit-pit season, the sago season, the taro season, the banana season, the *mami* season, and the yam season. In spite of this succession of ripening crops, however, there is a period of possible dearth from late November to the middle of January. Wanitzir suffers most because the land there is too dry to support much sago. The remaining three neighbourhoods, on the other hand, have adequate resources of sago and they ride the dearth quite easily—using their advantage for trading with Wanitzir.

In all their economic activities, in hunting, clearing the garden site, fencing it, cultivating crops, building houses and lodges, carving slit-gongs, hand-drums, food bowls, and wooden hafts, fashioning 'grass' skirts, bark-cloth breech-clouts, string bags, and cane work waist-belts, anklets, and wristlets, Tangu use traditional tools: the spear, adze, axe, knife, digging stick, and tomahawk. In the old days before the European came to New Guinea cutting edges were made of stone hafted to wooden handles by binding with cane. Today, the same tools have iron or steel cutting edges. In addition, there are a variety of bush and hunting knives, and a few saws, hammers, and nails which Tangu have obtained either by bartering or with the cash they earn by going away to the coast on contract labour.

Though iron and finished steel tools have replaced the old stone tools, there has been very little substantial change either in the techniques of work, or in the purposes for which the tools are used. Old men say that the steel bladed spear kills pigs more certainly than the old stone bladed spear; forest trees take a few days rather than a week or so to fell; a steel bladed adze is more efficient than a stone one. Only a few digging sticks are pointed with iron, and in truth the difference between one that is shod and one that is not is small. Iron nails rust very quickly and give way without warning—cane lashings are more trusty; and in the circumstances prevailing an axe or adze or knife is more useful and more efficient than a saw. And while one cannot say that the time saved by having more efficient tools has been put to any other specific purpose, it may be that in co-operative tasks stone tools implied more people working together for longer periods. However, exchange and trading relationships still occur in each neighbourhood across the brother and sister link, between households where the wife in the one is regarded as the sister to the husband in another. And since each neighbourhood produces goods and commodities which the others lack or require in greater quantities, economic ends are satisfied by inter-marriages across neighbourhood boundaries.

Wanitzir and the hither, neighbouring parts of Biampitzir

51

enjoy a near monopoly in the region of the manufacture of clay cooking pots. Made by the 'coil' method, sun-dried and roughly fired, most of the pots find their way into other Tangu settlements across brother and sister relationships against tobacco, string bags, sago, yams, and now in recent years, cash. The remainder goes to outsiders for cash and also for goods. Tangu need hunting dogs, iron, salt, and sometimes pigs for *ad hoc* feasts: their own clay pots, string bags, areca nuts, tobacco and sago are in demand in neighbouring areas. Manufactured knick-knacks bought from the local mission store are an attraction. Mostly, external trading relationships remain fairly constant. Individuals, either through a marriage, or by finding a common ancestor or ancestress, make for themselves a network of 'brothers' and 'sisters' in the surrounding villages through whom they can obtain the goods they need. Gradually, however, the traditional necessity to combine a trading relationship with a kin relationship is beginning to lapse as the opportunities for occasional, chance deals increase.

Tangu lies astride one of the main routes from the coast to the hinterland, and Wanitzir particularly is well placed to control the more valuable traffic going inland. Kanakas from the hinterland, from the coast, and even from as far away as Manam island, come to Tangu in transit, to trade, to exchange news. Every Sunday Tangu from all four neighbourhoods repair to the mission to attend Mass. Pagans accompany Christians. Mass over, people stop awhile, gossip with friends and relations, make arrangements, and, if they have a few pennies they buy a little something from the trade store. Catechists report progress to the missionary, collect their stipends, quarry out any relevant news from the coast, and pass it on to their friends.

Though Tangu are merely a part of a much larger cultural unit including Diawatitzir, Igamukitzir, Andarumitzir, Tangwattitzir, Jumpitzir, and to a certain extent Mariap and Kangwan, in themselves they form a reasonably compact and interdependent social and economic community. The mission, drawing together the Christians of each neighbourhood into a religious community, and an economic focus for all, has done much to strengthen interior links. Rather more important, however, is the fact that Tangu express the values they hold in common through a political institution known to themselves as *br'ngun'guni* which, though found in the same form among surrounding peoples, is virtually exclusively participated in by Tangu, in Tangu, irrespective of neighbourhood or settlement affiliation. Tangu form a polity. They feel their own unity and relative exclusiveness, and they insist upon it. They articulate it in the phrase, '*Nai 'gunwan! Nai kam ungunwan!* We are one! We are one tongue (people)!' Nevertheless, on the cultural level, and being empirically minded, Tangu are always prepared to adopt strange activities and ideas and substitute them for their own if they appear to serve better. Tangu are self-evidently proud of being Tangu though little is actually required of them as such today. They are individualists, suspicious of each other and more so of strangers. The atmosphere in which they live is obstinate and closely textured: courtesies are clearly stamped with reservation. A man's primary loyalty tends to be to himself, and then to his immediate family, his household: active allegiances to other kinds of group follow behind. Yet, coming more and more to the fore, especially so when the context or occasion includes a white man, Tangu are wont to identify themselves with all Kanakas in New Guinea, as black-skinned men in opposition to white-skinned men. '*Nai Kanakatzir!*' they say with some vehemence. 'We are Kanakas, people of New Guinea!'

THE DISTRIBUTIVE SYSTEM

In Tangu the processes of production and distribution, based on a subsistence economy, are rooted in a traditional but still firmly held division of labour between the sexes which requires that any efficient working group shall be based upon males and females in partnership. Men are accustomed to the more aggressive kinds of work. They cut down trees, make garden fences, build houses, dig, plant, and hunt. Women, generally submissive and hard working, carry out the duller, more laborious work of weeding the garden, carrying produce, cooking, drawing water, clearing underbrush, making string bags, and looking after the children. A man feels it degrading to weed, carry, cook, or draw water. His traditional role, which he sees no reason to relinquish, is to direct the work of his household, and to remain unencumbered, ready with the spear. Currently, since warfare has ceased, a woman can do some of the man's work and *vice versa*. But, however strapping they are, women cannot for long survive without the help of a man, and men are ashamed to do the work associated with women. Tangu say that a man must have a wife else how would he eat, and that a woman must have a husband else how would she live. Sometimes middle-aged widows are looked after and protected by their mature, unmarried sons; or brother and sister will help each other; and a daughter will do the woman's work for a widower father. Nevertheless, such and other partnerships are regarded as makeshifts. The ideal basis for a working team remains the marital union at the centre of a household.

Everywhere in Tangu, the basic and definitive social and economic unit is the household which, with the married couple at the centre, normally includes natural and adopted children, an aged parent of either spouse, and, perhaps, a husband's brother or wife's sister. Where a man has more than one wife, each, with her children, forms a parti-household dependent on the husband they have in common. Households are commensal and co-operative units: the claims on persons, property and movables adhering to each of the individuals composing the households are put to work for it; members garden, hunt, and gather as a unit; when youths go away to the coast on contract labour the goods and earnings they bring back with them are put at the disposal of the household; within the household mutual obligations cannot normally be put in issue before an assembly of other households. When a son or daughter marries, however, he or she leaves the natal household to help form the nucleus of a new and independent household. Subtly, sibling relationships change. Though considered most unseemly and improper, brothers may then dispute in public assembly.

For a variety of economic tasks, as well as on ritual and festive occasions, households co-operate with one another. For administrative purposes, when cultivating the rice field, digging latrines, or cleaning the village, Luluai, Tultul, and Doctor boy attempt to recruit to the labour as many households as they can physically lay hands on, or cajole into willing co-operation. The work is unpopular, and most households try to slip off through the bush to their own gardens. In general Tangu feel that the labour involved is only worthwhile when an administrative officer on patrol is expected—in order to avoid punishment or wordy castigation. The rice can only be sold in Bogia after a long walk to the coast, and having sold it there remains the problem of how to distribute and share the profit. For thus far Tangu have not developed a method of fairly reaping the rewards of work done on a total community basis. Christian households are expected to co-operate under a catechist or mission boss boy for such occasional tasks as building and maintaining chapels and school houses; and they can usually be relied on to do so voluntarily though from time to time the missionary will shoot a pig and feast the workers, or make a distribution of cloth or other small goods. In such traditional activities as house-building, clearing and fencing garden sites, providing feasts, making food exchanges, and dancing, on the other hand, households combine with each other in terms of their own internal sectionalisms.

Normally, as a matter of course, each household has trading or exchange relationships with those households formed by the married men who stand as brothers to the wife, and those in which the wives stand as sisters to the husband.[1] Where the relationship between the spouses of a household can be expressed as a brother-sister relationship those households are, or might potentially be, in a trading or exchange relationship.

[1] The relationships are classificatory—what a European might distinguish as first, second, or third cousins. Ultimately, 'brothers' and 'sisters' are men and women of one's own generation—but not exclusively. They may be 'spouses', 'possible spouses', 'sweethearts', or 'friends', for example.

Conversely, where a trading or exchange relationship exists between households, those households are described as standing to each other as brother to sister. The co-operative relationship is similarly described as existing between siblings of the same sex. The households formed by sisters, or brothers, should be in a co-operative relationship; and where households are in a co-operative relationship the husbands are regarded as brothers and the wives as sisters. In the old days, before the turn of the century, there was probably a much greater degree of congruence between the kin and economic relationship, and combinations of households almost certainly coincided with the corporate groups which were recruited under particularized criteria of kin affiliation and residence. Today, however, partly perhaps as a result of having more efficient tools—which makes stable combinations not so important a matter—and partly for other reasons,[1] households come together into temporary alliances not necessarily because the husbands or wives concerned are paternal or maternal siblings, but because it is economically and politically advantageous to be allied with households whose husbands are managers, men who are renownedly productive, hard working, shrewd, and persuasive. That is, unusually for a primitive or generally non-literate people, kin allegiances do not necessarily reflect political or quasi-political unities.

Though kin relationships and residential contiguity certainly do play a part in the formation of these alliances, and though as a model of the way in which households should co-operate, exchange, and trade with one another the kinship idiom is always used to describe the economic relationship, actual physiological conformity with the expressed kin relationship is by no means invariable. Those who co-operate with each other are behaving as brothers, or sisters, should: therefore they are described as brothers or sisters. And those who trade with each other, or make exchanges, are behaving as though they were linked in the brother-sister relationship: so they are thought of and described as being related as brother to sister. If a certain kind of economic relationship is

---

[1] *Vide infra*, p. 73.

implied in a kin relationship, it is also true that a kin relationship is implied in an economic: the two kinds of relationship belong together.

Households gather leaves and nuts in the forest, hunt, and cultivate their gardens as separate, independent units; and as such they also participate in kin and economic occasions by trading and exchanging across an actual or putative brother and sister link. They are brought together for work on certain tasks by the administration and mission, and they help each other either as, or as though they were, brothers or sisters. But for feasts, feasting exchanges, dances, and participation in *br'ngun'guni*, the political activity, households co-operate and exchange in a more significant way. They behave politically, they ally themselves to managers. For their part managers create co-operative groups, bring husbands and wives together as brothers and sisters, by their ability to persuade, and through their reputations for industry in the field. Normally, in each Tangu community—which does not necessarily coincide with a mission, or administrative unit under Luluai, Tultul, and Doctor boy—alliances are formed at the beginning of each horticultural cycle so that those households participating in feasting and dancing exchanges form two approximately equivalent groups in mutual opposition to each other. Not all the households within a community necessarily take part: rather is the community defined in any one year by the households which do co-operate in making feasting and dancing exchanges. The core of the community thus defined may consist of men and women in the requisite categories of siblingship for co-operating and exchanging, but the majority are those who are persuaded into, or see some kind of advantage in, joining one or other co-operative group or alliance. Managers, having formed the core of their co-operative groups, have the further tasks of persuading these others to join them, and aligning themselves with other managers. And the end to which these energies are channelled is a political occasion: a feasting and dancing exchange in which *br'ngun'guni* takes place.

Finally, besides co-operating, exchanging, and trading with

one another, particular pairs of households may be what is known as *mngwotngwotiki*—an agreement by free and mutual consent neither to trade, nor to exchange, nor co-operate. In its substance the meaning of *mngwotngwotiki* could be translated as 'equal', 'equivalent', 'all-square', 'unconstrained to obligation'.[1] Since in Tangu personal, social, and politico-economic rivalries, friendships,[2] and hostilities are developed and worked out through food exchanges as well as in the co-operative activity, households which are *mngwotngwotiki* are, in theory, morally or truly equivalent[3] with one another and not in rivalrous or co-operative social, economic, or political relationships. Nor, so long as they are *mngwotngwotiki*, may any pair of households take any action in respect to each other which would imply either the co-operative or exchange relationship. If a member of either one or other household of a pair which is *mngwotngwotiki* does act in such a way as to preclude the moral equivalence between them, the two households come into an exchange or co-operative relationship and the peculiar relationship between them lapses. On the whole it is when the underlying emotional relationship between the husbands and wives of two households which are *mngwotngwotiki* develops so as to preclude a true moral equivalence between them that little time is lost in allowing the relationship to lapse, and co-operating or exchanging with one another. In turn, the maturation of the emotional relationship tends to hinge on other, economic and political developments within the community as a whole.

Each household in Tangu has some kind of theoretical contact with every other household: it can trace an actual or putative kin relationship, or a connexion through institutionalized friendship.[4] On the average, however, no household has regular relationships with more than about forty others. Of these ten to fifteen, on the peripheries of the local community, will be in dormant or potential exchange or co-operative

---

[1] Dealt with further *infra*, p. 81.

[2] Friendship in Tangu is institutionalized. *Vide:* Friendship in Tangu, *Oceania*, Vol. XXVII, No. 3, March 1957, p. 177.

[3] Dealt with further *infra*, p. 83.   [4] See note 2, above.

relationships, and from time to time, for a variety of purposes and as occasion demands, a particular relationship may be invoked. Within the range of between twenty-five and thirty households relationships are more active and definite. At the other extreme, during any one horticultural cycle, three to five households will be in a well defined co-operative relationship, and these will combine with other similar co-operative groups—to make a total of anything between twelve and twenty households—to make feasting and dancing exchanges with a group of roughly equivalent size. One, two, or three pairs of households in a local community will be *mngwotngwotiki*.

SORCERY

The problem of evil in Tangu, particularly the evil in men, is posed by the several meanings attached to the word *ranguma*. The word is here translated as 'sorcerer' though a more accurate rendering in many contexts would be 'witch', 'criminal', 'crook', 'scapegoat', or simply 'nasty and unwholesome fellow'. 'When [the] sorcerer came into the world,' Tangu say, quoting a myth, 'he was the last man out of the hole. He brought with him poison and [the means to cause] sickness and death. He was arrogant and proud, and proclaimed that all things were his.'

A sorcerer is a man, not a woman; almost always a particular man at a specified time, less often a particular man all the time, and though the plural may be used generically only rarely today does it connote an organized group of men.[1] A man may be thought of as a sorcerer but only in certain situations does the thought become explicit: in other circumstances he may be regarded as a hard worker, a thoughtful father, or a careful husband. Yet though a man may not be identified as a sorcerer the label itself connotes a particular kind of person. He is first an odd or eccentric fellow, a non-conformist, a broody and surly man who is always something

---

[1] In former days sorcerers might be organized into groups or gangs— when they had an almost sacerdotal role.

of a stranger, outside the social circle. And the more a man is a stranger, both socially and morally, the more likely he is to be a sorcerer. The Tangu word for stranger is *rangama*, so close to *ranguma* that the more cynical like to play on the words, equating stranger with sorcerer. A sorcerer is habitually thought of as a tall, bony man, with red-rimmed eyes and the splay hand and long fingers of a strangler. Not all red-eyed men are sorcerers, but one should be careful in dealing with such men. A secretive, churlish man is quickly suspected of being a sorcerer—Why else, Tangu ask, should he not feel himself free in the company of others? Lonely men with grudges to nurse tend to brood over their fires, smoking, and their eyes become bloodshot: such men, Tangu say, are surely dangerous. A sorcerer is a thief, not one who seizes the opportunity to pick up an axe carelessly left lying, but the sort who is prepared to break open and enter a hut when the owner is away. Unlike the common adulterer who shares his wrong-doing with the woman, and who is willing to shoulder the responsibilities which may flow from the act, a sorcerer deliberately, with intent to do harm, lures a good wife into his arms. Only a sorcerer could, or would, intentionally and maliciously cause sickness in another or initiate a killing outside open warfare or feud. A sorcerer has within him what others have not: both the desire and the ability to do such things, either for his own ends, or on behalf of those who may have his desires but not his abilities.

The means a sorcerer uses may be mystical or pragmatic or a mixture of both: he may use charms, spells, gestures, actual poisons to be found in the bush, strangulation, or the spear. But because he is a man a sorcerer is vulnerable: he may be speared, clubbed, beaten up, or persuaded to make restitution and compensation. Nevertheless, a sorcerer is feared, especially at night when counter action is difficult; and women and children who cannot in any case retaliate themselves are considered to be particularly vulnerable. In the daytime a sorcerer may hide near the gardens or walk in the bush on the lookout for unaccompanied women and children. At night he is supposed to creep into the environs of a settlement—and he may crawl under the floorboards of a hut to entice the women-folk out. A prudent man whose wife or daughters are not sleeping well, or who hears a rustle under his hut, thrusts his spear down through gaps in the flooring. No man walks abroad after nightfall, not even to answer a call of nature, without a light or a weapon. To be without a light is sugges-tive of covert designs, and having a light is both evidence of good intentions as well as an aid to seeing a sorcerer and so being able to retaliate if attacked.

For example, one evening, towards dusk, some girls and small boys were playing near the perimeter of the village. One of the girls thought she saw someone lurking in the long grass about thirty yards off—'Who's there?' she shouted.

The others stopped their play and looked out over the grass in silence. Then, 'Sorcerer!' they screamed.

A man who was sitting close by immediately leapt to his feet, grasped a spear, and sprinted into the grass. Other men and youths joined him. They searched but could find no one. They declared that either the sorcerer had made good his escape, or that the girl had been imagining things.

If there had been a man in the grass he would have been beaten up or killed. Good men, innocent men, just do not prowl round the edges of a village at dusk. Bad men, men up to some mischief, sorcerers, do. The men who dashed off into the grass to deal with the suspected sorcerer were not to know they would not find anybody. Since it was dusk the odds were on the side of the many against one. Had it been full night, however, few men would have stirred: the odds would have been heavily in favour of the sorcerer. There are men in Tangu, on the other hand, who would have taken the risk. These men specialize in killing sorcerers. They are bold men, skilled in bushcraft, cunning, and with the patience to wait for the right moment to strike. They take their work seriously and they may attain some notoriety. On some nights such men cannot sleep. Their skins become 'hot', or 'creep', and they roam the village keeping watch and ward. They know mystical ways of detecting the approach of a sorcerer, and so, being forewarned, they may ambush and kill him. Such a man is, of course, suspected of being very much like a sorcerer, and some, indeed, are 'retired' sorcerers, men who were once evilly disposed but who have turned over a new leaf, men who can use their knowledge of a sorcerer's methods to counterattack him effectively. Like a sorcerer he has little compunction about killing and he has the ability to do so; unlike a sorcerer he kills to thwart the initiative of an evil man and to defend good men.

The sorcerer killer is not a regular night watchman. He only stands his guard on certain occasions. Tangu expect trouble from a sorcerer when they know that a sorcerer is near; and they expect a visitation from a sorcerer when there is trouble in the village, or when there is likely to be trouble in the village—particularly during a feasting and dancing exchange. The two ideas are associated and work intimately together. A sorcerer means trouble, and when, for example, two men of the village have quarrelled, then Tangu expect a sorcerer. So a guard is set. Normally, villagers prefer to think of the sorcerer as someone coming from outside, from another village or from another neighbourhood, or from outside Tangu altogether. But it is also true that the presence of a sorcerer killer keeping his watch prevents the two men who have quarrelled from surprising each other during the night and doing an irreparable mischief. In this way, too, a quarrel within the village is deflected outside it whilst at the same time effective internal measures are taken to prevent the quarrel from spreading or becoming inflamed.

Few events in Tangu are considered to be accidents in the European sense. They are, mostly, considered to be the results of men's activities. What we would call an 'act of God' is morally irrelevant: it happens, it has to be accepted, its effects may be mitigated. But there can be no retaliation, no positive return to conditions as they were. Thus, when somebody falls sick, or dies, or if there is an earthquake, Tangu ask first not What is responsible? but Who is responsible?[1]

---

[1] After a small earthquake which occurred in Tangu whilst I was there responsibility was first laid on me—Tangu had just told me of their cult activities and it was thought that I might be giving them some kind of sign, retaliatory or congratulatory was not quite clear. Then

And since some events—sickness, death, theft, adultery, wounding insult—continually recur Tangu have developed ways of dealing with them. They tie the label sorcerer to a man. Only a sorcerer will steal in spite of locked doors, so a man who steals in spite of locked doors must be a sorcerer. Only a sorcerer can induce sickness in another, kill in cold blood, or commit adultery in a particular way: therefore a man who does any of these things must be a sorcerer. Sorcerers are criminals because criminals are sorcerers. Further, since Tangu consider that no man is totally exempted from participating in evil, any man might be, or might be like, a sorcerer. Their problem is to find out who is the sorcerer causing this trouble at this time. And actual identification is as urgent as the trouble is serious: if the trouble blows over there is little point in looking any further for the sorcerer. He is no longer being a nuisance. By insisting that a sorcerer is a man, not a concept, Tangu are able to exert a measure of control over what one might be tempted to call the principle of Evil; and because a sorcerer is a man of flesh and blood, a moral being however immorally he may behave, Tangu are able to deal with him in terms of themselves. As an abstraction 'he' could only be dealt with in terms of abstraction. As things are Tangu have the choice of dealing with a sorcerer morally or immorally, boldly, in fear, or charitably.

When a man falls sick he hopes he will be better on the morrow. If he is not he calls in a specialist to see what can be done. But if the specialist fails to effect a cure, if the sick man vomits, suffers from continuing eruptions of boils, cannot eat, has diarrhoea, and begins slowly to waste away—then assuredly a sorcerer is causing the sickness. Having diagnosed the cause of the illness, a sorcerer, the next step is to ask the sick man to make a full and complete confession. Any sickness or accident will make a man or a woman search his or her conscience and confess his or her misdeeds.[1] For no such

it was laid at the door of a man who had just killed a large snake. Finally, it was hazarded that Yali (*vide infra* p. 196) might have been responsible.

[1] To a kinsman, an institutionalized friend, or to an old man who has retired and who is no longer involved in making exchanges.

disability is considered to be wholly an accident or wholly undeserved: a prior transgression is probably responsible. Whether a sickness is considered to flow directly from a wrongdoing,[1] or from defying the powers of a protective spell,[2] the act of confession both expunges and externalizes the guilt of the one, and also, where a spell or human originator is involved, it obliges the other to negative the power of the spell. But once a sickness has been diagnosed as the work of a sorcerer it becomes more and more imperative to identify him and force him to stop his wicked ways. A sorcerer is a man who, typically, may not feel obliged by another's confession—though a man who may be employing a sorcerer to cause the illness is expected to feel so obliged. In making his confession the sick man names those he has wronged—so providing a list of suspects. It is then advisable to wait for a few days: he has made explicit to himself and to others who might be making him sick; and in so far as the sickness is a punishment for prior transgression he has confessed his guilt. His conscience is clear, he does not deserve sickness any more, he ought to get better. He is in a strong moral position to retaliate.

If the sick man does not get better after his confession, but begins slowly to sink, skilled dreamers and sorcerer killers get to work. First suspects are those most strange or distant, a circumstance which usually leads to strained relations between the village of the strongest suspect and the village of the sick man. Trade, travel, and exchanges are held up. In the event of the victim's recovery normal relations are resumed; but if he continues sick relations are likely to be broken off altogether. Since, however, both villages suffer equally from the interruption of normal social and economic intercourse, both communities feel it necessary to bring the trouble between them to an end as soon as possible. Should the sick man die relations are, perforce, resumed in an atmosphere of distinct uneasiness: the search for the guilty party continues, perhaps for several years, until someone admits his guilt—in which case

---

[1] As it does from a sexual misdemeanour.
[2] As may happen to a thief or trespasser.

compensation is made by an exchange of valuables—or until the relatives of the victim, sure of the identity of the sorcerer, or of the man who has hired the sorcerer, either force him to confess, or dispatch him outright; or alternatively, hire another sorcerer to make *him* sick. On the other hand, should the victim remain sick, not dying, it may then be reasoned that because a stranger would not hesitate to kill, the sorcerer responsible must be a fellow villager. Accordingly, the most likely suspect—having regard to the sort of man a sorcerer is, and the pointers provided by the confession—is identified by specialists, dreamers,[1] sought out, accused, and forced to confess. When he does so an exchange of valuables is carried out and the matter is finished. Usually, the sick man then gets better. But if he does not it is clear that someone else apart from the fellow who has confessed is also at work. So the task of trying to identify the guilty man goes on.

When a man supposedly responsible for inducing sickness confesses he gains notoriety, and a certain amount of power. People are afraid of him because he can induce sickness in others. Consequently, a man who confesses once is usually asked or forced to confess on other occasions. Because he has confessed on one occasion he becomes more suspect when other incidents occur. He becomes a known sorcerer, dangerous, but not so dangerous as sorcerers who remain unidentified. The known sorcerer acts within the conventions. He always confesses. He gains by so doing. And if a sick man dies after a known sorcerer has confessed, because it is then assumed that the responsibility for killing has come from elsewhere, the blood of the dead man is not on his head. It is worthwhile confessing before death occurs because by so doing the known sorcerer clears himself of responsibility for the death itself. In this way a man who is known to be a sorcerer remains a member of the community, feared, but healthily respected and treated with a certain magnanimity because he obeys the rules. Often, too, he becomes a scapegoat. He can be induced to confess when attempts to extract a confession from

---

[1] These men claim to be skilled at identifying sorcerers by dreaming about the suspects.

elsewhere would embroil the whole village in troublesome vendettas and reprisals.

The life histories of known sorcerers show that the community plays a large part in forcing them into their role. As a child the known sorcerer was an odd little boy. When children play at identifying and retaliating against a sorcerer the shy, rather uncommunicative boy is chosen to be the sorcerer. Often, his parents are thought to be rather strange, or even suspect; he himself is more than usually silent, retracted into his shell. Frequently, he is the child of a 'mixed', or at the time disapproved, marriage. Later in life, when the children are grown men, the peculiar little boy becomes the queer cuss brooding alone over his fire. Inevitably, suspicions centre around him. In acquiescing to confession the known sorcerer is securing prestige by doing, or claiming to do, evil things. He is a sorcerer because the community thinks he is and because he claims to be one. In dealing generously with such a man the community acknowledges that his being a sorcerer is not wholly his fault. Besides, the existence of known sorcerers does not mean that the consequences of their existence and activities are necessarily bad. The facts that a sick man is expected to confess his misdeeds, and that an exchange of valuables is made, are clear evidence that the sickness is considered to be a retribution which is not undeserved.

When a man begins to have doubts concerning the fidelity of his wife he begins to dream about sorcerers, to suspect their presence, and occasionally to see one. It is difficult for an adulterer to get at his wife in the daytime. She is at work in the gardens, the husband is close at hand, and besides, there are usually others working nearby and he would be seen. The opportunity is lacking. At night, on the other hand, the case is different. Generally, Tangu sleep very soundly. One man, for example, admitted that the sore on his foot was due to a rat which had gnawed it and failed to wake him. He was a well satisfied man sleeping the sleep of the just. In such circumstances, therefore, it is not so very difficult for an adulterous pair to make an assignation at night. But the moment a husband begins to suspect he sleeps less soundly. And as soon as his suspicions are aroused he begins to take precautions against sorcerers. He doesn't necessarily beat his wife because he believes that the sorcerer has rendered her helpless to his advances and charms by the aid of mystical techniques. He does not think of the adulterer as an ordinary man but he thinks of him as a sorcerer. And when he announces that he thinks a sorcerer is creeping around his hut after dark, trying to entice his wife, he at once enlists the sympathies of his co-villagers, who help him in his precautions. Such action may solve the problem, for things become too difficult for the would-be adulterer.

It is fairly clear why an adulterer is a sorcerer. He is a man of evil intent. If he were not, if he was honest, he would not make advances to a married woman. If he honestly wanted to marry the woman, and if the woman wanted to marry him, then there are proper and conventional ways of going about the business. Providing that everyone is agreeable it can all be arranged without loss of face and without much harm coming to anyone. And because it can be done, because there is a conventional procedure for doing so, a man who tries to take a short cut, who takes no count of the feelings and rights of others, who tries to find enjoyment without accepting the full range of accepted social responsibilities—such a man is obviously acting improperly. He is a sorcerer.

Tangu are few in numbers, leading a life which is, technologically, very simple. There are not numerous classes of men among whom the blame for troubles may be apportioned. They live close together within an ambience of kin relationships. They can either blame themselves or those who are not quite of themselves—sorcerers. Trouble must stem from trouble makers, from men who want to, or who do, make trouble; from odd and secretive men who appear to think and brood too much, who think in a way that is different, and who do not do the things other men do. Such men are called sorcerers, and sorcerers are such men. Generally, Tangu prefer to live at a certain distance from their fellows: 'In that way we do not have trouble from sorcerers', they say. At the same time they are parts of a community and community life and community values bring them together. But certain men, a man who leads too lonely a life—he is suspected of being a sorcerer. Conformity pulls very strongly and is 'good': non-conformity is 'bad', probably evil. When a man meets trouble, and becomes sick, he confesses, examines his conscience and so, in terms of his own and the community vocabulary of what is fitting, analyses himself and his motives. As a non-conformist a sorcerer is not considered to accept community values as binding on his own thoughts and activities.

Tangu do not think of, or conceptualize, Good and Evil ever at war. They think of themselves as living a traditional kind of life, gardening, hunting, gathering, having feasts, dancing, making love, marrying, and having children. Into this life trouble, evil, and non-conformity come through a sorcerer, bringing envy, hatred, sickness, and death, causing quarrels and disturbing the even tenor of life. In most ways a sorcerer is the physical embodiment of evil, and Christians find it easy to regard him as the Devil in person. Most men, say Tangu, are ordinary men, good fellows. Here and there, however, are men who either want to be different, non-conformist, or evil, or who are these things in spite of themselves. Any man is liable to be bad, to want to do wicked things, and sometimes he falls into temptation. He becomes a sorcerer, temporarily; or he hires a sorcerer. What Tangu can never be sure of, as a matter of principle, is whether a particular man does what he is doing in spite of himself or because he wants to do them. And though in theory such a statement poses a number of problems, in action Tangu find fairly simple solutions. When a sorcerer is identified as being a fellow villager he is given full benefit of the doubt. He is treated leniently. If he comes from another village he is rather less likely to be nasty in spite of himself. And if he is thought to be from a village outside Tangu—especially if that village is in Dia-watitzir or Tangwattitzir—he is surely a very wicked person who wants to be odious in the eyes of good men, and likes to make trouble.

Realizing that sickness and death are so closely allied to beliefs in and about sorcerers and sorcery, the administration through its officers makes every effort to maintain a high standard of hygiene in the villages. Digging latrines is part of the battle against sorcery. Administrative officers try very hard, too, to have cases of sickness brought into a base hospital for treatment. By so doing, some feel, they may be able slowly to eradicate sorcery. Currently, however, no Tangu is willing to carry a sick man to hospital. Apart from the arrangements and labour involved, it is considered that such an act might anger the sorcerer and so bring harm on others as well. Besides, as has been pointed out, the fact that the man is sick is considered to be partly his own fault. It is right and proper to help a sick man, but not right and proper to sidestep the real issue—helping the sick man to purge himself of his wrong-doings—by recruiting outside help. Beliefs in sorcerers and what they can do are axiomatic. If a European doctor does effect a cure it is not considered that the sorcerer has been worsted, but that the sorcerer has allowed the doctor to make the sick man well. And while this factor allows Tangu a loophole, a hope that the sorcerer will be generous and permit the white man to use his skill to effect, it has to be balanced against the more pressing alternative that the sorcerer may be goaded into killing the sick man from pique. After all, a sorcerer is considered to be an evil man with evil intentions: it is just this kind of thing he is expected to do. Finally, the failures of European doctors stand out with alarming clarity—proving to Tangu that sorcerers can, if they wish, outwit the European doctor.

The belief in sorcerers and what they can do cannot simply be called a habit of thought that dies hard. Sickness and death may be the chief contexts of relevance, but in truth sorcerers and what they do impinge everywhere. Tangu talk about sorcerers as other people talk about kinship. Sorcery is central to the moral order, intimately concerned with life and death, linking bad with good, guilt with innocence, wrong-doing with rightdoing, and the development of the self in relation to society. No ambition or ascription of motive may leave sorcery out of account.

Tangu themselves are aware of the extent to which problems

69

of sorcery are questions of belief, upbringing, and social understanding. White men, say Tangu, are immune from sorcerers because they do not understand about them. But, it is added, Europeans are concerned with other things called *jems* (germs): and they take all kinds of precautions against them. Indeed, to Tangu the elaborate apparatus used by Europeans to protect themselves from germs appears as very impressive beside their own meagre techniques for countering sorcerers. When I, a European, began to speak in the vernacular, and was conversing quite freely, thinking in their idiom, Tangu became alarmed at my apparent carelessness regarding sorcerers. I reminded them that as a white man I was immune.

'No more!' they replied. 'You can speak our language. You understand.'

And, of course, they were quite right. I was immune no longer. Clandestine intrusions into my hut, and suspicious noises at night—including a chase across the village and into the bush—persuaded me to take note of what may have been a friendly warning that I could not expect to be privileged as a European and as one of themselves at the same time.

The anecdote also points up the nature of sorcery. To examine sorcery in full would be to analyse a total series of mental and physical activities which take their departure from a set of beliefs which remain axiomatic for the large majority of Tangu at any rate. To understand Tangu, to think the way they do, is to think in their language. The axioms and ideas contained within Tangu sorcery beliefs and activities are best expressed in the Tangu language which itself expresses the way in which Tangu think about themselves and the world outside. Realizing this, that 'sorcery' is a European category inadequately describing a particular aspect of a whole mode of thought, and convinced that in the long run the most significant approach is through the mind, the mission in Tangu has proscribed sorcery as a 'work of the Devil'. The mission does not ingenuously deny, as many white men do, that in Tangu sorcery exists. On the contrary, the dangers from sorcerers are admitted, and a protective technique, prayer, is offered to combat the evil. More positively, by teaching Pidgin English, and more recently, English, the mission hopes to draw Tangu out of the confines of their language into a broader field of understanding. Only by so doing, the mission feel, may Tangu be guided out of their chief moral problem—private evil-doing in opposition to good, public acts in conformity with custom and tradition—into an appreciation of what Christianity has to offer.

So far as it concerns a few of the more intelligent Christians in Tangu the mission can, indeed, show some results from its labour. For these few treat sorcerers in ways different from their fellows. They try to treat them rather as the missionary does—as bad men who happen to exist, as criminals. But for all Tangu, Christian or pagan, there remains the fact that if a sorcerer can be simply a criminal, he is also a man who has the capacity deliberately to act outside the moral conventions; who, being typically arrogant and unobliged by morality, usurps, and is therefore touched by, what is divine; who is culpable because he causes trouble, because his self-will, instead of transcending, eschews the community moral.

CHAPTER III

The People

[ii]

Tangu economic life, gardening, hunting, gathering, and the manufacture of such articles as string bags and clay pots, is largely—but not wholly—a matter of their own internal adaptations and traditional arrangements. So also is the distributive system, the organization of households into co-operative groups, and exchanging and trading across the brother and sister link. At the same time white men and their goods do, and have impinged on economic life in important ways. For the present three may be picked out. First, steel tools have replaced the old stone edged tools. But though these new tools are more efficient than the old ones their use has not involved any new kinds of work, purposes, or forms of organization. Time is saved, and the day is longer. Second, contract labour has drawn young men to the coast where they work on plantations for cash to buy the tools they need as well as other goods such as beads, pigment, cloth, wooden chests, and a variety of knick-knacks. Third, the introduction by the administration of rice to be grown as a cash crop has involved a quite different and separate arrangement for production and distribution without altering the indigenous system for dealing with traditional crops.

Tangu sorcery beliefs, on the other hand, remain virtually intact. In purposefully attacking the complex through the provision of hospitals and an insistence on standards of hygiene the administration may have lessened the frequency of opportunities for making accusations of sorcery, but the beliefs themselves seem in no way impaired. Sorcerers act in many other contexts besides those of sickness and death, and the beliefs about sorcerers and their activities are but a part of a larger whole which, by and large, remain axiomatic. The mission, however, rather than confine its efforts to a particular expression, or symptom, has embarked on a long term campaign directed to the area of belief itself. The first stage which may be identified, and in which it has been moderately successful, is the addition of a new technique to combat the effects of the activities of sorcerers: prayer. Prayer to God. The second stage, which some Tangu have reached, might be described very broadly as a more positive comprehension of God and Christianity which has the effect of stripping sorcerers of most of their traditional mystical attributes, relegating them, rather, to the category of criminal.

The political scene, with which this chapter is concerned, and into which both mission and administration have intruded much more, is best seen in the present context as one of leadership at the village level. It involves native officials, Luluai, Tultul, and Doctor boy, who are confirmed in their offices by the administration; the catechists and mission boss-boys appointed by the mission; and the managers, politico-economic bosses who emerge from the traditional structure.

LEADERSHIP

The duties of Luluai, Tultul, and Doctor boy have primarily to do with the maintenance of law and order by reporting misdemeanours to the European administrative officers, assembling the villagers for a census on the advent of a patrol, the upkeep of paths, working the rice field, the cleanliness of the village, maintaining the medical stores in the medicine hut, and reporting cases of acute sickness to the medical officer at Bogia. The Luluai is taken to be the senior, general supervisor; the Tultul is his aide and constable. The Doctor boy, who is given a short course in hygiene and simple therapy, is the junior partner. The position, power, and authority of each of these officials derive from the administration: each is a part of a hierarchically organized, authoritative system. Their duties involve recruiting households in a non-traditional way to a variety of unpopular tasks. The sanctions they can apply derive from the European environment: reporting to Bogia as a result of which an offender may be fined or imprisoned. Unpaid, precisely the same sanctions may be visited on them for neglecting their duties.

Catechists, who are carefully selected and trained as teachers in the mission headquarters at Alexishaven, enjoy a small regular stipend though their work is regarded as essentially vocational. Their influence in local affairs is much coloured by their connexion with the mission, and they have also their own achievements as lettered men. Their responsibilities are mainly to the Christians of a community and to the missionary himself. Helped by the mission boss-boys, catechists usually have little difficulty in recruiting Christian households for occasional tasks. Common values in Christianity override economic and political sectionalisms. Finally, there are the managers, men whose capacities for influence and leadership have no European based supports, who are entirely dependent on their own abilities to create certain kinds of relationships with those among whom they live, and who are our main concern here.

Native administrative officials have roles and occupy political offices; the tasks of mission personnel, more diffuse, may have political consequences. Managers carry out economic tasks and occupy political roles without the aid of an office. In action on the ground each category is qualified by personal abilities and idiosyncrasies; and the roles of administrative officials and mission employees cannot but be influenced by the traditional managerial values. Though a single man may combine in his person the acknowledged capacities of a manager, the powers of an administrative official, the education of a catechist, or the connexions of a boss-boy, many managers are not native officials, some of the latter have few managerial gifts, and catechists—who are not eligible for the administrative offices—usually find it too onerous to establish themselves as managers. Each category of leader has a well defined role, but those of manager and native official often cut across each other personally, and, when it is a question of organizing households in different ways for dissimilar and unevenly weighted ends, politically.

Tangu call a manager *wunika ruma*, big man. The primary qualification is productive ability, the capacity to provide quantities of meat, tubers, fruits, and other kinds of foodstuffs. From this it follows that a manager must be physically robust, in good health, a cunning hunter, and an industrious gardener with a mastery of the techniques, mystical and pragmatic, which are necessary to take game and harvest good and plentiful crops. He must be married. He must have a wife, or wives, to do the many essential tasks which only a woman can do well, and which it would be shaming for a man to perform. He must have children to help in the household work, and in whose name he may give feasts. He must have sisters and wife's brothers with whom he can make exchanges and so advertise his productive capacity. He must have allies to help him, and an opposition which will provide him with the opportunity for showing his qualities. Since, also, the primary expression of productive ability is in feasting and dancing exchanges, a manager must be able to dance correctly, with verve, and have a wide knowledge of the various melodies, rhythms, and choreographies that are associated with each dance through the numerous myths which sanction and justify them.

During feasting and dancing exchanges, in the intervals between different phases of the dance, as food is placed before the exhausted dancers, men from either group of participating households make speeches. This is formal *br'ngun'guni*: the political activity. The oratory is accompanied by staccato beats on the hand-drum, thwacking the buttocks, and, if a man is well roused, wild leaps into the air. Men boast of their prowess in the gardens and bush, comment on the dancing, and remark on the productive abilities of others. Some take the opportunity to remind the gathering that it is time to harvest yams or taros, or that work in the rice field is lagging behind; others bring up grievances relating to hunting, or fishing, gardening, administrative, mission, or kin matters, exchange obligations or suspicions of sorcery. Visitors from other communities in Tangu come along, not only because they enjoy a party, and can eat and smoke and talk and gossip with friends, but because during formal *br'ngun'guni* they have a favourable opportunity for publicizing, or putting in issue, a claim or grievance.

Br'ngun'guni may also occur contingently, as the result of an expression of anger, after the announcement of a betrothal, or following the discovery of a theft, trespass, or insult. In the unexpectedness and heat of the moment many of the niceties of the feasting, formal *br'ngun'guni* may be omitted; but the procedure, ends, and means are much the same. Accusation is met with counter-accusation; disputants boast of the feasts they have provided, draw attention to the meanness or disreputable motives of the other, and seek the events in their relationship with each other that will be scored to their credit. Bystanders may be drawn in to support one side or the other; some use their own initiative and enter the fray to equivocate and balance the issues. At the finish nothing is said or made explicit. There is no adjudication. It is for the disputants and each man present to make their own judgements and order their lives accordingly. For, in *br'ngun'guni*, whether contingent or formal, managerial ability is brought into full focus and receives its severest test: through *br'ngun'-guni* young men become managers, gain prestige and influence; older men may be seen to be losing their touch. Householders are left to decide where their best interests lie.

Management in Tangu is leadership without the definable authority of an office, or the security of a specified status. Some managers are endowed with a brief share of the qualities we call charismatic, but those last longest who use their knowledge and experience of the people they live among, who know the interrelationships of others, the activities they engage in, their interests, and the possible or probable consequences of particular acts and events. Besides advertising their production in feasts, managers must score points in *br'ngun'-guni*. They should be quick to take advantage from a slip of the tongue, and seal it with a timely phrase. They must lend support where it seems advantageous, remain aloof if necessary, equivocate, arbitrate, or play off other managers against each other. But on no account may they offend the personal pride of another. Such an act will bring mystical retribution in the form of sorcery. The word or act that goes through to the heart and lodges in the vitals hurts the doer himself, for even if he is oblivious his allies and supporters cannot afford to ignore the danger of sorcery: they will secede, or opt out of the alliance.

A manager cannot retain his influence for long without a solidarity of public opinion behind him; nor, without a clear cast of inclination within the community, has a manager any basis for foresight in planning his own moves. Wholly withdrawing from situations which seem to contain too many variables, and then waiting for public opinion to assume a firm tone, is a typical managerial technique. When I had been in Tangu some time I learned that when I had first arrived those managers who were not native administrative officials absented themselves. They were faced with an unknown quantity—neither *kiap*, nor *misin*, nor *kampanimasta*. As public opinion began to adjust to the new situation, and to express itself, managers began to put in a few tentative appearances, coming to see me in my hut. Later on, as soon as it became clear that the community as a whole had accepted my presence in the village, managers began to compete with each other to carry acceptance a stage further by proceeding to adoption. Three main prizes seem to have been at stake. First, inevitably, there was access to tools, stores, and equipment. Second, talk and rumours about a European who had assumed an unusual role by staying in a Kanaka village almost indefinitely would scarcely exclude mention of the manager who had adopted him. All in the region would come to know the name of the manager as the man who had adopted a European, who had '*bossed*' a white man. Such prestige, especially in the backwash of a Cargo movement, was not to be lightly forsaken. Lastly, as all the members of a Tangu community must be known to each other in terms of categories of kinship, adoption of a European was not only carrying the general will—acceptance—to its logical conclusion, but it was also an innovation in tune with the times.

Normally, though managers first try to meet, and then steer the general sentiment of the community, they also attempt to create opportunities and force issues. If some unforeseen event makes a situation susceptible to manipulation, managers who perceive it leap to take advantage. If a manager is confident enough he may seize upon some petty act or accident—such as a bruised yam in a food exchange, or the misbehaviour of a child, or a misunderstanding—and attempt to engineer a major dispute. He has the initiative by taking it. Whatever the short term result, if he is vociferous and violent enough his name will become known. He will gain the reputation of a man willing to go to some lengths in defence of his pride and honour, and with whom it would be best to tread warily. His challenge, for that is what it is, is really a challenge to himself: it provides him with the chance of putting to the public test and approbation—without which they are as nothing—those qualities and abilities he believes himself to have.

A manager must be, as Tangu describe it, *gtangi*, hard, strong-willed, obdurate, not easily persuaded by other individuals. He must be generous with his wealth and sociable, but also, in certain senses, mean. Since a manager is relatively prosperous, some will want to milk him. There are those who have claims on him, and he should not behave so as to disappoint their expectations. Full brothers will extract the half-chewed betel from each other's mouths and share it in turn; cousins or even second cousins will calmly take the tobacco leaf from the armlet of another and roll it into a cigarette or stuff it into a pipe; nephews and nieces like to be spoiled with gifts. Such conventions dissipate hard earned produce among a circle of kinsfolk without necessarily raising him in the estimation of the community, and a manager has to be a man removed from the ordinary run if he is both to prevent this drain on his resources and avoid a reputation for petty meanness. So, managers take pains to avoid those situations where generosity may be asked of them and yet count for little. They avoid the daily gossip group, when everyone is being a little generous and to be over-generous is merely to be vulgar. In this wise managers preserve their substance and can afford to be overwhelmingly generous on the occasions that count—when a traveller stops by, when a missionary passes through, when a manager from another settlement makes a surprise visit in the hope of catching him unprepared. It takes managerial capacities to foresee such occasions and not miss them. Then again, partly in order to maintain a large production, and partly to avoid being unnecessarily generous, or becoming too involved, managers spend much of their time in comparative isolation in their gardens or hunting lodges.

The dilemma is clear. Managers have to be sociable and maintain contacts with the community in order to keep abreast of events and informed of the way opinion is moving. They have to work hard to produce food. They cannot afford a reputation for petty meanness, and they have to avoid occasions which might dissipate their produce without profit. Finally, if any man, and a manager is more noticeable than others, leads too solitary a life others will at once assume he has taken to sorcery. In general, part of the solution is to develop an air which will restrain relatives from making explicit demands whilst at the same time making it quite clear to others that no such request would fall on deaf ears. In such a way a manager isolates those who would milk him, and also ensures their support. For no other manager would care to have as a supporter a householder with the reputation of a parasite. Otherwise, the only alternative to skill in handling people is more and more hard work in the gardens and bush.

As soon as a manager's physical abilities fall into decline he begins to produce less and, eventually, he cannot cope with his problem. Without the solid productive achievement which must be seen at a feast his area of influence contracts: he has to rely more and more on other kinds of skill. But the latter by themselves do not take him very far. Allies prefer to be linked to a sufficiency of yams in the present than to a reputation built on a productive ability that no longer exists. So, at last, the ageing manager goes into retirement, a miserable, lonely existence. Younger, stronger, and more energetic men take his place. Similarly, since the basis of influence is productive achievement, the sickness which prevents a young or middle aged manager from hunting or tending his garden will cause at least a temporary decline in his influence. And, as we have seen, sicknesses in Tangu are not accidental: they are conceived as consequences of wrongdoing, and are most often thought of as due to the mystical measures taken by one who himself has been wronged in some way. To anger a man, to puncture his pride, to deprive him of what he considers to be his, to reveal in public defects of character—such acts are thought to entail a resort to sorcery, to mystical means of retaliation the object of which is to secure the sickness or death of the offender. Since Tangu know, and themselves make the (to them) logical connexion between offence, mystical retaliation, and sickness, both before the fact and after it, it behoves a manager to act carefully, with circumspection and forethought. It is unwise for a manager to make enemies either of rivals or allies,[1] for by so doing he risks mystical retaliation, tends to distance himself from his supporters, broods on his predicament, loses time from the garden, and produces less. As a manager he is on the way out.

At the simplest evaluation the managerial task is a difficult one. It requires experience, the ability to learn a lesson, and the courage to act on conclusions. It does not depend on mysterious 'powers of leadership' but on hard work and painstaking attention to detail. Unlike the native official who gives orders, and who is obeyed because he can touch the springs of physical coercion, a manager wields influence because he is what he has made of himself. Ideally, he is the very best kind of conformist—but the sorcerer is ever at his elbow, suggesting a tempting short cut. And because the temptation is known to be great a manager is the more readily suspected by rivals and others. To resist resorts into sorcery, to avoid hiring a sorcerer and yet retain that initiative which encompasses community values and at the same time goes a little beyond them is to meet a heavy demand.

[1] A rival is not necessarily a personal enemy, nor an ally a friend.

AMITY AND EQUIVALENCE

Among Tangu a manager should not only know others, he must know himself as a moral being. Each rung in the ladder to maximum influence is embedded in certain prime notions and associated activities which should form a unity as adequate reflections each of the other. Managers should weld activity to notion: in their behaviour they should demonstrate the unity. Managers may act, but without moral understanding they cannot make their actions mirror an ideal.

All Tangu, howsoever related, assent to the notion of amity. Amity exists within its own moral right: it is the critical norm by which all relationships are judged, and with which all relationships should coincide or approximate. Whether a relationship is economic, political, or one of kinship, the activities within which either party is engaged in relation to the other are limited and determined by the notion that the relationship should be characterized by amity. The breach of amity immediately sets in motion procedures designed to ensure a return to amity. As a result, in action on the ground, amity entails relationships shifting until the mutual obligations contained within them can approximate at least to an overt conformity with amity. If A and B are not able to co-operate in amity they may yet achieve an amicable relationship through the mutual respect that comes from exchanging with each other; if X and Y are enemies they should only encounter each other in situations where they can be amicable. So far as a relationship is reflected in the activities two parties undertake in common it tends to alter from a given datum until the activities themselves conform overtly with amity.

Amity is itself most significantly manifested in the idea of equivalence; in the idea that individuals are in a state of moral equality, one human being, as a whole, being neither morally worse nor morally better than another. Amity is a function of equivalence: through equivalence the most perfect kind of amity may be found. In action, equivalence, and

81

therefore amity, finds primary expression in formal exchanges of foodstuffs whether they are between individuals, households, or groups of households. All such exchanges should be equivalent. If they are not, expectations are disappointed, trouble results, and a breach of amity occurs. Yet, in the nature of things, no food exchange can be precisely equivalent. And because resources are limited households are forced to establish a scale of priorities, necessarily disappointing some to satisfy others. Since, in such circumstances, there is always room to find fault, exchanges that are regarded as equivalent reflect a true moral equivalence between the parties to the exchange. Normally, when this occurs households become *mngwotngwotiki*. Having achieved a conclusive equivalence they express it by neither exchanging nor co-operating.

An exchange which is not regarded as precisely equivalent, or which remains not honoured in full too long, is taken to indicate a lack of moral equivalence. A sense of grievance cannot imply either amity or equivalence. One or other party to the exchange is thought to be attempting a dominance or moral superiority. He who produces more is suspected of endeavouring to assume a loftier moral status in virtue of what may be a simple physical competence: which is deplorable. Brute strength may help towards attaining a higher social standing, but it can only reflect degrees of moral perfection when used in particular ways for certain ends. He who produces less may be suspected of contumely, of behaviour which is essentially contemptuous and therefore not in conformity with amity. And either may be suspected by the other, or by members of the community, to be resorting to a technique which is meant to shroud the other in obloquy. The ideal is equivalence, neither more nor less, neither 'one-up' nor 'one-down'. To be 'one-up' is to offend and therefore to invite mystical retaliation. To be 'one-down' and remain content is almost unforgivable: it implies a complete retreat into sorcery, a resolve to maintain equivalence by doing evil only.

The accepted, public device for finding and maintaining

equivalence is *br'ngun'guni*. Behind the talk is a feasting exchange, a needling envy, perhaps a suspicion of trespass, or cheating. The seemingly careless remark strikes home: and a riposte is immediate. Does the cap fit? One man probes to find out a weakness; then thrusts, retreating for the parry. The language flickers to sting and annoy; it should not draw blood. There should be just enough room for one to advance, just enough room to fall back. To press an opponent into a corner leaves him with little alternative but to take refuge, later, in sorcery. If a man appears to be going 'one-up' by so hurting another he is only hurting himself. Sensibly, support falls away. By retiring a little, by parrying the consequent onslaught with a whoop and thump on the buttocks, the ball comes back into play. The victory is never to the dominant; it goes to the man who knows when to sit down, to the man who can look through his audience and know that nobody is certain who is 'one-up'.

All transgressions in Tangu may be seen as attacks on equivalence; and where possible the wrongdoing is related to an individual's potential for producing foodstuffs in an exchange. In this way public equivalence may be reached through *br'ngun'guni* and a series of feasting exchanges. Theft and trespass, the most frequent offences, are automatically regarded as attacks on food producing potential; those emotionally at odds can always take the opportunity to find fault with a food exchange; if adultery is not to slide into sorcery, or plain killing, it must be reduced to a matter of food production. Food is the conventional pretext for a quarrel; and *br'ngun'guni* is the accepted procedure for returning to amity. Just as a denial of equivalence can be formulated in terms of behaviour relating to food, so is it re-established through activities directly connected with the production of foodstuffs: *br'ngun'guni* and a series of feasting and dancing exchanges. Moral relationships, therefore, are reflected in the way people behave over food; food is economic wealth; the amount produced and the way in which it is distributed yield political power; and each is geared to equivalence, the primary expression of amity.

The most transparent breach of equivalence is an expression of anger. Tangu have no noun to denote anger: it does not exist as an abstraction. Men are angry with one another, or with something, not merely angry; the word that is used is a transitive verb. Anger kept in the heart leads on to sorcery, and may mean sickness or death for some other person. Anger made public, normally by a rapid onomatopoeic drumming on a slit-gong, may lead into a complaint and thence into *br'ngun'guni*. An angry man is a dangerous man, and the signal on the slit-gong is both a warning to keep clear and an invitation to a close friend or kinsman to inquire what the matter might be. And, whatever the underlying cause of the anger, almost invariably the reason that is made explicit has something to do with food. By regarding theft and trespass as inroads on food producing potential wrongdoer and injured man are enabled to quarrel on conventional lines without resorting to personal assault or sorcery. It brings a quarrel out into the open, making it socially relevant, and enables disputants to make social and political issues out of what might be a personal antagonism. That is, to restate, personal issues are translated into public issues and made subject to the community moral. The only way to settle a score in private is by sorcery. Or, the moral system forms an indivisible whole which individuals may not contract out of without doing wrong. And because the prime norm, amity, is directly expressed in food production and exchanges, the conventional pretext for resolving a quarrel, a breach of amity, again concerns food.

In order to make their names as producers would-be managers are forced to challenge particular exchanges and so involve themselves in a series of equalizing feasts. They have to seek a breach of the ideal, or fabricate one, in order to furnish a further positive expression of it that will redound to their own personal advantage. Yet, equivalence still binds them. Managers challenge other managers of roughly equivalent abilities and resources. To challenge a lazy, or poor, man would be fruitless. If the resulting exchange is equivalent little evidence of superior industry or productive ability can emerge; if not, the manager lays himself open to mystical attack. In consequence, allies withdraw their support. And, since a man knows or must presume that sorcery is going to be used against him, he begins to lose his self-assurance. He becomes moody, retires to the bush to brood on his predicament, and so loses his touch. Even if he is not actually sick he begins to spend more time on reflecting how he may break even than in his gardens. Productivity falls off, friends and relations tend to avoid him, and in a short while he has spelt his own ruin.

Selection of the opposition does not mean that managers only come into effective relationships with other managers. It is true that the focus of their climb to greatest influence lies within this context, but they have also to maintain equivalence with others around them. Tangu do not have grades of equivalence. It is not enough that manager A should be equivalent with manager B. He must create a moral equivalence with all in the community. Only on such a basis will others co-operate or exchange with him. The most prodigious worker may, through a kin relationship, be forced to make exchanges with a lazy good-for-nothing. But it is no excuse for the former to lord it over the latter. Indeed, it requires tact, foresight, a reliable network of informants, and a meticulous attention to detail to find out how much the other is going to produce for the exchange and to match it precisely. To do otherwise is to offend: and for a manager, more so than for other men, to offend is to start a train of disasters.

For Tangu the concrete symbol of true amity in the heart is the exchange which both parties deem to be equivalent, and concerning which neither party is swayed by the malicious gossip and pinpricks of others. In a more absolute sense such an exchange, which no one else questioned or tried to mar, would stand as a model for all, the exchange *par excellence*. Carried to its logical conclusion the implication is that in the best of all possible worlds, since all exchanges would be equivalent and true amity reign over all, there would no longer be any need to make exchanges. And precisely this is involved in being *mngwotngwotiki*, truly equivalent.

85

SOME DISPUTES

In order to see how Tangu work out their equivalences, and to appreciate the flavour of their disputes, summaries of four recorded during fieldwork are presented below.[1]

I

One afternoon two teams of brothers were building houses for their sisters, Juatak, wife of Kwaling, and Nuongweram, Turai's wife and Kwaling's half-sister. Kwaling and Juatak were distributing food to the latter's brothers, and Nuongweram's brothers were working. The atmosphere was one of quiet and cheerful industry as men and women went about their tasks, smoked, talked, or chewed betel nut.

Presently Meakriz, the Luluai, was approached by Igamas, his natural son, and Bunjerai, his adopted son. There was a short whispered conversation, and then all three ran off into the bush.

The incident created a small stir. People deduced that a pig had been trapped, and since no one in Tangu eats himself what he has killed in the hunt, but divides it between those to whom he has obligations, expectations were aroused. To whom would the pig be given—from among the many who believed they had claims?

Sure enough, half an hour later the cries and halloos of a party returning with a pig were heard. Reamai, Meakriz's half-brother, had killed the beast, and it was taken to a small group of homesteads on a hillock, separated by about fifty yards from the main settlement. There was a short pause as the pig was laid down on the ground, and then came the deep tones of the slit-gong announcing to whom the pig was going to be given. It was Bwatam, Reamai's sister.

[1] The disputes described in this chapter have been abstracted from Disputing in Tangu, *American Anthropologist*, Vol. 59, No. 5, October 1957, pp. 763–80.

Mureg, who is sister to Meakriz and his half-brother Reamai, and who, since Meakriz is a widower, normally cooks for him and his sons, was disappointed. She said in a loud voice to her husband, Nuok, 'What is this? Why does not Meakriz have Reamai bring the pig down here, carve it under my porch and give it to me to distribute? Why is he giving it to Bwatam? I, not Bwatam, cook for him every day.'

Nuok, friend[1] of Kwaling and brother to Juatak, stepped out into the dancing space to support his wife. 'Why was the pig going to Bwatam? Why not to Mureg who cooked for Meakriz daily? Gasai, Nuongweram's brother, had killed a pig the day before and had given it to Nuongweram to distribute to the brothers building her house. It was appropriate that Meakriz and Reamai should give their pig to their sister Mureg to divide between the brothers building Juatak's house. Were not Kwaling, Meakriz, and Reamai brothers?'

Reamai, who had actually trapped the pig and who was annoyed that his choice should be questioned, came down from the upper portion of the village and confronted Nuok. 'We will do what we like with our pig,' he said truculently. 'We are giving it to our sister Bwatam.'

'Who cooks for Meakriz?' asked Nuok. 'Bwatam?'

Reamai did not answer. He strode away angrily, vigorously asserting that the pig would be given to Bwatam. Nuok walked off in disgust.

Suddenly—perhaps Mureg had fired a parting shot— Reamai lost his temper. Turning swiftly on his heel he ran back to Mureg's house, forced his way in, and started to thrash her.

Mureg screamed. She was still screaming when Nuok, hurrying to the rescue, confronted Reamai emerging from the hut. Nuok stooped, picked up a clod of dried earth and flung it at Reamai. He missed.

Reamai sprang to the attack. Being smaller and frailer, Nuok fled. Reamai gave chase and grappled. Meakriz, the Luluai, pounced on them both, trying to separate them.

[1] The friendship between Kwaling and Nuok is one of institutionalized friendship. They are bound to help each other when in trouble.

Reamai whooped in triumph, raining blows. Nuok cried for help, and others rushed yelling to the scene.

Kwaling was among them, a heavy digging stick in his hands. Bounding into the mêlée with a shout, he cracked Reamai across the head. Reamai staggered back, blood spurting from his temples and pouring down his chest. Nuok broke free. Gaiap, Juatak's full brother, supported Reamai and helped him out of harm's way. Kwaling retreated. Women scuttled around to the backs of their huts. The village was in uproar.

Br'ngun'guni commenced.

Why has brother struck brother? Both Kwaling and Reamai are managers. They are classificatory brothers who ought to be in an amicable co-operative relationship, but they have been quarrelling since boyhood and they dislike each other intensely. Reamai is the younger of the two, boastful, hot tempered, and very proud of being the son of a famous father. He is an excellent gardener, hunter, and dancer. Nevertheless, he is jealous of Kwaling who is quiet, withdrawn, cool, well known and respected far beyond the boundaries of Tangu. As Luluai of the village, Meakriz is responsible for keeping order, apprehending wrongdoers, and reporting misdemeanours to the administration. Because he is a widower with children, his sister Mureg has given him shelter, and has cooked for him and generally looked after him. She can reasonably expect generosity in return. However, Meakriz cannot find a new wife and he had been thinking of having his sons adopted by either Mureg or Bwatam on a more or less permanent basis. This means putting his potential as a food producer at the disposal of either Bwatam or Mureg —a matter on which the two women had come to blows a few days previously, and which had resulted in Bwatam moving her house from the main part of the village to the upper, outlying cluster of homesteads.

Even apart from the economic issue Bwatam and Mureg have little love for each other. The former is an attractive creature, well liked by the men of the community; it is no

Village in Wanitzir

Village in Riekitzir

Catechist going to a dance. This man died recently, and is believed to have been killed by sorcerers hired by the 'old conservatives'.

Tangu mission station on a Sunday

An administrative officer on his rounds. Officials are on the left, with their caps on: villagers have been lined up to be registered and counted.

secret that Meakriz expresses his affection for her by many small favours. Having eaten a meal cooked by Mureg, Meakriz is wont to stroll over to Bwatam's house and there enjoy his leisure with tobacco and betel nut. Mureg herself swings her hips to some effect and enjoys the reputation she has among men of being somebody else's mistress. Reamai, however, regards Mureg's notoriety as a blot on his name. He has had words with her before, and he has beaten her. Quite recently, too, Reamai had embroiled himself over an alleged theft of areca nuts and, since the popular suspect stood to him as son, he had attempted to clinch matters by threatening to beat up anyone who continued to speak of his 'son' as a thief.

Into this generally uneasy situation, then, has come a stroke of good fortune—the capture of a pig. Meakriz and Reamai are burdened with a choice, and their decision has angered and disappointed Mureg. Nuok, her husband, has made a complaint, and the impending dispute is across the brother and sister link. Reamai was presented with a second choice, for he might have returned with dignity to his pig and carved it notwithstanding. Instead, angered, he chose to beat Mureg. In consequence Nuok was angry and the two men start fighting. Meakriz, as Luluai, tries to separate them. Kwaling has the choice of helping Reamai who is his brother, or Nuok who is his friend, or, like Meakriz, he might have tried to make peace. He chose deliberately to strike Reamai. Gaiap, Juatak's full brother, has already limited the range of the dispute and taken the first step towards a return to amicable relations— to amity. By ostensibly supporting Reamai and shielding him from Kwaling—his brother-in-law—and incidentally shielding Nuok from Reamai, he has shown that this need not be a matter involving all of Juatak's brothers. It is a personal issue.

Nevertheless, a number of expectations have been disappointed, several relationships have been thoroughly disturbed, equivalence has been breached, and, personal issue or not, the whole dispute must be worked out in public.

Shouting, leaping, whooping, beating their buttocks with the palms of their hands, Kwaling, Reamai, and Meakriz ran up and down the dancing space, sweating, furious, livid with anger; boasting, threatening, calling witness. Nuok had made himself scarce, for Kwaling had taken the quarrel out of his hands and made it his own.

The blood streaming down Reamai's body was *prima facie* evidence of a breach of amity. Meakriz, running, leaping, and thwacking his buttocks, said it was a deliberate assault and that he would take Kwaling to the administrative court at Bogia on the morrow.

Reamai passionately endorsed the proposal. Dizzy, eyes glazed, rubbing his hands in the blood, he demanded the court.

Kwaling countered. Reamai had beaten his sister, he said, and was in the act of assaulting Nuok when the blow was delivered. Should a man not go to the aid of his friend? His father and Reamai's father had been very close to each other. They had lived together in amity and co-operation, and their sons should behave in the same way. Right. Go to court. Tell the white men how they behaved—how a man of the village had beaten his sister, fought the husband who came to the rescue, and had, in the past—how many days ago?—threatened to beat others.

Meakriz withdrew from *br'ngun'guni*, sitting down in silence.

Reamai and he, continued Kwaling, had been brought up together in Kimaimwenk. They were brothers. Was it necessary to fight?

Still dazed by the blow, Reamai stuck doggedly to court, rebutting the appeal to amity by stressing the deeper issues between them. Kwaling disliked him and had hit him on purpose from spite. He, Reamai, had left Kimaimwenk and settled on his own—all because of Kwaling. From there he had gone elsewhere, and it was Kwaling who had stopped him from settling in the village now. Court was the only way to settle the matter.

Kwaling, however, continued to conjure moral or 'ought to be' relationships. By doing so he was looking ahead and placing himself in the stream of public opinion. He had taken advantage of the opportunity to give Reamai a knock and had everything to gain by returning to amity as quickly as possible. Reamai, on the other hand, was handicapped. He had suffered—albeit by his own fault—and he wanted redress. But it was hardly a fruitful course to pursue. If he was in earnest in calling for the court, and succeeded, it could only further postpone the eventual return to amity. If he was bluffing—and threatening to go to court is a stock manœuvring weapon—he was also invoking non-traditional values and procedures: a tactic in strong contrast to Kwaling who was referring the quarrel only to what was traditional, and who had also pointed out that the court might be equally severe about Mureg's bruises. Meakriz's withdrawal was a tacit admission that going to court was not a practical solution. By revealing the real relationship between himself and Kwaling, Reamai was deepening the rift and flying in the face of public opinion by making it so much the harder to return to amity. Kwaling, too, withdrew from *br'ngun'guni* from time to time to have a smoke, a manœuvre which made it quite plain who was upset. Other things came up.

Each accused the other of cheating in food exchanges. Each boasted of his own ability in producing food and accused the other of trying to steal the limelight when they had co-operated. Reamai called Mangai, his wife's brother. Mangai, an old manager, pointed to the blood, remonstrated with Kwaling, pleaded with Reamai not to make too much of it, and was emphatic that the affair should not go to court. Womak, a close friend of Kwaling, tried to pacify Reamai— What other way was there? Kusai, mother's brother to Kwaling and father to Reamai, scolded Kwaling as he was in duty bound to do, saying he ought to go into the deep bush and stay there a while. Then, turning on Reamai, he entreated him to be more reasonable. Dimunk, called by Kwaling, remarked only that this was an affair between brothers. The matter of the adoption of Meakriz's sons was brought up, and the incident between Bwatam and Mureg was discussed. Previous assaults by Reamai on Mureg were remembered, and the recent theft of betel and its consequences were thrown in as makeweights. The air was clearing.

As the examples show, those who interjected remarks—and many did so whether they were asked or not—did not take sides. Explicitly supporting neither party, or blaming both, the remarks were designed to mollify anger, soothe hurt pride, and prepare the ground for re-establishing equivalence and amity. The specific issues which triggered the incident could not be considered as isolated acts, for each formed part of a complex of disappointments and grievances. At the same time, the focal issue in the *br'ngun'guni* is clearly the personal rivalry between Kwaling and Reamai—a rivalry which has become politically relevant. The principal disputants interacted with each other and also with the community, the former attempting to influence and to manage, the latter to mediate—a process which may be described as a 'mutual steering' to equivalence and amity. What is also evident is a 'looking to consequences'. From the moment he grasped his digging stick Kwaling seems to have been looking several moves ahead, and Meakriz's behaviour reveals the same concern for what the future might have in store. Juatak and Nuongweram had fled from the scene as soon as the fracas started. As far as the trapped pig was concerned Nuok's complaint had ranged their brothers in opposition, and the presence of the sisters might have provided concrete mobilizing points. After it was all over Nuongweram said, 'We went away because we might have had to say something which would have made more trouble.' Gaiap, it will be remembered, had made the first move to limit the range of the dispute by ostensibly protecting Reamai. Only Reamai himself seems to have been hopelessly entangled in the events of his own making.

The present explosion may be taken to have ended when Gaiap, with two coconuts, and Gasai, with a bunch of areca nuts, placed their offerings in the middle of the dancing space —to be shared among both sets of brothers. And this attempt to demonstrate 'no quarrel' as between the groups of brothers was echoed in the way the pig was eventually disposed of: it was shared between all those who came to work in the rice field the next day. That is, it came from Meakriz, the administrative representative, to all those who engaged in an

administrative task, irrespective of kin affiliation or co-operative alliance. But the disposal of the pig that had triggered
the events only marked the end of a phase. Reamai and
Kwaling were committed to feasting each other and finding
public equivalence through hard work and recruiting help.
In the feasting exchanges more *br'ngun'guni* will occur.
Meakriz shifted his residence to a site almost a mile distant
from the larger settlement, and Bwatam and her husband went
with him. Bwatam will look after Igamas and Bunjerai
and Meakriz will work with Bwatam's husband in alliance
with Reamai.

After the dispute was over Reamai was left with the
opportunity for making good his claims to respect and managerial ability. He had something to win. Kwaling, on the
other hand, whose position before the incident had been fairly
secure, was shaken. First, he is past his peak in physical
energy and competence, and no amount of cunning or high
reputation will offset his smaller production. Second, by hit-
ting Reamai, and afterwards contriving to make him look
small in *br'ngun'guni*, Kwaling was beginning to dominate, to
become too big by far.

In the days that followed Kwaling began to brood, and to
think about sorcery. His life and work were coming unstuck.
Those who co-operated with him began to be apprehensive.
He had, with almost contemptuous ease, merely used the
community moral for his own personal amoral ends.

Reamai brightened and became cock-a-hoop.

II

Kwaling was too good for his nearest rival, Reamai, too cunning and too shrewd. He lost standing in the eyes of the
community, and in his own eyes, because by being too clever
he was unable to maintain equivalence. He was losing his
touch.

A fortnight later he exploded again.

Twambar, Kwaling's four-year-old son, was playing with
Geengai's young sons, Kandidi and Manduz. Seeing a small

piglet defecating they decided, as children will, to stone the animal for being thus ungracious. Kandidi struck hard and true, crushing the delicate skull. Death was almost instantaneous.

Geengai, the village jester, cackled with mirth, 'Oh, well hit, well hit!' he cried.

The owner of the pig, Luassi, Kwaling's aged mother, started to grieve, complain, and scold. Kwaling himself tucked his pipe into his armlet, leaped to his feet, and grasping a large chunk of firewood started after the children. With a whoop he hurled his log, hit Twambar in the back of the neck, and brought him down. Juatak hurried to the rescue and dragged the screaming child to a safe place.

Br'ngun'guni commenced.

Whooping, yelling, leaping into the air, and thwacking his buttocks, Kwaling had everyone's attention. Children fled from the dancing space, women sought out their huts, and a few men who were stitching sago fronds into roofing strips continued their work with studied concentration.

Geengai made a few half-hearted runs and then retired to his hut. Kwaling wanted to know what Geengai was about. Did he want a fight? What then? Did he think he had a garden of worth? Did he want a feasting exchange? Ha!

Luassi intervened. This, she said, was a fuss about little. The pig was dead. Kandidi was only a child.

Gently, but firmly, Kwaling hustled her off and returned to the dancing space. Meakriz, the Luluai, who had been sitting near by, rose to his feet to speak.

Barely had he opened his mouth when Kwaling let fly at him. The Luluai sat down in silence.

Luassi came forward again, imploring her son to desist. Kwaling only took her by the shoulders and led her, protesting, back to her hut.

Geengai, who is an easy-going man with no pretensions to managerial ability, had seemed transfixed. At last he gave voice. He pointed out that the piglet deserved stoning: it should not foul the village. Everyone stoned piglets that defecated in the village. Who could tell it would be killed?

Besides, Kwaling ought to take more care of his pigs. Kwaling's pig had been into his garden, rooting and eating his yams.

'Come out of your hut!' Kwaling cried, livid and bouncing with rage. 'Come out into the open!'

Geengai refused. He has a big enough garden, but as the village jester he is wont to laugh at the things others take seriously. He is not interested in prestige and influence. His metier is gossip, turning the phrase, mimicry, making fun of the pompous. He likes his joke.

'Ha!' With a last flourish and thwack of the buttocks, Kwaling sat down to relight his pipe. The village fell silent.

Seconds later, Geengai emerged from his hut, axe in hand. Walking deliberately, he went round to the back of his hut— to his coconuts.

Immediately there was uproar. Geengai's wife's brothers rushed down and pushed Geengai away from his coconuts. They argued, they placed themselves between Geengai and his coconuts, hugging the trees. Gently, they relieved him of his axe. No, he must not cut down his coconuts.

Geengai said little. With a gesture of resignation he turned and went into his hut. In a few moments he came out, spear on his shoulder, and, with Manduz following, he walked disdainfully out of the village.

Though the incident arose from the irresponsible act of a small boy who had not reached years of discretion, the critical choices cleared the way for a speedy return to amity. Kwaling had an interest in the piglet and there is no doubt he was angry over its death. But he is in no kind of competitive relationship with Geengai. He struck Twambar, his own son, not Kandidi who had done the deed. By so doing he avoided a major issue with Kandidi's mother's brothers. Nor was the action an accident: it was done, as Kwaling afterwards explained, specifically to avoid further entanglements. He was looking to consequences. The *br'ngun'guni* had to happen. The pig was dead, killed in public, and Geengai had laughed. Something had to be done. Nothing could bring the pig back to life but, especially in view of what had happened with Reamai, there had to be a retort.

Geengai refused to accommodate Kwaling. In his way a philosopher, and a Christian, Geengai had spent the last two weeks bringing out the funny side of the Reamai affair, and he had even succeeded in making it look ridiculous—a joke hardly appreciated by Kwaling. Yet, though Geengai refused to meet Kwaling on a ground of his own choice, he is so far locked in traditional values that the reply he made referred to the ravages of Kwaling's pig in his garden. And his final act, an apparent attempt to sever his connexion with the village by cutting his coconuts, shows that he felt keenly his inability or reluctance to maintain equivalence in the traditional way. In the eyes of his friends and relations he was failing quite miserably.

Nobody will ever know whether Geengai was bluffing or whether he really meant to cut his coconuts. He had more to lose than to gain by so doing, but points in his hand if someone would stop him: his wife's brothers could hardly have been more timely. Kwaling had dominated in *br'ngun'guni*, but this was only because Geengai had refused to accept. If Geengai had wholly submitted, sympathy would have gone to Kwaling because Geengai's behaviour would have been thought contemptuous and therefore a deliberate breach of equivalence. Further, no one in the community would have failed to impute to Geengai a purposeful and malicious intent to get his own back by sorcery—a flagrant intent to do evil which would have made him most unpopular and even an outlaw. If Geengai had succeeded in cutting his coconuts, the community would have fallen to pieces: many households would have gone off into the bush to found new settlements where they might be able to live uninvolved in such an outrageous affair. Kwaling's reaction to the death of the pig was expectable and, in the circumstances, natural. Geengai ought to have engaged in *br'ngun'guni*. Yet no one would have had sympathy either for Geengai or for Kwaling had the coconuts fallen. Geengai should not have done it, nor should Kwaling have driven him to it. On the other hand, the evidence of intent served to equalize. Kwaling and Geengai, both, went off into the bush and kept out of each other's way. Three weeks later relations between them seemed to have returned to normal. Geengai was as cheerful as ever, and Kwaling had recovered his confidence. They had finished equivalent.

III

It was thought in the neighbourhood of Mangigumitzir that a man from the neighbourhood of Biampitzir—who was a renowned and skilful hunter and who had been giving a series of feasts—had been taking game from bush habitually used by a man of Mangigumitzir. Private representations had been made in Biampitzir, but still the game was elusive. The conclusion in Mangigumitzir was that the trespasser was continuing his mischief.

One night, at the start of a regular community dancing and feasting exchange in Mangigumitzir, Ndori, the Luluai, who was leading the dance, became dissatisfied with some of his team who were blowing whistles. So Ndori stopped the dance, asking his brothers to stop blowing their whistles. They nodded compliance and the dance continued.

A few minutes later, quite firmly, the whistlers piped up again.

Again, Ndori stopped the dance. It was his favourite dance, and as a leading conservative or traditionalist he disliked trade store whistles being blown in the dance. Was it clear that he didn't want any whistling? Yes, it was. The dancers resumed their places in the line and the dance recommenced.

But those with whistles wanted to whistle. Gradually the soft little 'peeps' grew into a chorus of shrill, fully blown screams. Ndori was obviously under some strain. Glowering, stamping too hard, and cracking his hand-drum in temper, he said nothing. Nearly everyone in the line was whistling.

Suddenly, Ndori straightened. Tearing off his headdress of cockatoo plumes, he flung it to the ground, stamped it to pieces, and strode off to his hut.

The dance stopped. Nobody spoke. Seconds later the rapid tattoo on a slit-gong and the clatter of the wand being flung into the body of the instrument informed all within earshot that Ndori was very angry indeed.

After a hasty consultation the dancers decided that the mission boss-boy should go to Ndori and try to persuade him to rejoin the dance. But when he returned a few minutes later he could only report complete failure. Ndori had shut himself in his hut, was very angry, and would speak to no one. 'Let us stop dancing,' suggested the boss-boy. 'If we go on it will make him angrier.'

The opposition was general. Someone struck up a hand-drum and the dancers resumed.

An hour later the boss-boy again repaired to the Luluai. He returned with the news that Ndori had gone to the stream to wash himself of his decorative, dancing paint. Speaking in formal *br'ngun'guni* the boss-boy exhorted all those present to abandon the dance. They refused. He started to lobby individuals, pointing out that Ndori could use his office of Luluai to stop dancing for the year. He went again to see Ndori, and spoke twice more in formal *br'ngun'guni*. But to no effect. Someone always struck up on a drum and the dance continued.

A little after midnight Kavak, Tultul of Biampitzir, who was attending the dance, rose to speak in formal *br'ngun'guni*. He was sorry, he said, very sorry indeed to see Ndori so angry. Why was Ndori so angry? There was nothing to be angry about. Perhaps it was the matter of——? But no! Allegations of trespass could be settled in amity, by talking. True, there had been a little wild talk, but it could never be meant seriously. True, men of Biampitzir were tired of being accused of trespassing, and there were some silly and irresponsible people who had spoken of stopping the trade in cooking pots if the accusations went on in this way. But now? Now it was different. Ndori was angry, angry in a dance! Angry because he had seen a man of Biampitzir, himself, at the dance! Right! Kavak thwacked his buttocks and leapt into the air— Biampitzir would let no more cooking pots into Mangigumitzir: they would smash them to make sure! Anger such as this over an unproven trespass!

Kavak did not get through his speech without interruption. It was pointed out that Ndori's anger had nothing to do with the trespass, nor was it a reply to the supposed threat of an embargo on cooking pots. It had to do with the whistling.

'Whistling?' cried Kavak, apparently incredulous. 'Bah!'

Many muttered expletives under their breath. Others shouted, 'You are a good fellow—come again next week!'

Or, 'Speak up—I cannot hear.'

Or, ironically, 'We like you. You're all right. Let us get on with the dance.'

Or, 'Oh true, oh true!'—a phrase always carrying explicit agreement but importing overtones of scepticism, or frank or aggressive disagreement.

Nevertheless, the position was serious. No one in Mangigumitzir could make a clay cooking pot. They had to get them from Biampitzir. The threat of an embargo was a fair weapon to use in reply to the allegations of trespass, but failure to establish Ndori's anger as resulting from the threat—followed up by carrying out the threat—was answering a pinprick with a bombshell. Mangigumitzir was to be without pots, and unless Biampitzir could establish anger in Mangigumitzir, Kavak, as representative of Biampitzir, had overreached himself.

The dance ended in general uneasiness.

The following night there was a dance in Biampitzir, and to it went several men from Mangigumitzir, including Ndori. The Luluai had recovered his poise, but even so the men of Biampitzir studiously avoided him during the feast. Towards dawn, however, Wapai, Luluai of Biampitzir, approached Ndori, offering betel and tobacco. Cautiously, he felt his way into a conversation. He joked, mentioning casually that there was no need for anger in this matter. He laughed with spirited gaiety. As tactfully, and quite as obstinately, Ndori refused to be drawn. In a few minutes Kavak joined them and contributed his quip. It was soon evident that he had abandoned his position of the previous night, and that his kinsmen in Mangigumitzir had persuaded him that Ndori had been angry over the whistling and not over the threat to place an embargo on pots. Without taking sides, he had become a mediator.

He tried to show both Wapai—who, sincerely convinced or otherwise, would have liked the anger pinned to the trespass— and Ndori that it was an understandable mistake that Ndori's anger should have been connected with the trespass. Ndori said little.

Nor were they the only men talking. It had become recognized that although Biampitzir was committed to stopping the trade in pots, the individuals concerned would like to recant without climbing down. If Ndori, or someone in Mangigumitzir, would admit Ndori's anger to have been over the trespass all would have been clear sailing. But no one in Mangigumitzir was willing to do it. Nevertheless, reconciliation had entered the decisive stage when it was agreed that Biampitzir should come to dance in Mangigumitzir. Throughout the interval between the feast in Biampitzir and that to be held in Mangigumitzir there were meetings between private individuals. Kin links between the two neighbourhoods facilitated the talks, but one factor stood out: How, in the circumstances, could one neighbourhood reach equivalence with the other?

During the feast in Mangigumitzir the men from Biampitzir danced very well. But when food was placed before them there was no meat and the tubers were not so well cooked as they might have been. Biampitzir were highly indignant. One after the other they spoke in formal *br'ngun'guni*. Why was there no meat? What had they done? Were the men of Mangigumitzir really so impossible? First there were allegations of trespass, then Ndori had been angry, and now there was no meat!

No one from Mangigumitzir spoke a word. They gathered the empty food bowls in silence, and the dance petered to an end.

As soon as the dance was abandoned there was jubilation in both camps. 'Now all the trouble is over,' said a man from Mangigumitzir. 'We gave them no meat.' A man from Biampitzir said, 'We shall have another feast. It is finished already, but another feast will finish it properly.' One insult had cancelled the other.

With the parties roughly equivalent there remained only a few niceties of wit to show how close to one-up equivalence can be.

Two days after the feast in Mangigumitzir the slit-gongs in Biampitzir announced the concluding feast together with the dance named Surai. When he heard the slit-gongs the Tultul of Mangigumitzir, who was to lead the dancers, at once let it be known in Biampitzir that he had a sore toe and would be unable to dance Surai. In Biampitzir there was much indignation since the Tultul's refusal was good for all Mangigumitzir. It was then noted, however, that the refusal had not been communicated by slit-gong, a public refusal in 'writing' as it were, but had been sent by messengers. In Biampitzir, therefore, those with kinsfolk in Mangigumitzir took up their spears, girded their betel bags, and set off for Mangigumitzir to make play with friendly intentions, and to confirm their suspicions of what lay behind the refusal.

Meanwhile, the Tultul sat on the platform of his hut, legs spread wide so that anyone who wished might inspect his sore toe. 'I do not like Surai,' he confided to me in a whisper. 'Besides, I haven't got the right regalia.'

It was also common knowledge in both neighbourhoods that the Tultul was an expert at the dance named Dumari.

As men from Biampitzir began arriving in Mangigumitzir to visit their kinsfolk, they passed by the Tultul. Some inspected the toe, clucking their sympathy, and went on their way. Others may have noted the Dumari plumes carelessly hung in the doorway. . . .

A couple of hours later the slit-gongs rang out again from Biampitzir. Surai was cancelled and Dumari was on.

Dumari in Biampitzir was a great occasion. The Mangigumitzir man who had first complained of a trespass went, and the alleged trespasser provided most of the food. All the speeches in *br'ngun'guni* were conciliatory. The quarrel, the 'talk', was dead. Both neighbourhoods appeared to have clean sheets before them. The atmosphere was gay, the food excellent and prodigious, the dancing superb.

Then Ndori made a speech in formal *br'ngun'guni*, the last to be made. He praised the food, soberly approving its quality and quantity, and he remarked on the skill, industry, and generosity that had gone into the preparation of such a feast. There had been some trouble, he said, the beat of his hand-drum beginning to quicken. There had been some talk. But now it was over. Ndori thwacked his buttocks for emphasis. He leaped into the air, bounding up and down the dancing space. 'Ha—what a feast!' he cried. 'But let the men of Biampitzir come to Mangigumitzir! Let them come to show how they could dance! Let them come and see if they could eat all that Mangigumitzir could provide!'

A chorus of yells greeted this outburst. 'Have you no shame? The talk is dead! There is no quarrel between us!'

Ndori sat down, gleeful and unchastened. The hubbub died down.

With the dawn came the end of the feast. As men and women stole away to their huts or their gardens to sleep, one or two remarked on the portent of Ndori's speech. Two months later men's ears were pricking as they reminded one another of what Ndori had said. For, though the two neighbourhoods are separate entities, only fifteen minutes' walk lies between them, the kin links are many and strong, and both sides enjoy having reasons to entertain each other at feasts—even when the reasons are of substance.

Besides being a Luluai, Ndori is also a manager. He had failed to get his way with the whistling, but in his final speech in Biampitzir he equalized personally and he also opened the door for another series of issues to be settled by inter-neighbourhood feasting. His last speech is the peg on which future issues will be hung. Other managers, looking to consequences and susceptible to mediation, also tried to influence the course of events. The mission boss-boy, not a Christian but inclined to be one, also a manager, was anxious because Ndori was angry and might have stopped dancing altogether. So he tried to have the first dance abandoned. Kavak used Ndori's anger to bring the bush dispute into the open, and to crystallize and justify what hitherto had only been rumoured —an embargo on cooking pots. Later, knowing he had overreached himself, he was among the first to attempt to restore equivalence through mediation, particularly choosing Ndori who had become, as it were, the fulcrum of the dispute. Others, in other directions, were not slow to follow his example. Some managers in Mangigumitzir felt that huge quantities of meat in the third dance, rather than no meat, was the proper response. Either would have neutralized the insult of placing an embargo on pots. But the scarcity of game at the time forced them to select the cheaper way. Wapai, manager as well as Luluai, called for dance Surai. In Biampitzir they were experts at Surai, well qualified to criticize others who attempted the dance. Knowing this, the Tultul of Mangigumitzir, also a manager, manœuvred Wapai into cancelling Surai and substituting Dumari, thereby serving a political as well as a personal interest. Finally, although Ndori's anger was over the whistling, a matter to be settled between a group of co-operating brothers, it started the whole train of events, was used to make other issues explicit, and was directly responsible for reopening further possibilities between the two neighbourhoods.

IV

The following incident provides a brief glance at Tangu in their relations with outsiders, and illustrates the basic theme of Tangu disputes: whither equivalence?

A dog belonging to a man from Andarumitzir—where they speak a variant of the Tangu language not intelligible to Tangu themselves—fell into a pig trap dug by a Tangu from the neighbourhood of Riekitzir. The dog died.

Grieved and angry at the loss of his dog the stranger repaired to the hunting lodge of the owner of the trap and demanded compensation of one pound (£1). Saying he would consider the matter, the owner of the trap returned to his settlement, spread the news, and started an informal discussion. A co-villager, just returned from hunting, joined them. He reported that he had fallen in with some men from Andarumitzir and they had urged him to tell the others in Riekitzir to forget about the demand for compensation. For Andarumitzir had no quarrel with Riekitzir.

One of those present said, 'Pay the compensation and have done with it.'

The latest arrival objected, 'There is no quarrel,' he said. 'It is best to forget all about it.'

'He was angry with me and demanded compensation,' said the owner of the trap.

The argument continued.

Payment of one pound is a fair and recognized compensation for causing the death of a hunting dog. But who was responsible for the death? Surely the dog was trespassing? The plain demand for compensation was a simple enough matter. It could be argued about and so mixed into other events that equivalence could be reached without actually making a payment. Withdrawing the demand after having made it makes the situation extremely complex. To pay or not to pay?

Riekitzir might insist upon paying, but in doing so they would offend Andarumitzir where there are considered to be many sorcerers much feared by Tangu. It would be asking for trouble. Not to pay puts Riekitzir at a decided disadvantage, for in any future *contretemps* men from Andarumitzir will say, 'Remember how we let you off that compensation you owed us?'

Even if the aggrieved party had not asked for compensation the death of the dog would have become known and nobody in Riekitzir could have imagined that the owner was not angry about it. Failing the open expression of anger the only other reasonable construction would be that the owner of the dog was resorting to sorcery. So men from Riekitzir would have gone to Andarumitzir to ask for sorcery to cease. In Andarumitzir they would have been suitably indignant, and counter-accusations would have been made. Other incidents would have been remembered.

From the moment that the man from Andarumitzir suffered his loss, some involvement with others was inevitable. And since it happened that a dog from Andarumitzir had died in Riekitzir the affair could not but involve Riekitzir in opposition to Andarumitzir. In the old days such an issue would

Old man of Riekitzir

A mother teaches her child to walk

Babe asleep in the gardens

have been resolved by armed demonstrations or warfare.
Today, since warfare is forbidden by the administration, and
neither party can or will *br'ngun'guni* in the settlements of the
other, the only way to 'settle' issues between them is to steer
clear, bicker intermittently, and resort to mystical attack.

The last dispute fairly describes the quality of relations
between households, communities, and neighbourhoods within
Tangu. Any event can, or is made to, precipitate a moral
issue related to personal integrity, equivalence, and amity.
Households are not organized into permanent corporate
groups, and co-operators one year may be in an exchange
relationship the next. All issues are basically matters for
consideration by the independent household, and expectations between households are only definable in terms of those
claims—which themselves are vulnerable to challenge—that
are actually being made good. The claims of individuals are
put to work for the household and, in a crucial conflict, the
household itself may split. When anger—which is evidence of
a conflict of claims and a breach of amity—can be related to
food and its production it is possible to maintain an equilibrium
as between households through *br'ngun'guni* and so establishing equivalence in order to return to amity. In Tangu no quarrel
is considered to have 'right' on one side. Each individual has
a way of retaliating to what is seen as a breach of equivalence.
In such circumstances, therefore, 'right' is merely a claim
temporarily made good in the teeth of possible or actual
opposition, and the extent to which a claim can actually be
exercised is only limited by what other individuals, having
counter claims, choose to do about it. On the other hand, any
action or attempt to exert a claim is subject to equivalence;
it has to allow for the counter and, if possible, leave room
for maintaining equivalence without forcing a resort into
sorcery.

Though, in Tangu, 'right' is in no way a theoretical absolute,
when Tangu become involved with the administration and its
officers, or its court, as Reamai threatened in the first dispute,

an explicit decision—implying a theoretical absolute—is normally made. And since such a decision must, in some way, detract from the total personality of one or the other interested party, it is a breach of equivalence and cannot predicate amity. So though Tangu often threaten to go to court they rarely go through with it; they know that to do so will only further delay the return to amity. If an issue does go to the administration and a decision is made, failing physical enforcement on the ground by policemen—which cannot be done effectively—Tangu proceed much as they would have done otherwise. They have feasting exchanges and *br'ngun'guni*. The administrative decision becomes a factor on the level of Ndori's anger or the Tultul's toe: it is used to work for equivalence. By resorting to the administration a second time, a return to amity is still further delayed. For, in order to return to amity it is necessary to establish equivalence, and the latter is as much dependent on the co-operation of the whole community as on the mutual respect of the individuals concerned. As we have seen, too, unless a native official is a manager in his own right, in a traditional context his influence is small. Meakriz tried his best but he was silenced. He came into his own when engaged on administrative business: working the rice field.

Br'ngun'guni is an activity designed not to make explicit decisions. It allows personal relationships to work themselves out in relation to the community. Brothers such as Kwaling and Reamai should, ideally, be in a co-operative relationship. But it so happens that, first, they are the two best food producers in the community and, second, there is a personal antagonism between them. In a co-operative relationship the discord becomes vicious and cannot conform to amity. In an exchange relationship, on the other hand, personal animosity becomes larded with mutual respect, which in turn lays the basis for equivalence. It may even be that Kwaling and Reamai will end up *mngwotngwotiki*—precisely equivalent. Finally, since Kwaling and Reamai are the two best producers —With whom can they exchange and at the same time maintain equivalence and a reputation for productive ability if they co-operate? What appears as personally desirable also emerges as a 'structural necessity'. Only by shifting from the co-operative to the exchange relationship can they work towards a personal equivalence. Other households will join them, help them towards their personal equivalence, and also work out their own personal equivalences. In the first dispute Meakriz, as Luluai, had to try to make peace. As Reamai's half-brother he came to his aid; as Luluai he demanded the court; and as Meakriz, the Luluai, a member of the community with a personal interest in it, he abandoned the idea. His behaviour in the second dispute, where he might have made an ass of himself by trying to be Luluai, as well as the behaviour of Kwaling, Reamai, Ndori, Kavak, Wapai, and the Tultul of Mangigumitzir, show a close coincidence of personal interest and political ends as well as revealing a more abstract conformity with the demands of the system itself.

As individuals managers are certainly restrained by the fear of sorcerers. A sorcerer may make a man sick, and if a manager is sick he cannot work. Being unable to hunt or spend time in the gardens his production will fall off, and accordingly his influence will decline. At the same time so long as equivalence remains a firm value expressed in equivalent exchanges of foodstuffs, it is evident that no manager can possibly attain an outright dominance. His own production must be reflected in the production of another. That is, even without the belief in sorcery the summit of power, the range of influence, and the amount produced by any one manager is no more than that which adheres to another manager also. Nevertheless, managers more than others are more keenly aware of the possibilities of sorcerers. To hire a sorcerer to make a rival sick might be advantageous; but to overreach oneself and so fall sick at the critical moment in a series of feasting exchanges would be disastrous. For even after a successful recovery others will bear the experience in mind, feeling that the same weakness might express itself in the same or a worse way. If, in short, the working out of equivalence might be expressed, abstractly, in terms of interest merely, in real life the belief in sorcerers forces a man to forward his interests and find his equivalences while also looking into his conscience.

AN IDEAL OF MANHOOD

Tangu managers have no exclusive control over particular techniques which are taken to account for their greater productive ability. The vast part of the body of pragmatic and mystical techniques are common to all: and each individual has a few private spells which have been passed on to him by a father, mother's brother, or friend. No one in Tangu will admit that his own private spells or techniques are in themselves less efficacious than those of another—though managers, of course, may claim that their own spells and techniques have special efficacy. When they are asked disinterestedly to account for differences in productive capacity Tangu either deny that differences exist, or they say, quite simply, that one man works hard and another does not; that one applies himself more than another. And so it seems to be in fact. A manager chooses his new garden site with great care; he remembers as others do not which sites have produced good crops in the past; he looks over the ground, seeking the signs, testing the mulch of the rotting leaves, observing the growth of wild vegetation. Mere convenience to the settlement is not the imperative with him that it may be for others.

Though a manager has no more knowledge than other men, he is able to use it. A man who produces less than a manager will not account for the difference in terms of any inherent disability or lack of knowledge. Instead, he will draw attention to the variety of circumstances that, for the time being, are preventing him from giving of his best. Or, he will laugh and say that he has enough. All men are considered to be equal one to another as whole beings, moral entities. A may have many advantages over B, but they do not provide him with grounds to behave as though he were better than B. A man dogged by ill fortune can either muddle along in terms of what is approved, or wholesome, or, being envious in his heart, he can resort to sorcery and make himself big out of evil. Then, as we have seen, Tangu are in a dilemma. Is such

108

a man taken by Evil in spite of himself, or has he chosen, with full cognizance, to do evil? Tangu are generous and charitable to sorcerers not only because they are afraid of them, and cannot know exactly what has happened, but also because he is a man, an equivalent being. In action amity and equivalence win out. Who knows, Tangu say, but that the sorcerer's victim deserves his fate?

For the majority of Tangu a manager embodies the ideal of what a man should be or should aspire to. Boys and young men see in him the realization of their best ambitions, and it is thought that all women prefer their husbands to be managers. Tangu have good reason to hold to such an ideal, for a manager is in himself an individual acting out community values, maintaining equivalence and amity through competition and rivalry, sensitive to internal community pressures. His capacities for industry, knowledge and judgement might be the envy of any elsewhere. But in expressing himself and his abilities he may not outrun the presumption of common and equal humanity. At the same time there are some in Tangu who are beginning to reject the managerial ideal. The more thoughtful and sophisticated Christians can see for themselves that maintaining equivalence demands constant disputing. And, bluntly, they do not want to dispute. The unities associated with the mission, and with Christianity itself—membership of a world wide body—cut across traditional sectionalisms and invite other and large loyalties. Catechists, able men, a new intelligentsia and outwardly the most knowledgeable Christians, feel they must fight an ideal that pushes them to the peripheries of the community, leaves them small scope for making use of their gifts in a political context, identifies them as partial outsiders, and denies them a full and developing part in the life of the community. Administrative officials, too, looking to the future and, perhaps, to their own interests, are conscious that they cannot carry out their duties in the face of the traditional managerial ideal. They know they are the chief agents of change through the administration, that particular changes must be imposed from above, and that this cannot be done within a society where leadership and influence are dependent, traditionally, on riding community sentiment.

Nevertheless, despite the seeds sown by missionary teaching and the demands of the administration, the twin values of amity and equivalence still dominate Tangu life in a very real sense. They are the keys to the understanding of the community structure, the composition of co-operative groups, the forms of political leadership, the process of becoming influential, the distribution of wealth, and to the ways in which individuals behave when they are in accord, or when they have differences. From early youth until retirement men are at pains to put to the proof their assumption that all men are equal, and that only by proving it to be so by disputing is it possible to live in amity. As canons of behaviour, however, both amity and equivalence are easily bruised. Moral equality is an easy, delicate premise which is difficult to perceive through variations of ability. And since amity is possible— as far as Tangu are concerned—only through equivalence, it is with the latter that they mostly concern themselves. They dispute frequently.[1] Neither ideal can be taken simply for granted. Both are individual and personal as well as community values which must be expressed and reiterated, first, as principles, and second, as socio-political factors affecting the content of particular relationships. And although for the few amity and equivalence appear as feeble impostors when compared either with Christian love, or the capacities and power of white men, an individual living in Tangu who was to allow either amity or equivalence to lapse by presuming they existed as given would suffer real consequences in the form of mystical attack, and loss of support in his efforts to wrest a living and prestige from the soil.

Equivalence entails a premium on personal sovereignty; an imperative which is easily transferable to the household since it is the latter which provides the child with a secure environment, subsistence, and, later on, enables the adult to fulfil

[1] One year of residence in Tangu produced twenty major disputes and many more minor ones. In addition, there must have been others taking place in those settlements in which I was not living at a particular time.

himself socially and politically through exchanges and
br'ngun'guni. Outside the household loyalties are not axiomatic. Permanent loyalties to this or that combination of households do not exist. Neighbourhood loyalties as well as the
feeling of being Tangu are largely matters of emotion, of oral
expression, comparatively rarely tying a man down to act, or
sacrifice himself on behalf of either. Loyalty to the household
is complementary to loyalty to oneself: each develops in
virtue of the other. Loyalty to other kinds of group within
Tangu, on the other hand, entails surrenders of personal
sovereignty. A man's social worth as expressed in the food he
produces himself becomes merely part of a whole contribution,
a combined effort. He, the unique combination of qualities
which make him a man equal to others, is submerged in the
whole in virtue of only a part of himself; he who, in an ideally
amicable and equivalent world, might be wholly self-sufficient
and independent of others, is yet forced to give and to
receive. Between the whole omnicompetent individual which
does not need to give anything to, or receive anything from,
anyone, and the man or woman who must do these things,
there is an inevitable tension: a tension—temporarily but
institutionally resolved in being *mngwotngwotiki*—between
self-will and morality, between the self as Lord and mere
constituent, which is clearly expressed in the action of
br'ngun'guni; in the shouting, drumming, running, leaping,
slapping the buttocks, and quivering limbs of the participants; in the calm, phlegmatic dignity of those who watch
and wait. It is a tension, too, which is expressed when
Tangu are given an order. To acquiesce in obeying a white
man, or a native official, is a denial of equivalence. To give an
order is partly cheating oneself of a birthright. Only partly
because Tangu believe that a new birthright is coming; only
partly because if the order is recognized as not arising directly
out of the administrative role it is an insult which, when
given by an official, can and must be made good in *br'ngun'guni*
and a feasting exchange.

CHAPTER IV

The People

[iii]

Behind Tangu as we find them today lie many years of continuous change and development. Before the grandparents of the present generation had seen a white man, and possibly before they had heard there were such people, a series of far-reaching changes were already in train. Indeed, to argue from a presumption of stability in Tangu during the last century and a half would be most ill-advised.

Sixty years ago Tangu were very much more numerous than they are today, a factor of some importance in relation to the distributive system and the forms of leadership. The dominating springs of action so far as they can be seen in terms of sorcery, amity, and equivalence were probably very much the same although they would have been filled out and qualified by the notions and activities pertaining to such institutions as the clubhouse and corporate kin group.[1] The managerial ideal, the politico-economic boss who is not only considered to be, simply, good, but capable withal, would have been balanced by the warrior, the military organizer, the specialists in herbal medicine, the ritual experts, as well as by artists and craftsmen. It is fairly clear, too, that the partial antithesis of the manager, the lazy man, was not only tolerated in communities large enough to 'carry' him, but that he probably had an important role as a man who reflected, ironically, on what others—more absorbed by community life—were doing. Or he may have been a jester, in the sense that Geengai, whom we have met, is a jester—a welcome relief from conformity and serious things.

[1] For the variety of corporate kin groups see The *Gagai* in Tangu, *Oceania*, September 1957, Vol. XXVIII, No. 1, p. 56.

Today, however, Geengai cannot spare the time to be lazy. Though he need not be a manager he cannot afford to be poor. No one else will feed him. But the image of the bad man— perhaps more clearly defined as an unlooked for result of missionary teaching in recent years—was probably always the sorcerer, the man who cannot, or will not order his affairs and ambitions plainly and openly within the accepted conventions but must needs resort to means considered underhand and evil. Nevertheless, it is possible to see through the talk of old men to a time when 'badness' in men had many more shades of meaning; when sorcerers were organized into small groups of men who, on special occasions, had a sacerdotal role; when death was not so much a sorrow as an opportunity for vengeance.

History seems to have had the effect of streamlining Tangu society. Once upon a time their houses were decorated with fine paintings; now they are plain, and the conventions and style of traditional art forms are dying out.[1] Making a slit-gong used to be a great socio-ritual occasion, involving several craftsmen and much feasting. For the slit-gong, the instrument that spoke for oneself across the ravines and down the valleys on public matters, was regarded as an extension of the self. Now slit-gongs are being made—when they are made— as a matter of course, roughly finished and undecorated: an expendable instrument. From a people enjoying a rich and variegated culture Tangu have developed into a reasonably busy people occupied with gardening and hunting, trading and exchanging, and feasting and dancing within the limits imposed by their resources and simple technology. Though today their tools are more efficient their clay pots, spear and adze hafts, string bags, grass skirts, hand-drums, slit-gongs, and decorative paraphernalia have neither the form nor the

[1] Just how rich Tangu culture might have been may be imagined by glancing through the sketches and paintings of Baron N. N. Miklucho-Maclay, who spent fifteen months on the Maclay coast (Rai coast) in 1871–2. These sketches are contained in Volume 5 of the series *N. N. Miklucho-Maclay* published for the Institute of Ethnography by Academia Nauk SSSR, Moscow and Leningrad 1954 (Academy of Sciences U.S.S.R.).

beauty they once had. And if the administration has seen to it that houses are more stoutly built than they used to be, they have tended to become buildings rather than homes.

This general process from diversity of occupation to participation in a few selected activities has not been entirely a result of the influence of white men. Specialization has also its indigenous roots. What is missing today, and conspicuously so, is an integrative or 'cross-cutting' institution in which competitive roles in the politico-economic process would, or could, become for the moment co-operative; the explicit occasion when sorcerer and manager could meet on equal terms; where fathers, mother's brothers, and sister's sons, normally relationships of tension, could meet on common ground; where all who were present could be enabled to admit, explicitly, to common humanity, community values, and interests. In short, the ritual or religious occasion. For let there be no mistake. The politico-economic process, its activities and associated notions, dominate Tangu life and thought to an inordinate degree. There is no break, no respite. The recognized opportunities for stepping off the treadmill of producing foodstuffs and competing in amity are few. Hidden rivalries, the quest for equivalence within competing and co-operative groups, and the fear of what sorcerers may do are ever present. Each individual must find his own opportunity to rest, to draw back with a laugh when he finds himself scanning another's garden in order to compare it with his own, to appreciate the irony of knowing that his ears are cocked for the insult, or the piece of information he is after. There is no specific community occasion today, having general consent, when the tensions engendered by the politico-economic process may have some temporary release or pause.

Once upon a time this specific occasion was provided by not one but several clubhouse organizations and secret societies; and a number of activities and institutions were associated with them. Initiation, circumcision, the teaching of ritual, the institution of friendship, ritual music on flutes, the teaching of crafts, painting, and the secret organization of sorcerers and sorcerer killers are a few of the activities which

114

used to be connected with clubhouses and secret societies. Their importance and significance were already on the wane, however, when the mission, backed by the administration, anathematized them. Today they are no more. But the mission itself is slowly providing a substitute. Every Sunday the Christians—and many others who are not Christians— make their way to the mission chapel to hear Mass. For a brief space, both during and after Mass, sectionalisms and rivalries are forgotten. The atmosphere is jolly, and the air is filled with laughter and joking as men, women, and children sit in the sun dressed in clean loin-cloth, grass skirt, or breech-clout, idly chattering, meeting friends, relations, and acquaintances. It is the only community occasion on which there is no food laid out, no need to worry about the return feast, no covert glances to see who has produced how much, or whether the meat is bad, or the tubers indifferently cooked. Those present are relaxed, and even the pagans enjoy themselves.

Nevertheless, although it seems to be fulfilling a need, the mission and its activities command no general consent. For a variety of reasons—arising largely from the implications of the triangle—the administration does not look kindly on extensions of mission influence. Opposition comes, too, from the pagan managers, the conservative element. One or two, it is true, are trying to interest their communities in reviving some of the old forms and traditions. But, for the most part, these men grumble about the present, and while they like to talk about the 'good old days' they actually do very little to preserve traditional ways. To them the existence of the mission in Tangu, and its teaching, are painful even to consider. Luluai, Tultul, and Doctor boy normally try to steer clear of the mission in case the missionary might seize the opportunity to remind them of work they have not done and ought to have done. Catechists, on the other hand, mission boss-boys, and those few who have begun to identify themselves with the particular kinds of change being introduced by the mission, do what they can to encourage attendance. For the majority, however, for the largely inarticulate mass over whom managers, native officials, mission employees, progressives, conservatives, missionaries, and administrative officers would like to exert a decisive influence, the mission station is somewhere one goes on a Sunday simply because one can go there. It makes a change and a joyful one.

Nevertheless, for all Tangu when they stop in their tracks to consider the matter, the mission evokes mixed emotions. It is a part of the new Europeanized environment. And as such it poses apparently intractable problems.

The difficulties Tangu have in accepting European institutional forms, and the more recent developments in the movement from diversity to uniformity, are intertwined with the formation and growth of the Cargo myth-dream. For the myth-dream was born when Tangu first saw white men, and it began to mature as the disappearance of traditional forms accelerated and encounters with white men grew more and more frequent.

EARLY DAYS

Apart from what has survived in Patrol Reports, and in confidential missionary reports—most of which were destroyed during the Japanese invasion—Tangu have no documented history. Reconstruction has to depend upon memories, material remnants, and calculated inference. Nevertheless, a pattern emerges.

The word 'tangu' itself seems to belong to a remote past. Perhaps to the people who fashioned so finely the stone implements to be found in the clay today. Tangu themselves know nothing about these particular stone implements or who made them. Nor can they give any tale accounting for the origin and meaning of 'tangu'. To them Tangu is the name which connotes the unity of the four neighbourhoods, and, more specifically, it is the place-name of a small but high spur in Wanitzir which has 'always' been called thus. By inference, since the particles -tang- and -tangu- occur elsewhere in the hinterland and are always part of the place-name of a rising spur, the word probably means spur, or high place, or what is associated with a high place.

116

The sites of some of the settlements in Tangu are undoubtedly very ancient. Particularly so in the central parts of Wanitzir, Biampitzir, and Mangigumitzir where the soft rock has been worn into channels by the passage of many feet. But though these sites are considered by Tangu to have 'always' existed, most of the present generation are too conscious of ancestries which lead backwards through time into other Tangu settlements and into the neighbouring areas to feel that they truly belong to them in the sense that they and a direct line of ancestors were 'always' associated with them. It is true that some of the older and more obdurate conservatives in the places mentioned do claim such an association but, on the whole, only those whose ancestries lead them directly to the now deserted spur called *Tangu* seem to be really confident that they have no other known 'origin'.

Though we cannot know what kind of people once lived in the area, it is reasonably clear that Tangu as we know them today are a mixture of peoples and cultures, the resultant of two very gradual population movements, from the hinterland and from the coast, meeting in the clump of ridges where Tangu presently live. The Tangu language itself probably has its roots deep in the past, but though its grammar and syntax may be assumed to have been reasonably stable, words have been borrowed from neighbouring peoples, and are being borrowed from Pidgin and from English today. The most popular myths in Mangigumitzir and Biampitzir tell of origins in the hinterland; and the ancestries of many of the present inhabitants of these two neighbourhoods lead them thither. In physical type there is a general conformity with the hinterland peoples: dark skin, dolichocephalic heads, large, strong boned men. Culturally, too, with forest traditions and sharing many myths, they are akin. As for Riekitzir, we know with reasonable certainty from genealogies and from the stories of old men, that it was populated in comparatively recent times by men and women from Biampitzir who came across the intervening ravine. If there were people living in the country now called Riekitzir before the Biampitzir folk came there we can only make a calculated guess about them. Probably they were kin to the people of Andarumitzir, far to the west, or to those in Jumpitzir to the south.

The present inhabitants of Wanitzir, on the other hand, are typically copper skinned, brachycephalic, stringy, light, and with grassland traditions: their myths and genealogies reveal strong ties with coastwise folk. Their ancestors probably came from the coast. And that the two population movements from the hinterland and from the coast are still going on, or have only recently ceased, may be inferred from the facts that one Wanitzir community has only been speaking Tangu for two generations—and speaks it with the glottal stop characteristic of the coastwise peoples; and that in Biampitzir, Riekitzir, and Mangigumitzir many ancestries of shallow depth lead westward into the hinterland. In the former case men can point to the coconuts, hunting lands, and settlements of their grandfathers some miles to the north-east, and they can remember them as being unable to speak the Tangu language. In the latter case a few men and women still visit their kinsfolk in the hinterland.

Though the argument as to ethnological origins can never be firmly based without documents and authentic records, what we can be reasonably certain of is that the polity we now know as Tangu was going through its birth pangs in the 'eighties and 'nineties of last century. Very first beginnings might, perhaps, be placed a generation earlier, in the 'fifties and 'sixties. At any rate, to take a date calculated on genealogies, between 1880 and 1890 the peoples living in the four neighbourhoods of Wanitzir, Biampitzir, Mangigumitzir, and Riekitzir certainly seem to have embarked on the process of becoming Tangu. They were beginning to know each other well, to intermarry regularly, to trade across the kin links so formed, to fight in a variety of combinations, and to interchange a number of cultural traits. Mangigumitzir, Biampitzir, and Riekitzir were very like to each other and closely homogeneous. Each of these three neighbourhoods consisted of very large collections of almost contiguously grouped hamlets of some four to seven dwelling houses sited on the spurs and crests of two parallel ridges: Mangigumitzir and Biampitzir on the same, northernmost ridge, nearly a mile apart, and Riekitzir south across the valley within sight and slit-gong range of the other two. Almost certainly they were organized in matrilineal groups, each hamlet being built round a dominant, localized matrilineage which served as a basic jural group.

The main Wanitzir communities were embedded in the outer curve of an escarpment which, rising steeply from the downlands to the east, turns north and west to Biampitzir and Mangigumitzir, and south and west to Riekitzir. These settlements were relatively compact, and divided into two topographical and social halves. A form of dual organization seems to have been characteristic. At the same time, however, there seem to have been at least three different kinds of social organization. One was based mainly upon patrilineal descent, another depended on a system of double unilineal descent, and in a third membership of the jural group depended upon placement in a line of siblings: first son to A, second to B, third to A—and so on.

That there was fighting, mainly on the level of the localized jural group, between members of the same neighbourhood, between representatives from Biampitzir, Riekitzir, and Mangigumitzir, between Riekitzir and Wanitzir, and between Wanitzir and Biampitzir, one may not doubt. But even of this early stage one is inclined to believe the claims of old men that Mangigumitzir, Biampitzir, and Riekitzir would combine with each other to ward off forays made from the north, west, and south. This does not mean that the three neighbourhoods fielded all their fighting men together. Such an operation would have been organizationally impossible, impracticable, and logistically improbable over the steep, thickly forested hillsides, narrow ravines, and marshy flats. But it does mean that members of each of these three neighbourhoods could expect help from kinsfolk in the other two. Wanitzir was rather more exclusive. Spatially separated from the other three neighbourhoods, more tightly organized, and almost certainly enjoying richer and more developed cultural forms, two main factors seem to have drawn the Wanitzir communities into active alliance with the other neighbourhoods.

First, population pressures from the north and west seem to have been far greater than those from the coast: only small fractionated parties trickled in from the east. If Wanitzir had not been overrun by the more numerous and vigorous peoples of Diawatitzir, it might still have been submerged by the peoples of Biampitzir, Mangigumitzir, and Riekitzir who were themselves being repeatedly harried from the north and west. As it was, Diawatitzir, still regarded today as the most danger- ous enemies of Tangu, almost outflanked Wanitzir and cut off their trade route to the coast. In fact, the four neighbourhoods, Wanitzir, Mangigumitzir, Biampitzir, and Riekitzir came together as a unit and combined with each other to fight Diawatitzir, Igamukitzir, Andarumitzir, and Jumpitzir. Second, together with the fight for survival enforced from outside went an underpinning of the military alliance by kin and economic ties.

Old men of Mangigumitzir, Biampitzir, and Riekitzir remember their fathers and grandfathers telling them of a time when they had no clay cooking pots, when they always cooked their yams and taros in barrels of green bamboo. Even today, in disputes,[1] Tangu refer to the time when cook- ing pots were exclusive to Wanitzir, when unity and friendship were sealed by the intermarriages necessary to maintain exchange and trading links. Bamboo does not grow well in Tangu though it is to be found in large quantities further to the west and north. And while Biampitzir, Mangigumitzir, and Riekitzir have plenty of sago, and pandanus fibre for making string bags and grass skirts, the land in Wanitzir is too dry either for sago or pandanus. Thus, economic and political needs seem to have drawn the four neighbourhoods closer together. The intermarriages necessary for trading and exchanging could not but weld more tightly the fighting alliances, and through kinsfolk in Wanitzir the peoples of the other neighbourhoods gained a safe route to the sea.

If some problems were solved by coming into a unity, along

[1] *Vide supra* p. 98.

with the extension of horizons, an interchange of cultural traits, and a higher standard of living, a number of further problems began to appear. The chief institution determining both internal community relationships, and the relations between local groups, was marriage.[1] Internally the composition of the jural groups was largely dependent on rules of exogamy, and it was through kinsfolk deriving from inter-marriages that local communities within Tangu could bespeak each other and settle disputes over land and sorcery without necessarily resorting to feud and physical force. In Wanitzir, so old men say, trouble had already started over the residual choice which lay, explicitly, in the children of a marriage as to which 'half' of the community they should belong to. Youths and maidens who had been betrothed in their infancies by their parents were kicking against the pricks. There were quarrels over the earnests of bridewealth paid over at the betrothals—quarrels which were going more and more often to points of no return. Intermarriages between the constituent neighbourhoods cemented political and economic ties but on other scores they were causing much unrest. In Biampitzir and Riekitzir new ideas of patriliny seem to have been attractive to many, and disagreements between traditionalists and others over marriageable brides and inheritance of hunting and garden lands began more and more to lead to serious quarrels. Furthermore, since the children of mixed marriages began to insist on trying to make good claims they might derive from either parent, small groups split off from the large parent communities and settled in the bush where they might more easily exercise claims both patrilineally and matrilineally based.

These factors apart, the payment of bridewealth was also becoming an acute problem. Traditionally, part of the pay-ment was the transference of chaplets of dogs' teeth; and the supply of dogs' teeth, a balance between the value of a live hunting dog and its teeth when dead, had, until the 'nineties,

[1] For additional details see The *Gagai* in Tangu, loc. cit.; Descent in Tangu, *Oceania*, Vol. XXVIII, No. 2, December 1957; Marriage in Tangu, *Oceania*, Vol. XXIX, No. 1, September 1958.

been reasonably steady. When the Germans came to New Guinea, however, they introduced quantities of manufactured 'dogs' teeth' which began trickling through into Tangu. It cannot be said for certain that the value of natural dogs' teeth slumped: but the value set upon either article certainly varied considerably. Many rejected the glistening, white artificial teeth as unsuitable for a bridewealth: others, on the other hand, rated them more highly than the yellow, black grained, natural article; yet others thought the one suitable for a personal adornment but not for a bridewealth. Even today, though the supply of artificial teeth has ceased and the supply of natural teeth has continued, there is no general consent in Tangu upon relative values. The increasing rarity of the one has not, in any general sense, made it more valuable than the other.

With the mutations of values in dogs' teeth, artificial and natural, went local variations in the ascribed status or worth of particular men and their wives as well as doubts as to whether particular couples were in any sense 'truly' married. As a result, marriage being under attack from several quarters, and a popular solution being to opt out of the traditional norm and found a new settlement in the bush, there was a weakening of the solidarity of the jural groups and the start of a general dispersal. Both processes were hastened on at the turn of the century by an epidemic sickness, the 'great sickness' as Tangu call it today. Possibly it was a pulmonary ailment carried to Tangu through their inter-village contacts to and from the coast, and certainly common throughout the Melanesian archipelago at about that time. Whatever the epidemic was, however, with it quarrels over marriage rules, bridewealth payments, and inheritance of bush lands took a far more serious turn. To quarrel was one thing, but when men and women began to fall sick and die Tangu could only see the situation in terms of the activities of sorcerers employed by one or other interested party. Obligations to vengeance pushed all previous conceptions of the stable life still further away.

Even without the sickness it is probable that the jural groups would have collapsed simply under the pressure of the numbers of people taking advantage of the alternative choices. General consent to a single and valid norm had disappeared in the interchange of cultural values. As it was, in order to escape the dangers from sorcerers and vengeance killings, households and groups of households quit their traditional homes to settle elsewhere. The general movement was south, south-east, and south-west. The former large communities broke up and small groups expanded over lands that the members of the four neighbourhoods had hitherto regarded as distant hunting bush or even 'enemy' territory. Women seem to have been more vulnerable to the sickness, and the men, polygynous, fought to win, or regain stolen, wives. Small numbers of households formed local groups based on mutual trust and common interests rather than on particular criteria of kin affiliation.

It is possible that there were short periods of general and complete anarchy. But they could not have lasted for long. Internecine fighting went on for the next twenty years: nevertheless, attacks by outsiders could still evoke, according to Tangu, a united response. Wife stealing was endemic, but, through legitimization, it helped rather than interfered with intermarriages across neighbourhood boundaries. Trading, exchanging, dancing, feasting, and clubhouse life continued. So did the interchange of cultural traits. Yet, from what Tangu say of those years the fighting seems to have been more burdensome, more serious, and more disquieting than a mere institutionalized expression of mutual oppositions would warrant. Tangu knew they were faced with a problem. Over the years simple acceptance of the situation, and reacting to it in terms of current values, began to yield place to the more positive idea that fighting must stop. They had begun to think that they might themselves change the structure of values in which they were imprisoned. If there had been an institution through which individuals might have expressed new ideas without being thought unworthy of the ancestors it is possible that Tangu might have come to terms with their situation themselves. As it was, lacking a suitable organizational form, and being unable to invent one, the fighting went on until, in the 'twenties, the Australian administration and the S.V.D. mission finally established themselves in Tangu.

There were many in Tangu who hated the idea of white men interfering in their internal affairs. Some, as we shall see, had encountered Europeans already. But whatever the nature of their experiences even the most grudging could see the advantages of being managed by white men. Unable to extricate themselves from their troubles for the lack of an adequate political institution, the bits and pieces of an old knowledge were being forgotten in recurring crises, in living in scattered isolated groups; and the forms and rules relating to incest and marriage—essential to an ordered social life—seem to have become almost completely subject to circumstance, the strong arm, and guile. Women, especially, were to be the gainers from an enforced peace and ordered life. Over the preceding twenty years, due to the fluctuations in bridewealth, the sickness, the fighting, and the wife stealing, they had become as chattels. From a position of some influence in the social scene they had become almost entirely dependent on the fighting skill of their men. Peace was essential.

Throughout their many years of troubles, however, there can be little doubt that Tangu knew themselves to be men. Men who had a past, who knew that their ancestors had been honourable men, who wanted to live, and knew what to live for. They also knew themselves to be men who, for sufficient cause, were fit and willing to die on the end of a spear; who, pitted against similar beings with the same kinds of tools, felt their manhood in question if they were unwilling to defend what they thought was of value to them. The coming of the white man ushered in a period of doubt. A period during which Tangu felt themselves to be something rather less than men and closer kin to the beasts of the forest.

WHITE MEN

At about the same time as Tangu were suffering from the first effects of the 'great sickness' the German administration was beginning to make itself felt on Manam island and on the coasts of the mainland opposite. The S.V.D. mission was establishing a station near the village of Baliau on Manam island, and another was in the process of building on the northern curve of Bogia Bay. If the bulk of Tangu had not seen a white man they were probably beginning to hear about their existence and the kinds of opportunities they were offering. It is probable, too, that some few Tangu had seen a white man whilst on a journey to the coast for salt. And it is from this moment when, with troubles at home, Tangu first saw white men and their goods that we must record the birth of the Cargo myth-dream. White men and their goods had to be explained and accounted for.

About 1910 sufficient knowledge about white men and their doings had been gained to persuade a few Tangu to leave the strife of their homeland to seek their fortunes in distant plantations. Some years later the first missionaries and recruiters came up to Tangu. The missionaries came to explore, to see what was there, not to convert. The recruiters came to get men. Both brought with them objects, ideas, and ways of behaving that were, for Tangu, literally from another world. Tangu admit today that they were greedy for the trade goods the recruiters had. And they were impressed with the apparel and equipment of the missionaries. Tangu parents sold their young sons to the recruiters for a steel bush-knife and a few beads. And on several counts the bargain was satisfactory to both sides. As far as the parents were concerned they obtained possession of valuable tools which saved them the labour of chipping spear, adze, and knife blades from stone, and in the chronic situation of wife stealing coloured beads in the hand were worth several arms with a spear. Tangu admit, too, that they had few scruples regarding the honesty of the bargain. If the recruiter got his labour cheaply, it was thought that the children who were sold could be relied on to escape from the recruiter if they wanted to, and, if they wished to go with him, it was better that they should do so rather than remain in Tangu in peril.

The men who were once these youths sold to recruiters do not express themselves as having been dissatisfied at the time.

They were eager for adventure, to see new things. But when, eventually, they returned to Tangu not a few of them found that their fathers had been killed and that their mothers were the wives of other men. They had left Tangu at an age when they were just beginning to understand what life was about: they came back having learned of new ways and not well versed in the lore of their own kind. As well as they could they settled to the task of relearning their lives. They told stories of their adventures, firing others to follow their example. Meanwhile, clubhouse life, feuding, feasting, exchanging, trading, and disputing continued to flourish; and underlying all was the necessity for making new gardens each year, for hunting, for gathering, for wresting a living from the land.

German administration in Tangu was nominal merely. Tangu came across German administrative officers in the coastal areas, and there is a vague story of an administrative patrol which came to, but did not enter Tangu territory. Tangu are more certain, however, when, with a laugh, they tell the story of a police boy who, shaking with fright, came to Tangu one day and told them that henceforth they were to be subject to a 'Kukurai' living near the coast.

Nobody took any notice.

Though Tangu continued to trickle to and from the coastal areas it was not until after the first World War, after the Mandate was granted, during the middle 'twenties, that following hard on the heels of probing missionaries, an Australian administrative patrol penetrated to Tangu. Consisting of a Cadet Patrol Officer and some police boys and bearers, the patrol approached from the south-east and came to a halt at the foot of the high escarpment on whose spurs the Wanitzir settlements lie.

On the skyline the officer in charge could see a gathering of warriors, leaping, shouting, flourishing their spears. Long wooden war-shields protected their bodies from neck to shins, and palm fronds, cassowary plumes, and the feathers of the bird-of-paradise nodded to the rhythms of a war chant.

The administrative officer relates that it entered his mind

to turn back and wait for another day until the excitement had died down. He had heard the slit-gongs the evening before and he was expecting just such a reception. Instead, in the best traditions, he found himself advancing up the slope to the crest of the ridge, his right arm raised in a gesture of peaceful intention and his police boys following behind.

Tangu gave way and submitted to a parley in Pidgin English.

Tangu must have known that spears and bows and arrows were no match for rifles, and it need not be assumed that, at any time, they intended to attack the patrol. It is more probable that they were, in their own way, prefacing a political conference with a show of strength. And it was, also, a dramatic demonstration of that ambivalence which was to become typical of their relationships with white men in later years. For his part the administrative officer was in no position to assume anything more than he could see. Accordingly, and again typically, he pressed home his advantage. Those Tangu who were present were told that in future they were going to be governed by white men; that fighting between themselves must stop; that their settlements must be cleaned up; that villagers should dig latrines and defecate there to prevent sickness; that responsible officials would be appointed; and that further armed patrols would be coming up to Tangu to see that the people were doing these things.

After appointing temporary officials in Wanitzir the patrol returned to base in Bogia.

Knowing Tangu, and bearing their German experience in mind, it is difficult to believe that they took the parley overseriously. There were many other more important things to be done: gardens to be tended, game to be caught, feasts to prepare. It would have taken more than a little experience and imaginative insight to realize, effectively, that the administrative officer had meant what he had said even had his part in the parley been well understood. Besides, there was no authoritative institution through which the administrative officer could have conveyed his wishes to all Tangu or to a particular settlement; nor did Tangu possess a representative

127

empowered to accept terms for, or speak on behalf of, others. Each man was his own master, limited only by community values, by equivalence and amity, by the obligations other individuals could constrain him to honour. The terms of the parley were valid only for those Tangu who had personally and individually understood and accepted them. Others felt themselves free to do as they wished.

Subsequent patrols, which went through Tangu to More-sapa, had trouble. It became necessary to punish, to herd villagers together at rifle point and force them to dig latrines; to tear down insanitary huts and burn the ruins; to make it excruciatingly clear that orders were not words merely but words that predicated action. But to Tangu, of course, orders were incomprehensible: at most they might be interpreted as friendly advice which each man was free to ignore as he chose, having regard to the probable consequences. For the administrative officer, on the other hand, a solitary European in the midst of a population which had to be viewed as potentially hostile, it was both doctrinal and politic to ensure that the orders he gave were obeyed. He had to act firmly, drastically, and quickly. Not only his own life, but the lives of other administrative officers might depend upon it.

To say that there were misunderstandings is to imply the possibility of mutual comprehension: and of such there is scarcely a shred of evidence. Only by absolving the administrative officer from his duties as such, by giving him another role, might there have been a basis of common understanding. The following example, given by Tangu, demonstrates a typical impasse. We can see it from both sides.

In those days it used to be the custom for administrative officers to forbid the sounding of slit-gongs as he approached a particular area. In this way [so ran the theory] he could see what the villages were like when he was not there. The villagers would have had no warning of his approach.

One such administrative officer arrived one morning in Tangu. The villages were deserted and empty; no one was there to welcome him. Tangu were out in their gardens, doing their daily work. The officer happened to be hot, tired, and not a little irritated by the sight of the dirty settlement. His police boys searched the village, and, by chance, found one man who had decided to sleep off the effects of a feast in his hut.

Dragged from his hut, the man was told to fetch the other villagers. Not unnaturally, he went straight to his slit-gong and began to sound the recall for a *Kiap*. He was stopped, and punished on the spot for disobeying orders.

Out in their gardens some of the villagers decided to return to the village to find out what was happening. Others guessed the truth and thought they would remain well hidden in the bush.

The conscientious or over-curious folk who returned to the village were collared by police boys and put to work cleaning the approaches and digging latrines. Then, exasperated because only about half the village had come back, the officer decided to make an example of those who had returned. He made them work for three days.

The story, cross-checked, is substantially true. The chain of 'misunderstandings' derived directly from the attempt to be where one should not, or is not expected to, be. With the advantage of perspective it may be appreciated that to see what the village was like when he was not there put the administrative officer in the position of an eavesdropper who, having seen or heard something not to his liking, walks in to put matters right. At the same time, in the circumstances, what other course was open to an administrative officer who wanted to make sure that villages were maintained in a state of cleanliness and not simply cleaned up to celebrate the arrival of a patrol? However, once having envisaged, then created an impossible situation, the officer could not do otherwise than persevere. The only alternative would have been to do nothing and leave Tangu to themselves. Which, as a good officer attempting to do his duty, he could not do. Finally, it should be pointed out that the sole advantage of an administrative process anywhere is that it creates regularities by which those administered can order their lives in peace. To introduce surprises and irregularities is to negate the whole function of administration.

The point here is not that the officer might have acted imprudently, but that his duties, and zeal, involved him in being paternal to adults. His intention was to act in the interests of Tangu, to train them in certain techniques which would prevent sickness and consequent deaths. Nevertheless, arising directly out of the incident related, it early became evident to Tangu that it was going to be difficult to put a foot right. Whatever one did, it seemed, trouble would follow. The simplest thing to do was to keep quite clear and remain in the bush until the administrative officer was forced to move on. Alternatively, for fear of doing the wrong thing, it was best to do nothing until physical coercion made it obvious what was to be done. In consequence, Tangu gained a reputation in administrative offices for being intransigent. And successive Patrol Officers, having read the reports of previous patrols in the area, seem to have been over-ready to seize on further examples of Tangu obstinacy.

And in truth Tangu really are obdurate. Twenty years and more later there were still many who retreated into the bush on the approach of an administrative patrol. In 1952 most of the population—even if only to share vicariously in the excitement of their fathers—was still basing its responses and attitudes towards the administration and its officers on first experiences. Encounters during the intervening years should have led Tangu to qualify their expectations of administrative officers. But the vividness of a particular experience has had more effect than the statistical validity of numerous other and different kinds of experience. As a matter of basic principle, quite unreasonably in European eyes, Tangu still expect administrative officers to behave either arbitrarily, or forcefully, and certainly harshly; they expect imprisonment or forced labour for making mistakes. And while they know well what some mistakes are they feel there is a large area in which, through some entirely unpredictable caprice, an act will be a mistake if the administrative officer decides that it is.

The rather more gentle intrusion of the mission into Tangu was only possible—though a missionary himself would argue the contrary—under the cover of administrative protection. The first essays met with little positive response, and it was no inconsiderable feat to establish the first catechist in Wanitzir. Then, as Tangu migrant labourers passing through Bogia were persuaded into friendship, things became easier. European missionaries paid their visits more and more frequently, and plans were made to establish a permanent station. By the 'thirties a European priest had started to build himself a house and chapel, and by 1940 the station was almost complete.

Wanitzir people eventually took to the mission in fair numbers. The other neighbourhoods were more recalcitrant. And in all neighbourhoods there was, and still is, a hard core of active opposition. At the same time most Tangu are agreed today that the peace imposed by the administration has been of benefit; and that the mission, providing a concrete concentration point where all Tangu can meet at regular intervals, an ordered form of marriage, education for the children, and a secure channel through which Tangu can always find work on coastal mission plantations and maintain contact with their kinsfolk at home, has served them well. For the missionary priest himself all Tangu bear respect. He learned their language, could converse with them in their own idiom, and was there as friend and arbitrator both in their own internal troubles and in their relations with the administration. For many, too, Christianity itself, being a Christian, became worthwhile for its own sake, shedding on some a new dignity. But for those we have called the opposition mission and administration alike have always been anathema. Magnificent blimps, all pagans, they hanker after the future in a past grown glorious with telling and retelling. They resent the coming of the white man because he means change, because he is a stranger intruding in what they feel is not properly his business. Though they send their children to the mission schools they scoff at their Christianity and prevent them from attending when they feel like scoring off the missionary. To them the meaning of man is wholly derived from the past, and they feel their manhood slipping further away into history. They do not relish being the drying crust of the chrysalis from which the new man must come.

MORE TROUBLES

Overall, by 1940, so far as it concerns Tangu, and in spite of misunderstandings, both administrative officers and missionaries had cause to congratulate themselves—and earn deserved praise from others—on the work they had done within the limits of the means at their disposal. Nearly a half of the population of Wanitzir were practising Christians, and a few had been won from the other neighbourhoods. The peace was being enforced, standards of hygiene and housing were improving, and there seemed to be few urgent problems arising from the flow of migrant labour.

Yet there had been a warning of trouble ahead.

The first major event in the creation of the Cargo myth-dream was undoubtedly the first sighting of white men and their goods. The second was Mambu.

Mambu was a native of Apingam, fairly close to Bogia. He had been baptized a Catholic. In December of 1937, shortly after he had returned from a spell of contract labour, Mambu started to preach rebellion. His movement went along classical Cargo lines. Exiled by his own people he went from Apingam to Tangu. Expelled from thence by the missionary he eventually made his headquarters by Suaru bay about seven miles down the coast from Bogia. For two months the situation in the whole Bogia region was very unsettled. Mambu gained a large following. Then he was gaoled. In a few months, by June of 1938, everything appeared to have returned to 'normal'. Tangu returned to their gardening, hunting, and gathering; to feasting, quarrelling, and marrying. Sons of households continued to seek work on plantations in order to earn the cash that would buy them axes, knives, razor blades and beads—more efficient tools which would help them in their primary work, and decorative gewgaws for themselves

132

and their womenfolk to wear at dances. The missionary worked patiently at his teaching, enlarging his school, and attempting to combat the more evil effects of beliefs in sorcery. Sunday became a day to look forward to. And for their part, administrative officers continued to lay stress on hygiene, on counting the villagers, on regulating the flow of labourers to the coast, on combating sorcery.

But if Europeans tended to forget about Mambu, pushing him into a limbo of the past, Tangu did not. They talked about him a lot, what he had said, what he had done. And little by little the gossip was embellished. Mambu was something important in a way of life from which most of the salt had been taken away. European tools, being of steel, were more efficient than stone tools. But they were essentially substitutes. Nothing new had been added. Decorative paraphernalia filled out traditional values. The mission and administration, however, were striking at the roots of their moral and mystical notions. Clubhouse life, dancing, feasting, exchanging, quarrelling, and beliefs in sorcery allied to the obligation for vengeance were parts of one complex. The imposition of peace upon a people whose guiding ideal was linked to conventional quarrelling and fighting meant a complete reappraisal of the future.

From Mambu's imprisonment until the Japanese invasions, nothing seems to have occurred in Tangu to warrant particular remark. But the myth-dream was developing, foretelling a future, and resolving certain problems on the level of myth. Reappraisal was taking place—not as an intellectual activity cogitated, known to be known, but as a largely emotional or spiritual process expressing itself in myth. Tangu were, quite literally, feeling their way.

When the Japanese came administrative and mission programmes ceased abruptly. The Christians in Tangu regarded the event as an unmitigated catastrophe. They had come to rely on the missionary rather more than they had thought at the time, and now they were flung back into an ambience of traditional relationships with no mission organization to help them. The conservative opposition, pleased to be rid of the missionary, felt themselves ready and strong enough to eliminate the more important Christians by hiring sorcerers to kill them. At first, too, they seem to have been ready to welcome the Japanese. But the latter missed their opportunity: Tangu found that they were now going to be bossed by men who insisted on immediate obedience. New officials were appointed, and it was made clear that punishments would be far in excess of anything the white man had thought of. On the other hand, provided they could get men as carriers and labourers when and as they wanted them, the Japanese left Tangu more or less to themselves. Military patrols passed through Tangu, and native officials were used merely as labour recruiters. No positive administrative policy was enforced.

One consequence of leaving Tangu alone in this way was that standards of hygiene deteriorated, and increasing sickness was seen as an increase in the activities of sorcerers. There were deaths, and so loose was Japanese control that it was possible to follow out the old obligation to vengeance. Then, too, the conservative opposition never ceased nursing their grudges against the Christians and pressed forward in their attempts to bring about the deaths of some of them. Here and there assassins brought their plans to a successful conclusion.

Despite the fact that under the Japanese Tangu were beginning to slip back into the kind of state they were in before the white man came there, it is evident from what they say about them that Tangu did not wholly dislike the Japanese and what they did. By this time Tangu had begun to be familiar with the idea of obeying orders when these orders were given by strangers from outside their own environment. And, like the Germans, but unlike the more liberal Australians, the Japanese left Tangu in no doubt as to what might happen if their orders were not obeyed. This, Tangu appreciated. It relieved them of the mind-twisting subtleties of a system dominated by a notion of law and the legal. On the other hand, respect for this kind of downright self-knowledge was mingled with contempt for the way in which the Japanese behaved among themselves. Tangu say that the Japanese 'defecated where they slept, ate uncooked food, and never washed'. One man, thinking back, remarked that the Japanese had cargo—but not as much as white men.

As the war in New Guinea drew to its close, allied patrols came through Tangu—to the relief and gratification of the Christians. At about the same time, doubtless for sufficient reason, the mission buildings were bombed and machine-gunned by allied aircraft—to the not unmixed pleasure of the conservative opposition. Indeed, the destructive power and noise of 'modern' weapons of war appalled Tangu. They were more shocked and scared by their bombing than by any other wartime incident. It so affected them that in 1952 my map-making was held by some to be the first signs that the Japanese were intending to keep their promise to return to Tangu and so restart another war.

Some months after the military situation had been stabilized, so soon as the military authorities would allow him to do so, the same missionary who had resided in Tangu before the war returned there. He came to try to carry on from where he had left off. It was hard work. Without materials that he could not cut from the bush, without proper tools, he had to rebuild and refurbish the station itself, school huts, and the chapel. He sought out his old catechists, tried to recruit new ones, organized school classes. Many nominal Christians, and other backsliders, who as a result of their war experiences both in Tangu and as members of either the Japanese or Allied labour battalions, had become sceptical, had to be won back to the fold. Tangu clubhouses, which had been falling into disuse with the passage of years as the mission strengthened its grip before the war, and which had to go if the mission was to fulfil its programme and object, finally disappeared despite the misgivings of the old conservatives. And with the return of the mission regular administration through newly appointed native officials and patrolling by administrative officers was reinstituted. The medicine hut with its bandages and bottles of iodine, the insistence on hygiene, cleaning the village, digging latrines, counting heads, taking names, exhortations to improvements—all were back.

But though the triangle had reformed the balance of influence had changed. The missionary was still on the spot, but the organization which supported him hardly existed except in name. The church, school houses, workshops, and living quarters at Alexishaven had been razed. Mission vessels had either been sunk or commandeered. Plantations were overgrown, torn, and ragged. The administration, on the other hand, had first call on the quantities of equipment left over from the war. New policies had been formulated in Canberra, and large sums of money had been voted as compensation for war damages as well as to support a variety of new schemes. Administrative officers themselves, who had for years fought for more effective and enlightened support from Canberra, were on the crest of a wave of enthusiasm. Traders returned to the scene.

Nevertheless, for Tangu, it was, in effect, a return to the days of the Mandate.

It was not easy for Tangu to begin again from where they had left off. So much had happened in the meanwhile. And it was more than difficult for missionaries and administrative officers who were themselves adapting to different circumstances and new concepts of government to properly evaluate themselves in the eyes of their charges. For Tangu the Japanese period had been one of comparative freedom, a time during which—whatever the disadvantages—they had been more or less free to order their own lives. Now they were returned to that relatively close supervision of their lives which—despite the advantages—they cordially detested. Christians appreciated the presence of the missionary, the guiding hand. But they began to resent his enthusiasm, his popping up unexpectedly to inquire about this and exhort about that. Conservatives glowered over their fires, and the large majority—pagans, pagan Christians, and Christian pagans—went their several ways with a feeling of unease in the backs of their minds.

In the middle of this process of again finding their feet with missionaries and administrative officers, Tangu encountered a Kanaka named Yali.

Yali was the third major event in the myth-dream. Before the war he had been a Tultul on the Rai coast, south from Madang. Then he joined the police. During the war he served with distinction with the Australian military forces, and he reached the rank of serjeant-major. Then, in 1946, after he had been demobilized, Yali commenced his activities in the Bogia region. For four years he travelled round the villages of the Madang district, talking, preaching, exhorting, telling his audiences of a new way of life. At length, in 1950, after an extraordinary career, he was sentenced to a term of imprisonment.

Precisely what Yali said to Tangu is not known. But what is quite certain is that—without money, or goods, or soldiers, or armed police—Yali communicated to Tangu a sense of being in touch with a man whose stature was rather greater than their own, or that of an administrative officer or missionary. For Tangu Yali seemed to be beyond and above any other kind of man they had met. Although for years Tangu had successfully opposed the blandishments of mission and administration that they should leave their scattered settlements and concentrate into a few large villages, when Yali suggested they do so they started work almost immediately. They began to build new extensions to the most favourably situated of their old settlements, coming nearer to the mission station and to the main paths leading through Tangu from hinterland to coast. And if such a coming together seems a small matter let it be understood that Tangu did not like to do so: but they did what they did because he, Yali, had suggested it.

It is certain, too, that when Yali left the vicinity of Tangu he left behind him an atmosphere of expectation and excitement, of something in the wind, of great events moving to a predestined climax. He was saying much the same kind of things as Mambu had said a half generation earlier. It was an atmosphere which not only survived Yali's imprisonment, but which seemed to take on a new lease of life when it was learned in Tangu that he had been put behind bars. The air of tension and excited expectation seems to have increased.

The new settlement pattern greatly enhanced the speed and variety of rumours of what was happening and what might happen. There were comings and goings to and from Pariak-enam, a nearby village, where a youth was dreaming strange dreams. It must have been clear to Tangu that a climax was approaching.

It came in 1951. Following the oral publication in Tangu of a dream dreamed by the youth of Pariakenam, and taking their example from others in the Madang District, some—but not all—Tangu engaged in a series of Cargo rituals.

The Cargo myth-dream, developing over the years since first Tangu had come across white men and their goods, had found expression in physical ritual activity at last.

MANAM ISLAND

Having sketched in that part of the background that seems to be most relevant to the Cargo activities in Tangu, it is time to consider the situation in Manam.

Manam islanders were familiar with white men and their goods a full generation earlier than Tangu. The German administration had been in full control in the years before the first World War, and until the outbreak of the Japanese war the S.V.D. mission station, near the village of Baliau, had had a history of steady and vigorous development. Nearly the whole population had been baptized.

There are no records of unusual administrative difficulties in Manam, and the people seem to have constituted a rela-tively stable political entity enjoying a common tongue. In the early 'twenties, while Tangu were beginning to feel the first effects of white penetration, Manam islanders were being studied by a social anthropologist.[1]

Manam island is a large volcano whose crater, topped with a column of smoke and ruffed with a bank of cloud, may norm-ally be seen from the heights of Tangu. And the people who live there are settled in largish village communities on the lower slopes of the volcano, near the sea. Culturally, the

[1] The late Honourable Camilla Wedgwood.

138

strongest affinities of Manam islanders are with the peoples of that part of the mainland lying slightly to the north of west. Nevertheless, traditionally fishermen and sea traders, Manam islanders make voyages to neighbouring islands, to other parts of the Bogia region, and, as we have seen, they venture inland as far as Tangu. They cultivate taros and other root crops in their gardens, harvest the canarium almond in large quantities, and also grow many coconuts. Many go to work on European plantations, but generally they prefer to work on ships as seamen. Throughout the surrounding area Manam islanders are renowned as seamen and as rather fierce, hard-headed businessmen. They are also greatly feared. Tangu, for example, do not mind Manam islanders coming to Tangu, but they would not dare to set foot in Manam themselves.

Unlike those in Tangu, Manam communities contain two strata: *Tanepoa* or those of 'noble birth', and commoners. *Tanepoa* are traditional bosses and organizers who derive their positions and authority in the community from their birth and parentage. Commoners defer to *Tanepoa*; only those who are *Tanepoa* may wear their badges of rank or live in their large, distinctive, and specially decorated dwelling houses. The rank of *Tanepoa* is inherited through the patriline, and though all who are thus *Tanepoa* enjoy superior status they are not all of them bosses. Rather do they form a pool from whom *the Tanepoa*, or chief (commonly *Kukurai*), of a village may be selected, and from whom also the minor bosses may be chosen. As between *Tanepoa* and commoner there are mutual rights and obligations which entail, generally speaking, responsibilities on *Tanepoa* in exchange for privileges.

Manam islanders are a notoriously proud and independent people: they tend to look down upon other Kanakas as inferior breeds. Their own notions of moral egalitarianism are drawn from their own social model. All men are equal, but some are bosses and others are bossed. The bosses have privileges, but in return for those privileges they bear the burden of responsibility. Manam islanders would like to draw Europeans into their own system either as bosses with a range

139

of known and limited privileges together with defined responsibilities; or on a level with themselves, as *Tanepoa* or commoners with parallel limits of obligation. Manam islanders pay lip-service to the idea of *Kanakatzir*, but, unlike Tangu—who feel they are one with all other Kanakas, and who would like to be one with all white men—they cannot help thinking of themselves as a whole as the bosses or leaders of *Kanakatzir*.

Manam islanders knew Mambu: but they could not admit to being led or influenced by a mere bush-Kanaka. Tangu, on the other hand, not being able to admit to a leader among themselves, were ready to be influenced by a stranger. Manam islanders knew Yali; and Yali came from outside their own regular ambience. But Manam islanders were what they are, and whilst they could accept some of Yali's ideas the notion of being led by a stranger was still distasteful. Through 1951 and 1952 their own charismatic figure was emerging. In 1952 all the ingredients of a Cargo movement were present in Manam, but a definable cult did not seem to be crystallizing. Instead, Irakau, a *Tanepoa* of Baliau, was very shrewdly organizing his village into a commercial concern. All in Manam looked to him. He was planting coconuts, organizing the manufacture of copra, and exporting it in bulk on the European dominated market. It seemed, in December of 1952, as though a Cargo movement had been continuing, *sotto voce*, for many months.

THE TRIANGLE

It would be a mistake, I think, to regard the activities of Europeans in New Guinea as being the causes of Cargo movements. Rather are Europeans and the roles they play parts of a total complex from which Cargo movements may emerge. Europeans seem to have been almost as much involved in the notion of Cargo as Kanakas themselves. And to appreciate the parts played by the charismatic figures Mambu, Yali, Irakau, and the youth from Pariakenam, they should be viewed not only in relation to the peoples they influenced, but within a total relationship structure including missionaries, administrative officers, and Kanakas. Traders, planters, and recruiters may be ignored because, except when they have behaved as though they were missionaries or administrative officers, or when they have behaved like missionaries and administrative officers, their influence in relation to the growth of a Cargo movement seems to be minimal. What the charismatic figures said and did meant something to their audiences because of what missionaries and administrative officers were doing, and hardly relate to traders as such. Similarly, the reactions of administrative officers and missionaries seem to have been determined by their own relationships with each other, to Kanakas, and to the charismatic figure in question. On the whole, traders remain isolated from the basic situation.

It will be remembered that the administrative role is to keep the peace and supervise and regulate certain selected activities such as migrant labour to the coastal plantations, co-operative schemes—usually in places fairly close to the European bases—hygiene, cash crops, and a number of other matters. On patrol, when visiting the villages in his area—the sector of the administrative task most relevant to Tangu and to Manam islanders—most of an officer's time is taken up with inspecting latrines, checking the stores in the medicine hut, the general cleanliness of the village, census counts, and inquiring into land and sorcery disputes. He uses Pidgin English, and his channels of communication and information are usually the native officials. His connexion with any particular community must necessarily be temporary and brief. He has many other villages to visit, reports to write up, statistical data to tabulate. On the completion of a patrol he returns to his base, composes a full and all-embracing report, and turns to the backlog of paper work that has been accumulating while he has been on patrol. Two or three months later he may set off on another patrol.

The work entailed is extremely demanding, calling for the very best balance of qualities of character, initiative, and training. And the administrative service is fortunate in being

141

able to find the men that it needs.[1] Nevertheless, it is only just possible, always supposing that he is not suddenly transferred to another area, that an administrative officer may visit all the villages and settlements in his sub-District once during his tour of between two and three years before going on leave. He might stay in a village a day and a night, or he might stay a few hours. A minimum personal relationship is involved. For the Kanakas concerned the officer stands for the administration: unless he does something quite extraordinary he is just another *kiap* doing much the same things in much the same way as other *kiaps*. Yet, typically, administrative officers regard the Kanakas of their area with affectionate possessiveness: they are their people, whom they would like to help, for whom they are responsible.

The missionary, living in his station which has been conveniently situated to serve a group of villages, also regards the Kanakas of his area as his own. He lives close to them. He teaches the children, he speaks the local dialect, he knows people's names, who their parents are, their circumstances and kinsfolk. He meets his charges every day of a tour which may last for ten years. Some S.V.D. and Lutheran missionaries have been with the same people for upwards of twenty years. And although a missionary is where he is to teach, and to bring to pagans an awareness of God that will result in freely consenting conversion, for Kanakas he is a person as well as a role. Unlike the administrative officer who, essentially in a position of authority, can always dispose physical force, a missionary has to live out, in a Kanaka environment, the results of his own as well as any other European's mistakes. In order to earn in his everyday acts the moral trust and respect of the Kanakas of his neighbourhood a missionary has to enter, at least in part, the indigenous system of reciprocities. If he does not he forfeits a basic and mutual confidence:

[1] Candidates for the administrative service are carefully selected and given a course of preliminary training at the Australian School of Pacific Administration in Sydney. After a short tour of apprenticeship duties in the territory officers return to the School for a long and detailed course of study. Later in their careers officers may return to the School for 'refresher' courses.

he is nowhere in sight of his primary end, nor is he able to put into effect a variety of necessary means. He is ostracized, scorned; boys and girls do not come to school; mission stores are pilfered; when he wants to travel, or restock his stores, nobody will carry his equipment and supplies; youths catcall at night to prevent him from sleeping. The trust and confidence of his parishioners is a missionary's first task and last risk.

Assuming that he has established such a mutual confidence, however, a missionary finds himself awkwardly placed. Kanakas, who like to think they are the best judges of their interests, expect the missionary to support them against the administration. And there are many situations in which a missionary can strengthen his own position among his Kanakas by satisfying their expectations of him. Not unnaturally, administrative officers tend to view such actions as 'making trouble', as subverting their own ideal relationship with the Kanakas under their charge. Much more than administrative officers, missionaries are aware of the predicament, and, because there are occasions when they need the help of the administration against Kanakas, they are always willing to put their not inconsiderable logistic resources at the disposal of the administration. Mission mechanics are efficient; their ships, lorries, and wirelesses work; they can always feed and restock a patrol officer running short of supplies. Such actions do not necessarily impair a missionary's relationships with his Kanakas, but, however well intentioned, they cannot but sour the lot of an administrative officer who wants to be a missionary too.

Although Kanakas are aware of most of the implications of the triangle, it would be fair to say that they do not quite grasp that they themselves, and their confidence, make the prize for which both missions and administration are competing. They are not unwilling to play off mission against administration when it suits them, but on the whole a missionary is a better ally against the administration than vice versa. Only a few seek the aid of the administration against a missionary. The adventure is too risky. The necessary personal relationship between villager and officer may evaporate in an administrative replacement, and, in any case, the duties attached to the role of an administrative officer are so much more important than the incumbent that anything short of a genuine grievance might find the complainant dangerously out of his depth. Thus in spite of himself, a missionary will often find himself involved against the administration.

On the other hand, because they are white men and therefore of the caste of the bosses, missionaries are sometimes forced into the role of administrative officers. Take a simple case. A Kanaka comes to his local missionary and says that he has been threatened with murder by sorcery. Overtly, the course of the missionary is clear. He should stand aside and hand the case over to the administration. But can he afford to do so? If the complainant is a Christian it is his duty to help him; more so if the complainant is a pagan. If he hands the case to the administration he knows that in the nature of things the very best officer will have little hope of disentangling the maze of apparent irrelevances that go to make a case of sorcery. The administrative officer is bound by his Law, and the Kanaka by beliefs of his own. If, as is most probable, the case is dismissed, or is inconclusive, he, the missionary, will suffer from both sides. The Kanakas will be annoyed by the fuss and bother of the investigation—and simply because a European type of investigation does lay bare so many details which most would prefer to keep hidden they will not confide in the missionary in the same way again. For his part, quite naturally, the administrative officer will be vexed at 'so much trouble for nothing'—and he may even note in an official report that the missionary is unnecessarily alarmist. If, on the other hand, the investigation is successful and a man is arrested, the administrative officer will return to his base with his prisoner, well satisfied with a good day's work. And, alone in his village, the missionary wonders how and when the kin of the prisoner are going to take their revenge. Sadly, he must go to his more loyal parishioners and ask them if they will volunteer to stand guard. Whatever the result of the official investigation, therefore, the missionary tends to lose stature and ground.

The picture of a missionary being boiled in a cannibal cooking pot is not really so inapt as it might be. From the earliest days of European penetration into Melanesia missionaries have had to live out the results of their own and other peoples' follies in their chosen environment. They have had to identify themselves with their parishioners, protecting them from the abuses practised by traders, slavers or 'blackbirders', in the early days as well as more recently; and with the coming of administrative officers they have felt it their duty to take their parishioners' part against what often seemed to be uninformed and unimaginative officialdom. If a trader survives a mistake, or sharp practice, in one place he will take care about going there again. An administrative officer can, and could, always withdraw under the cover of rifles, confident at worst that he will be posted elsewhere soon. Not so the missionary who, often maligned by trader and administrative officer alike because he must take the part of the Kanaka against either, has to live through his troubles whether he caused them or not.

In practice, of course, missionaries have to weigh up the merits of each particular case which may involve them with administrative officers. They learn to live with sorcery as do Kanakas themselves, and they learn to deal with the variety of problems that arise in their own ways. They have to. Nevertheless, by doing so a missionary cannot but be an obstacle in the path of an administrative officer who feels, quite rightly from the point of view of the role put upon him, that he and not the missionary is the man properly fitted to deal with such cases.

Not necessarily involving a conflict of personalities, but certainly implying a conflict of roles, a missionary, who is subject to the pulls of both environments, must first evoke the values of the local environment if he is to bring his charges to an appreciation of the values of the environment of which he himself is a child; and in cases of conflict he must choose according to his conscience and to his role—which are not always compatible. Having made his choice he must accept the consequences which must inevitably flow from the values of both environments. He is so placed that he must be maligned whether he is helping one side or other, both, or neither. He is a favourite target, not least because he cannot riposte without damaging himself. An administrative officer, on the other hand, enjoys power limited only by his conscience and the vigilance of his superior officers. He may invoke the values of either or both environments without necessarily being bound to face the consequences flowing from either. Sanctions on his behaviour derive only from a part of one environment: the administrative system. That there are so very few abuses within a complex that so lends itself to them says much for the quality and calibre of officers in the administrative service. As for Kanakas, they are bound by their own traditional values when living in their villages. But when Europeans are involved they may invoke the values of either the European or local environment as opportunity suits. When outside their villages they are bound only by the loose camaraderie of fellow workers reinforced by the vigilance of employers and policemen. Yet, whatever their circumstances, when a European is involved Kanakas can have no clear idea what kinds of consequences particular acts may set in train. They feel they have no basis for accurate prediction.

Inevitably, because it implies the constituents of a complex of political power, the triangle is the framework within which Cargo movements develop, and within which charismatic figures must carry out their tasks. We shall see in later chapters how Mambu tried to solve the pushes and pulls of the triangle by attempting to expunge it altogether; how Yali started by trying to turn the triangle into a one-to-one relationship by inflating the administrative role and ignoring the part played by missionaries, and how he ended, like Mambu, in endeavouring to destroy it; how the youth of Pariakenam simply disregarded both administrative officers and missionaries—and so failed to provoke and sustain a movement of any consequence; and finally, how Irakau, wiser than any of the three we have mentioned, consciously or by some instinct, has realized the present inevitability of the triangle and, against great pressures from his own people, seems to be feeling his way within terms of its implications.

CHAPTER V

The Myth-dream

[i]

For a period of some seventy years leading up to the events narrated in the *Prologue*, then, Tangu were a developing political entity who suffered a series of crises traceable both to internal and external sources. Conflicts concerning the rules of descent and who were marriageable mates; a deterioration in the status of women combined with doubts as to the legitimacy of marriages contracted after the introduction on a large scale of manufactured dogs' teeth, the medium in which bridewealth was paid; and an epidemic sickness seen by Tangu as an excessive increase in the activities of sorcerers seem to have been the main factors associated with the destruction of the major hinge of political, social, economic, and domestic relationships: stable marriage. Manufactured dogs' teeth, with social not merely technological value, wrought vast changes in Tangu social relationships. Other goods of European origin, on the other hand, filled out traditional values without substantially affecting the totality of social relationships.

With the exception of dogs' teeth, much more important than European goods were encounters with white men themselves and the appraisal of European notions which, whether commercial, political, religious, or moral, took place through traders, missionaries, and administrative officers, as well as through other Kanakas. Further, by far the most significant part of the transmission of European values seems to have taken place within the interrelationships implied in the roles of Kanakas, missionaries, and administrative officers, in which, more importantly, administrative officers and missionaries have been competing for the moral trust and confidence of Kanakas.

Though, therefore, Tangu had become involved in a series of far-reaching changes before the advent of the white man—which goes some way towards explaining the birth of the myth-dream—the development and growth of the Cargo myth-dream may be explained largely in terms of the tensions engendered by the triangle.

As a concept 'myth-dream' does not lend itself to precise definition. Nevertheless, myth-dreams exist, and they may be reduced to a series of themes, propositions, and problems which are to be found in myths, in dreams, in the half-lights of conversation, and in the emotional responses to a variety of actions, and questions asked. Through this kind of intellectualization myth-dreams become 'aspirations'.

All peoples participate in particular myth-dreams: they are not only to be found amongst pre-literate peoples. Myth-dreams are not intellectually articulate, for they exist in an area of emotionalized mental activity which is not private to any particular individual but which is shared by many. A community day-dream as it were. But among literate peoples portions of the myth-dream may be intellectualized and set down in writing. And though through the process of intellectualization some of the themes in the myth-dream tend to be so interpreted that they serve a sectional interest, they nevertheless assume the form of aspirations which may be both comprehended and apprehended, and which feed back into the myth-dream, giving it matter on which to develop. Eventually, such intellectualizations as are made may become the definitive principles upon which a group of persons may organize themselves into a viable party or movement. And by so organizing themselves the group concerned puts itself into a position from which it may 'capture' the myth-dream by symbolizing and putting into effect the propositions contained in the myth-dream. Having done so, having captured what appears as a mainspring of community action, the group concerned may harness this power to serve a community or sectional interest.

In New Guinea intellectual articulation of the myth-dream is rare. But from time to time a charismatic figure brings portions of the myth-dream out of the area of day-dream, and, for a relatively short period of time, transforms—and externalizes—these portions of the myth-dream into the word. Such charismatic articulation brings the myth-dream into a position where its meaning may be apprehended by the participants, and where it is capable of being comprehended by the intellect. And then, so it would seem, the catalyst of the charismatic figure has the effect of reducing the myth-dream from emotionalized mental activity to physical activity —the rites and ceremonials of a Cargo movement. Further, if the rites and ceremonials of a Cargo movement express the themes of the Cargo myth-dream, when the charismatic experience is over significant portions of the articulation which has taken place find their way back into the myth-dream, refining and developing the themes already contained therein. That is, though the charismatic experience does not entail any necessary intellectual comprehension of the myth-dream, it may do so for some. For most of the participants, however, the experience simply externalizes the myth-dream and makes it capable of apprehension on the level of emotionalized mental activity. And, still on the level of the day-dream, what has been appreciated through the charismatic experience feeds back into the myth-dream.

Though both Tangu and Manam islanders seem to have shared and participated in much the same Cargo myth-dream, we shall only follow out the maturation of the Cargo myth-dream in relation to Tangu. Four milestones in the developmental process have been selected: the first apprehension of white men and their goods, the activities of Mambu, and of Yali, and the ritual activities precipitated by the youth from Pariakenam. In this chapter we shall consider the implications of the first event. To do so something must first be said about the way in which Tangu appreciate their myths.

MYTHS

When Tangu recount myths or tell stories they participate in a social convention, an art form, ostensibly historical or even evolutionary, to project a future, to explain or account for the whole, or part, of a current situation, or to see through the present into the past. There is no story that does not carry a quality of myth, and few myths do not have direct doctrinal or dogmatic force.

Tangu consider their myths to be repositories of truth. When asked to explain a part of their culture they resort to the myth in which it is contained: '*Keyaki*, that is the way of it, thus', they say. For, for Tangu as well as for a European observer, the content of a myth formulates connexions between various kinds of experience, and attempts to express relations between past, present, and future. And even those myths and stories called by Tangu, in Pidgin, *sitori nating*, just a story, a phrase which indicates that the events and circumstances of the story are considered to be simply fictitious, contain truth: the validity of the moral principles revealed by the events narrated.

Interpretation, the task of eliciting the meanings of a myth, may be carried out on several different levels depending on the context. As an example we may paraphrase the opening passages of a particular origin myth:

The central character of the myth, while still a baby, is taken by his parents to the new garden site they are preparing by burning off the dried scrub. The baby is put into a string-bag cradle and suspended from a branch in the shade. A short while later a hawk swoops down through the smoke of the burning underbush and carries the babe to the top of a high tree. The parents, try as they might with the help of babe's mother's brother, cannot rescue their child.

By and by the babe becomes hungry and begins to cry. He puts his little finger into his mouth and sucks. He is comforted but not nourished. Still fretting, he exchanges little finger for thumb and goes peacefully to sleep. But when he wakes again he is ravenous. So the hawk introduces its penis into the mouth of the child and ejaculates. The child sleeps, is nourished, grows large and strong.

The story continues. . . .

It will be clear, firstly, that going to the garden site, burning the underbush, putting the baby to sleep in a string bag, and the sucking of finger and thumb are taken directly from life. They are truths which, for Tangu, are reflected on a simple level of everyday life. That a hawk steals the child, sets him on a high tree where he cannot be rescued by father, mother, and mother's brother, and then, as a result of oral ejaculation makes the child grow strong—these are not so easily explained. They are symbolic representations whose meanings become plainer within the vocabulary of Tangu cultural values.

The hawk is the only fierce bird of prey in Tangu. It is a symbol of masculinity, and once upon a time it was a clan or moiety totem. We need go no further on that score. And what the hawk does to the child can be directly related to Tangu ideas concerning birth. The germ of being, Tangu believe, is contained in the woman. And it remains such until it is 'fed'— the Tangu word is *brami*, to eat, used of food, drink, tobacco, and suckling at the breast—by the spermatozoa of a man. Then, and only then, can the germ grow into a human being.

Now, there are numerous connexions that can be made here, but one in particular will suffice. When Tangu relate the myth, as soon as the hawk introduces his penis into the mouth of the babe it is no longer referred to as *namai*, hawk, but as *yapwerk* or *avai*, father. And since the more perceptive Tangu, when asked the meaning of the hawk's action, immediately talk about how a child is made in the womb, it is clear that what the hawk did—whatever other relevance it might have, and there are several—is a symbolic representation of the accepted theory of the procreative process. It is a neat, shorthand way of telling a young person how he or she came into the world. And in so far as the incident contains an accepted theory it is a truth. Those Tangu who can themselves connect the symbolism with the theory are at an advantage: the two truths check each other. Others in Tangu, not so percipient, although they do not see that theory and symbol are two faces of the same coin, yet regard symbol and theory, separately, as truths.

But if this short example has indicated the way in which myths contain truths, in order somewhat to discipline interpretation other considerations have to be taken into account.

Since Tangu lack durable records, and are, for practical purposes, non-literate, living memory and the present can be the only criteria of accuracy. Also, for Tangu, what 'my father' said, did, and said he did, is often 'more true' than the experiences of Ego himself. Ego has a number of contemporary living critics, father has less, and grandfather comparatively few. What is said or done today can be contradicted, qualified by other witnesses, or proved to be false. But what was said and done in the past, because it has survived to the present, has been through the test of criticism and emerges as truth. The present is a process of truth in creation, and what grandfather is said to have done or said is a more perfect truth than Ego's reflections today. When Ego's present reflections are communicated to his fellows, and then subjected to qualification and criticism, they may become accepted by the community. When they are so accepted they become truths. At any particular moment in time, therefore, since for a truth to be such it must be resilient to time, a universal, the whole body of truths is a present reality composed of truths with differing degrees of perfection. For Tangu, however, the past is remote; and the truths which derive from it tend to be well established and even encrusted. The present, the period of truth in creation, goes back three or four generations, the greatest span within which a living person could have seen, touched, or spoken to an ancestor.

What Tangu are doing when they recount a myth is to interrelate a variety of experiences which may seem disparate to a European, but which are not necessarily so to Tangu. In much the same way as certain scholars of the nineteenth century imposed an evolutionary time scale on what was, essentially, a typological classification, so Tangu use chronology as a quasi-logical connective. When in one myth, for example, a penis walks from village to village, and has successful intercourse in each, a man's seed is travelling and leaving descendants, spread over territory, who are agnatic kin to

In Tangu: a young traditionalist with bark-cloth in front and the jungle behind

On the coast: an older progressive with neck-tie, flowers, and a packing case

Gepam

each other. That is, one may explain a patriline that exists, or is thought to exist, in terms of a sequence of events that would have produced just such a result. Finally, the walking penis is not necessarily forgotten when agnatic or patri-relationships become unimportant to the ordering of social life. It is then a historical truth. A truth which was relevant in the past. None the less, it remains a truth. For once a truth exists as a truth, in a myth, its destruction is not, nor need it be, necessarily dependent on a reversal of the process that made it. And for Tangu a truth becomes such when, by community consent, it is contained in a myth.

There is a further matter. Over the past sixty years the truths contained within Tangu myths have been challenged with growing force and intensity. With fresh and significant experiences following one upon the other the task of interpretation and distillation into a myth, an intuitive rather than an explicitly intellectualized process, has led into emotional stress and anxiety combined with intellectual perplexity when the question is explicitly put to them. Tangu have heard the myths told by other natives of New Guinea, many are acquainted with the Bible stories told by missionaries, and a few repeat, rather nervously, a rigmarole about monkeys.[1] But since, for Tangu, myths still remain repositories of truth the problem for them, in face of an ever widening range of experience, is how to know what truths to place there, how to formulate criteria of consent. On the one hand they say, 'We are fools. We do not know the truth. Our fathers could not write like you white people. They had to use their memories and they forgot much. They deceived us. You white men seem to know everything, and now the mission is teaching us the truth.' On the other hand there is also much doubt. Tangu are reluctant to leave their own myths in order to take over others. On an intellectual level they cannot be sure where truth lies or how to recognize it. Emotional forces,

[1] Such crude Darwinian evolutionism is, of course, even more pernicious than the story of Ham in the Bible. For the hewers of wood and drawers of water are, at least, granted full moral status as moral beings —something that strict evolutionism, with its inevitable superior and inferior, higher and lower, forms cannot logically tolerate.

however, what Tangu feel about things, override intellectual scruples and, willy-nilly, find articulation in myths. It is, perhaps, just because underlying emotional forces find expression in myths that Tangu tend to regard the physical world about them as reflections of truths which themselves are to be found in myths. Certainly, it is in these introductory terms that the Primal Myth, presented in the next section, should be read and evaluated.

THE PRIMAL MYTH

Presented below are four versions of what may be taken to be a single myth. They were elicited when conversation teetered delicately on the edge of the writer's role as an investigator who had been assimilated into the culture, and the fact that he was a European and therefore outside it. The preface to each version was that it was a secret: something known to Tangu, knowable to other black men in New Guinea, but hidden from Europeans; hidden especially from missionaries and administrative officers.

Like all myths, each version contains truths: and each is retailed at length because it is necessary to show how these truths are expressed. Generally, they tell of a way in which man became bound in society and subject to the responsibilities involved in reproducing his kind. The myths are, basically, evolutionary stories revealing an origin of culture and its dependence upon an organized marital relationship. Such differences as there are may be related to structural factors, to different organizational forms. For, to achieve the same object, to reveal the same moral, a storyteller is forced to handle one set of people in one community, and another set of categories when his field of standard positional relationships is otherwise ordered. The similarities, on the other hand, reveal absolute truths, truths with general consent.

Though the myths may originate far back in the past, as they are told today they have current significances. Tangu say of each of the versions that they were 'always' thus. But the latter portions which are of primary interest here cannot, in fact, have had an origin much further back than the first decade of this century. In addition, it will be clear that very recent events have been worked into them. Nevertheless, by finding out when men and youths first heard the versions it is reasonable to presume that the basic contents of the latter halves had 'set' by about 1930. They have become accepted as truths; they reveal a relationship with white men based on first sightings; and they reflect the basis of the Cargo myth-dream.[1]

The first version, as told in W'tsiapet in Riekitzir, runs thus:

One day the men of the village decided to hunt a pig by burning off a tract of ginger [where pigs are unlikely to be]. Duongangwongar, an odd fellow[2] who had a mother but no father or mother's brother, went with them. When the party arrived at the place previously agreed upon the other men would have nothing to do with Duongangwongar. They told him to go away.

So Duongangwongar wandered off on his own. And presently, seeing a pig-run entering a patch of *kunai* grass [where pigs are likely to be], and following it, he was confronted almost at once by a pig. Quickly selecting an arrow from his quiver he set it to his bowstring, took aim, and loosed off. The pig was wounded.

Meanwhile, hearing Duongangwongar's cries for help, the

[1] These four myths have been abstracted from Social Implications of some Tangu Myths, *Southwestern Journal of Anthropology*, Vol. 12, No. 4, 1956, pp. 417–30.

[2] The Tangu word here is *'mbatekas* or *imbatekas*. As a key word in the culture it is impossible to translate directly and accurately. It describes the essence of a sorcerer, its meanings range through evil, bad, useless, odd, peculiar, strange, non-conformist, monstrosity, of unknown potential.

Duongangwongar is *imbatekas* because (i) he has no father and no mother's brother—he is virtually unplaceable in the system of community relationships; (ii) because he is non-conformist—all the lads whoop off together but he goes by himself; (iii) despite or because of his non-conformity he knows something which the others do not—where to find a pig, and (iv) because, like a sorcerer, he disturbs the *status quo* in the sense that his non-conformity forces the remainder of the community to think again and readjust themselves.

others ran from the ginger into the *kunai*, surrounded the pig and killed it with their spears. Then, as each man withdrew his spear from the corpse of the pig, he plunged it into Duongangwongar. Duongangwongar fell dead. Satisfied, the men placed the body on a small platform and hid it in the exposed roots of a tree [a form of burial not practised in Tangu today nor admitted to having been practised except in the remote past when the events occurred].

When the men returned to the village, Gundakar, the mother of Duongangwongar, asked where her son was. They said they did not know, they had not seen him.

That night Gundakar had a dream in which her son appeared to her and told her that he was dead and hidden in the roots of a tree. So, next morning Gundakar went out to look for the body of her son.

As she walked out of the village a little bird, the spirit of Duongangwongar, settled on her shoulders and showed her the path she should take. In this way she found the tree where the body of Duongangwongar had been hidden. She extricated it from the roots and she put it into her string bag and returned to the village. There she collected together some yams, taros, bananas, *mami*, and sweet potatoes [recently introduced into Tangu], put them with the body in the string bag, and left the village.

The first village she came to was W'tsiapet [the storyteller's own], and she asked if she might bury her son there. The villagers refused. So she went on to Amuk in Wanitzir. There they also refused her, sending her on to Mariap, outside Tangu (Figure 4). Despite her pleas Gundakar was sent from Mariap to Kangwan, and from Kangwan she was ordered to go on to Lilau on the coast. She rested by the sea, but not until she came to Dogoi, where a man copulated with her, was she able to stay and bury her son. The man was her helpmeet. He dug a hole for her, placed the body of Duongangwongar inside, and covered the grave with coconut fronds. Eventually he married Gundakar and she bore him sons.

Meanwhile the body of Duongangwongar rotted in the grave.

One day, when Gundakar was in the village alone and in need of some water, she went to the grave of her son. She drew aside the coconut fronds and, finding salt water

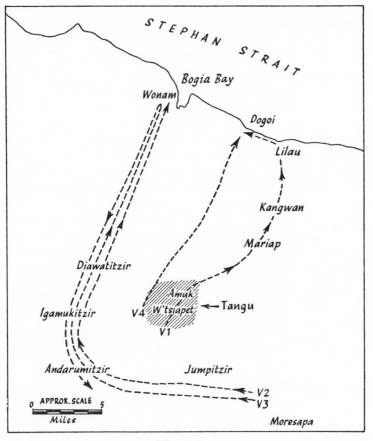

Figure 4

Routes taken in the four versions of the Primal Myth V_1 V_2 V_3 V_4

and fish coming from the nostrils of Duongangwongar, she filled her pot with the water and used it for cooking the evening meal. Her husband and son [*sic*] thought it good.

157

That night Gundakar's son grew tremendously. And next day when her husband's younger brother, *Tuman* (*tuman* = younger brother), came to visit them and saw his elder brother's son grown so much, he was surprised. 'Your son has grown so big!' he exclaimed to his elder brother, *Ambwerk* (*ambwerk* = elder brother).[1] 'My own sons are still small—what has happened?'

Nothing was said.

Next day Gundakar collected the skins of her taros, yams, and *mami* and flung them on to the garden plot which her husband had recently cleared and burned off. Wonderfully, the skins took root, reached back into the soil and became real tubers.

Then Gundakar returned to the grave of Duongangwongar and collected from his nostrils some water and one small fish which she put in a pot and boiled for her husband and son to eat.

That night the son grew into a man.

Next day *Tuman* was so surprised at the transformation that he insisted on knowing how it was done. Gundakar turned to *Tuman's* wife and told her what to do. 'Go to the grave of Duongangwongar,' she said. 'Take away the coconut fronds, draw some water from his nostrils, and take one small fish. You will see there other, larger kinds of fish. Do not take them. Take only one small fish.'

Tuman's wife repaired to the grave, removed the coconut fronds, and drew some water. Then, in the putrefying nostrils of Duongangwongar she saw a large *ramatzka*, a long fish like an eel. She speared it.

At once there was a loud rumbling in the earth like thunder. The water from Duongangwongar's nostrils came out in a seething torrent of foam and bubbling waves. And the water, which was the sea, rose up and came between *Ambwerk* and *Tuman*. They fled in different directions.

Afterwards, *Tuman*, who had found safety in a low lying place, killed a small bird and after cooking it threw the

[1] The words *tuman* and *ambwerk* are Tangu kinship terms meaning respectively, 'younger brother' and 'elder brother'.

bones into the sea. There was a small splash and soft sssshhh . . . like water running over pebbles. Then he killed a crested pigeon, cooked it, and threw the bones in the sea. There was a small splash and the sea remained calm. So he killed a hornbill and did as he had done with the other birds. The surface of the waters rippled. He killed a cockatoo and surf flecked the waters. Then he killed a cassowary, and on throwing the bones into the sea the waves rose with a roar and tumbled on the beach.

Tuman was satisfied.

Pondering on the fate of his elder brother *Tuman* took a leaf, directed it to the village of his elder brother, and threw it on the waters. *Ambwerk*, who had found refuge on high land, saw the floating leaf. He picked it up, exclaiming, 'Oh! My younger brother is well. He has sent this leaf to me to find out how I am. So I will send it back to him.' *Ambwerk* threw the leaf back in the sea.

When *Tuman* saw the leaf floating back to him he knew that *Ambwerk* was safe. So he took another leaf, and writing [clearly a recent addition] a message on it he despatched it to *Ambwerk*. *Ambwerk* received the note and sent an answer in return [a European practice].

Tuman felled a tree, hollowed it, made a canoe, and set off to visit his elder brother. *Ambwerk* saw *Tuman* in his canoe from afar, and he wondered what it was. When *Tuman* had beached his canoe and brought it near the village, *Ambwerk* looked at it and marvelled. 'Who showed you how to make this?' he asked. 'Surely you did not do it all by yourself?'

Tuman answered: 'I made it myself. I thought of it on my own.'

When *Tuman* had gone, *Ambwerk* copied his younger brother. He made a canoe of his own and went to visit *Tuman*. Then he returned to his village, content.

At once *Tuman* started work on a boat. Having made it and had some practice in it he went off to see *Ambwerk*, to show him the boat. *Ambwerk* was surprised, and to his question *Tuman* replied, 'I invented it myself. And I made it on my own.'

Then *Ambwerk*, not to be outdone, made a boat for himself and went in it to see his younger brother. *Tuman* complimented *Ambwerk* on his craftsmanship, and *Ambwerk* returned to his village content.

Then *Tuman* constructed a pinnace. He made an engine, fitted it, practised, and went off to show it to *Ambwerk*.

Ambwerk was dumbfounded. He commenced work on a pinnace at once.

Tuman made a motor car, a motor bike, and a large ship with tall masts and a siren which went 'Whooooo!' *Tuman's* ship was so big that it broke his elder brother's jetty and they had to secure it by ropes passed round coconut palms [exactly such an incident occurred in Bogia in late 1951]. *Tuman* made an aeroplane, canned goods, cloth, and all sorts of things. Each time he made something he went to show it to his elder brother. And each time he did so *Ambwerk* copied him.

At the end of his recitation the storyteller turned to me, the writer, and said: 'You see, *Tuman* could use his head—like you.' [The implication was that *Ambwerk*, like Kanakas, could not.]

The second version of what seems to be the same myth runs thus:

One day a woman who had no husband left her daughter alone [and thus especially vulnerable to sorcerers] in the village while she went to fish. A sorcerer came into the village, and, after beating the child, killed her and buried her.

When the woman returned to the village after fishing she could not find her daughter. 'Oh where is my daughter?' she wailed. 'I went to get some fish and she has disappeared!'

That night the woman had a dream, and in the dream she saw the burial place of her daughter. Rising at dawn she went a little way off into the bush. There she saw a bamboo

160

thicket which she recognized from her dream as the burial place of her daughter. [The form of burial is neither practised nor admitted to.] She dug in the earth, found the body and put it in her string bag. She went off towards Moresapa, came round by Sorkmung, and went on to Dimuk and Wonam.

At Wonam, Damzerai, the man who had killed the daughter, came to the mother, Matzia, and asked her what it was she had in her string bag.

'My daughter who is dead,' replied Matzia.

Damzerai took pity on her. He married her, dug a hole for the daughter, and buried the body.

Very soon the body rotted and there was a rumbling in the earth like thunder. And Matzia, who had had another dream, hastened to the grave to see her daughter. She saw the watery rottenness, and tasting it, she found it salty. She saw that there were fish there, too, and she thought she would cook some of the fish and salt water for Damzerai. So, telling him nothing of how she had come by the fish, she put some in a bowl and gave them to Damzarai to eat.

Damzerai was sick. But after he had taken some lime and pepper he returned to his meal. And he found it good.

Matzia showed Damzerai the grave and what she had found there. He thought it marvellous.

That night, their son, who had eaten the fish and water, grew large and fat.

Next day Damzerai's elder brother visited him and was surprised to see how the son had grown. 'What do you give him to eat?' he asked. 'My son is older than yours and yet your son is now bigger!'

'Eat some of this,' said Damzarai. 'We took it from the grave of my wife's daughter.'

Dwongi, the elder brother, ate some of the food. He thought it excellent. So good that he took some home to his wife.

The following day Dwongi returned for more. They all sat down to eat the fish and salt water. Afterwards, while

Damzerai and his family repaired to the garden, Dwongi went to the grave by himself. There, he speared one of the larger fish. At once there was a thundering noise, and the sea spurted up out of the grave with a rush of foam, separating the two brothers.

Damzerai made an armlet of dried grass and threw it into the sea. It drifted to Dwongi who picked it up and examined it. 'My younger brother is alive!' he exclaimed. 'He is somewhere over there!'

So Dwongi, *Ambwerk*, made a basket and threw it on the waters. It drifted to *Tuman*, Damzerai, who then knew that his elder brother was alive and well.

Tuman made a boat. *Ambwerk* made a canoe. *Tuman* set off in his boat but was sunk by a heavy sea. So he swam back to land and decided to build himself a large ship. He fitted a large mast to his ship, put in an engine, and then went off to see his elder brother—first warning him by a letter [*pas* (Pidgin) = letter] thrown on the waves that he was coming.

Ambwerk received the letter and said, 'Ha! I shall be seeing my younger brother soon.'

When *Tuman* arrived at the village of *Ambwerk* the two brothers shook hands [a European, not a Kanaka custom]. 'Well met!' said *Tuman*. 'I thought you might have died. Now I can see for myself that you are alive and well.'

'And I, too, thought you were dead,' *Ambwerk* replied. 'Now you have come to see me in your fine ship.'

Tuman returned from whence he had come, and *Ambwerk* stayed where he was, on the top of Manam island. *Tuman* made all the good things—clothes, knives, umbrellas, rifles, canned food, and so on.

One day *Tuman* came back again to see his brother. 'You stay where you are,' said *Ambwerk*. 'You stay where you are, and I will stay in my place.'

So *Tuman* came to Tangu while his elder brother stayed on the top of Manam island. And that is why some people have black skins that are dirty. That is why there are people like us.

The third version runs as follows:

A widow had a daughter who was killed and buried by a stranger. Although the widow searched everywhere, and cried aloud for her daughter, she could not find her anywhere. At nightfall, when the widow went into her hut to sleep, she dreamed that her daughter was buried in the cavity left by a tree that had been uprooted [neither practised nor admitted to]. So she went to such a place, and lo! upon digging she found her daughter.

The widow put the body in her string bag and went to Moresapa. There they told her to go to Andarum whence she was forced to go to Wonam. At Wonam she married the younger of two brothers, and after bearing two sons to her husband, she, her husband, and their sons returned to Andarum. The elder of the two brothers remained at Wonam with his wife and two sons.

Arrived at Andarum the woman went to the grave of her daughter. She removed the topsoil and found that the putrid flesh had turned into salt water and fish. She gave her husband and sons some of the fish boiled in the salt water. They were sick. But after they had chewed ginger for a few minutes they returned to their meal and found it good. That night the son [*sic*] grew big and strong.

Shortly afterwards the elder brother came from Wonam to visit them, and seeing the astonishing progress of his younger brother's sons, he asked what the secret was. They told him. So *Ambwerk* went off to get some of the marvellous stuff. Unfortunately, he speared a *ramatzka*—which was nothing less than the dead daughter herself. There was a thundering noise from underground and the sea spouted up, separating brother from brother.

From this point on the second version is followed precisely.

The fourth version is:

Rawvend came to Biamp from Andarum via Mangigum. He is the ancestor of all the men of Biampitzir. [If so, Rawvend's alternative name is Niangarai. Rawvend may also be a corruption of Yahweh (Jehovah), or of Reverend —the appellation preferred by Protestant missionaries.]

Rawvend went off to Kangwan where he found a small pool. But what he was looking for was a convenient hole. He found one in Dogoi near where Liliau now is. So he killed his daughter, Samaingi, who had been sick and who was covered with sores. Having run her through with a spear he buried her and covered the grave with coconut fronds. Samaingi rotted in her grave, and out of her putrid flesh came salt water and many fish. One of the fish was a *ramatzka*.

Tuman wanted to spear the *ramatzka*. But his mother prevented him, saying, 'You must not shoot the *ramatzka*. Take only the small fish.'

But *Tuman* did not heed her. He shot the *ramatzka* with his bow and arrow. There was a rumbling and a growling in the bowels of the earth, and the sea came rushing out. It came up around the Ramu valley, it came up the valley of the Iwarum. Up and up it came until Rawvend said, 'Enough!'

Now the sea had divided people into two parties. Samaingi arose from her grave and went to Se-wen-de [normally Pidgin for Seventh Day Adventist. Here regarded as a place—paradise?] where she built the habitations of the white men and government people. And she, Samaingi, was also the ancestress of Chinamen and brown people—related to us black folk.

Of the other party *Tuman* was on the mainland and *Ambwerk* was on Manam island. *Tuman*, who was short of firewood, wrote a letter and sent it off on a log to *Ambwerk*. Then he wrote another and sent it off by a bird. Then he chose a third messenger, a dog, which succeeded in reaching *Ambwerk*, and which also brought back some firewood for *Tuman*.

Tuman sounded his hand-drum, and *Ambwerk* replied on his slit-gong. As a result of this interchange of signals *Ambwerk* and *Tuman* met at the grave of Samaingi, Rawvend's daughter. They decided to settle together.

164

Ambwerk had paper. *Tuman* had yams and other tubers. Now, if it had been the other way about [if *Ambwerk*, not *Tuman*, had shot the *ramatzka*] you white skinned people would have had yams, and we black skinned people would have had paper and all the other good things.

Of the four versions the first was produced with the most confidence. The storyteller knew what he was saying and was allowed to get through with it without interruption or objection. The last, the fourth version, may be regarded as the least reliable though it is not unrevealing. The author made his delivery nervously and in a very muddled way. There were interruptions and objections, but it was *his* story that I was interested in. He was said to have been on the fringes of several Cargo cults that had occurred in the general area and, unlike the majority in Tangu, he had had dealings with Seventh Day Adventist teachers. The second and third versions were delivered with reasonable confidence, but since the authors knew that I had heard the first version they rather tended to hurry. The author of the first was certainly the best known to me, and the one least liable to be embarrassed or shy. The author of the last was a man I did not know well, and of the four the most likely to be embarrassed when telling a European something that was a secret to be kept from them.

THE PRIMAL MYTH: EVALUATION

If we ignore a few discrepancies the basic story may be re-written somewhat as follows:

The scene produced for the listener is that of a mother and child without male protection. The child is killed and the body is hidden. Nevertheless, through a dream the mother regains possession of the body. She places it in a string bag and she sets out on a journey. The journey ends when she finds a place where she can bury the body, and marry. After marriage, after bearing sons, the woman returns to the grave of her dead child and finds there salt water and fish, both of which are the products of the putrefying body. The woman takes a small fish, and some water, and makes a meal of them for her family. They find it good. More than that, a son quickly develops into manhood—a circumstance that occasions the curiosity and envy of the husband's brother and his family. Letting them into the secret, the woman warns her relatives by marriage that they must not shoot the *ramatzka* fish. But the warning goes unheeded, and the *ramatzka* is shot. The earth rumbles, and the sea rises up to divide brother from brother. Later, when the brothers get in touch with one another again, their relationship appears as a competitive one, and one of them emerges as much cleverer than the other. This explains why white men are different from, or are more masters of their environment than black men appear to be.

There are, here, a series of incidents involving four basic kinds of social relationship woven into a pattern of shifting roles. Parent and child where parent becomes wife (fourth version *contra*); wife and husband where husband is also brother; brother and brother where the latent antagonism symbolizes the relationship between white men and black. The mother-child relationship is set in a context of helplessness. There are no husband, no brothers, no mother's brothers to care for them. In the first, from a patrilineal group, where the child is a son, his helplessness is less obvious and it is made more explicit. The third story comes from an ambilineal group, but as in the first, where the child is killed by those who are explicitly not in an amicable relation with him, the child (in the third) is killed by strangers who, in Tangu, are also enemies. The second version, from a double unilineal group, follows the general idea, but the killer of the child later enters into an amicable relation with the mother by becoming her husband. In the fourth version the child is provided with a protector-father so that no one but he can kill her. And he does. This version comes from a locale where patrilineal and matrilineal peoples live in the same settlement; but since Rawvend is explicitly identified with Niangarai who, in another myth, brought forth human beings from the hole in the earth which he had made with a digging stick, a consistency may be elicited by the phrase, 'the child of a creative element is killed'. Each version provides an inner consistency by presenting situations in which it is to be expected that the child will inevitably be killed.

The dream through which the mother finds her child is, as we shall see in more detail in the next chapter,[1] a normal Tangu technique for solving a problem. For Tangu dreams provide answers, and they are also springboards of action. The incident occurring as it does in the myth is both evidence of, and a sanction for, the general efficacy of dreams. Consistently, the journey the mother then undertakes is a projection from the present. The solution of the isolate mother-and-child is a husband who will care for them both. Among Tangu widows do not remain such for long. They become second wives, usually joining the husband of a sister, or they form unions with widowers. If no man is available in the home village she is forced to travel abroad until she can find one. Sometimes, but rarely, not even a brother will find it convenient to care for her if other possible alternatives are available. During fieldwork I, the writer, chanced across a woman and her two children living a precarious animal-like life in the bush. Her husband, who had died, had been a noted sorcerer, and largely because of him no one would have anything to do with her. So, when she could gather a sufficient reserve of food she journeyed to the nearest settlements to offer her services as a wife—only to return to her lean-to in the forest. Tangu commented briefly: 'She ought to go farther away where nobody knows of her past.'

The particular routes selected by the woman reflect other factors. The first and fourth are the traditional paths taken by Tangu when, in the days before the white men came, they used to go down to the coast to fetch salt. They still use these routes when they want to go down to, the coast. Then, as now, it was essential when travelling far afield to pass through a chain of settlements in which there were women standing as 'sister' to the males of the party, or 'friends' of either sex. This not only ensured hospitality but also protection from sorcerers. The shorter and more direct route is used only by

[1] *Infra* p. 179.

people of Biampitzir—where the fourth version came from—
and the more popular route, always used by people of Riekitzir—who provided the first version—is the first.

The routings provided by the second and third versions are
more difficult to account for since they pass through country
known to most Tangu only by hearsay. Direct contacts with
Moresapa date only with the coming of mission and administration. And the Diawat people (Dimuk) as well as those from
Andarum are hereditary enemies. At the same time, however,
the relationship of enmity never prevented intercourse and
trading from time to time, and it never preven.ed inter-
marriages.

Wonam is the place where the Diawat people went for their
salt, and it is possible that the salt found its way to
Andarum through Diawat and the Igamuk area, where the
people, Tangu speakers, were at varying degrees of enmity
and friendship with Tangu, Andarum, and Diawat. 'Foreign'
wives would also have brought with them variations of routes.

The marital relationship into which the story leads us
describes a normal and settled relationship in which the wife
lives in the husband's village and bears him children. From
the norms of a relationship with which everybody might be
presumed to be familiar, the wife disturbs the grave of her
dead child. Even though Tangu visit the graves of dead kinsmen fairly frequently, there is no record of any custom entailing disturbance of a grave. And, more strange still, coming
from the nostrils of the rotting corpse are salt water and fish.
This is the gift which, though there are indications of reluctance—in the second and third versions husband and son are
sick—both husband and son eventually find good. Indeed, so
good is it for the boy that he grows big, or develops towards
manhood, overnight. Evidently, this gift, a gift which raises
the offspring of a union to adulthood, is the kernel of the
marital relationship; and since the gift *does* seem strange, and
is placed in the centre of a familiar workaday relationship, one
feels that the symbolism strikes deep and is only superficially
related to a series of other items: the vital need for salt, the
uterine line of descent providing safe conduct to the coast,

Manam islanders dancing

Manam island: after the dance, ready for prayers

Tangu dancing

Before the dance: examining harvest exchanges

fertility in terms of offspring in exchange for a husband's protection against marauders, the association of women with fishing (fish are not an important item of diet in Tangu), the duty of a wife to cook for her husband, economic co-operation in the household plot, the fertility of the crops, and a fair give-and-take within the household unit. Tangu social life today appears to provide no further clues as to the content of this gift, nor why it should bring the boy to manhood; nor can they themselves offer any deeper explanation of the symbolism. When taxed they say, 'That is the story. She gave him a fish.'

Moving in to the third relationship, the gift and its consequences arouse the envy of the husband's brother. He asks how it is done. He wants his own son to grow up as quickly. In the second and third versions husband is younger brother, *Tuman*; in the first he is elder brother, *Ambwerk*; and in the fourth, since no marital tie is mentioned, it is not clear how the brothers would have stood to Rawvend or Samaingi. Where the husband is *Tuman*, it is *Ambwerk* who kills the *ramatzka*, and who, later on, is presented as the denser of the two—in spite of the fact that in Version 2 it is *Tuman*, also husband, who committed the original murder. Although *Tuman* is not the husband of the 'mother' (M, see diagram, Figure 5) in the first version it is he who, eventually, turns out to be the brighter. And there is a certain consistency in the fact that it is his (*Tuman's*) wife and not *Tuman* himself who kills the *ramatzka*. In the fourth version it is 'mother' who tells *Tuman* not to kill the *ramatzka*, but it is left for the reader to decide for himself whether this 'mother' is the mother of the brothers, or the mother of the slain child (K) and the wife of one of the brothers. At any rate *Tuman* has initiative even though the honours seem to be more evenly distributed. In addition, however, *Tuman* in the fourth version has common ground with *Tuman* in the second in that while the latter is the murderer of K the child, the storyteller makes it explicit in the fourth that when *Tuman* is killing the *ramatzka* he does not know that he is actually killing the child or its spirit or ghost. Thus the shift into the isolated inter-brother relationship is occasioned by the act of the brother not married to the 'mother' (second and third), or by his wife (first version). In the fourth version this detail is lacking.

As soon as the forbidden act is done, the sea rises up and

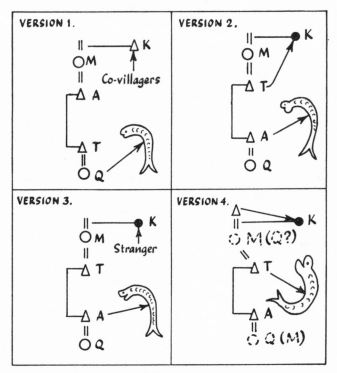

Figure 5

Relationships corresponding to the four versions of the Primal Myth.
K, the child who is killed; M, the mother; Q, a wife; A, *Ambwerk*; T, *Tuman*.
The arrows indicate direction and participants of killing.
The *ramatzka* fish is self-evident

separates brother from brother. The spousal and affinal relationships are dropped. M, K (and Q) (see diagram), have served their purpose. The story concentrates on the relationship between elder and younger brother, *Ambwerk* and *Tuman*.

And in this setting—essentially rivalrous or competitive within friendship—*Tuman* appears as better equipped for meeting the hazards of this life. There is no question of luck here; he is fundamentally better endowed. He is cunning. He can think. He can invent things. Moreover, in the first version he does these things on his own—and in the vernacular this is doubly emphatic. That is, he uses no ritual aids; he does not seek help from any spirit or godling, nor does any being or person outside of himself give him the inspiration. In other words the abilities of the successful brother reflect the claim made by Europeans that their own technical abilities are based in their own inventiveness, their own *nous*—which runs contrary to traditional modes of thought. For, in terms of the latter, most enterprises require ritual as well as pragmatic techniques to bring them to a successful conclusion. The other brother does not lack in industry, and he has an honoured position sitting on the volcano of Manam island; but initiative, the ability to think for himself, is lacking.

In the fourth version the brothers make a pact of friendship based either on apartheid or coexistence or both. Nevertheless, while the story is being told, even the monotonous recitation of the things that *Tuman* does, working up the scale from a dug-out canoe through motor boats and steam-ships to an aircraft, hardly prepares one for the climax—'And that is why white men are different from black men', or 'That is why white men have all the good things of this world and we have only yams'.

Stripped of cultural content and particular situational requirements, two things seem to spring from the inevitable death. First, associated with an exchange within the marital relationship, there is abundant life. Secondly, associated with a stupid act of disobedience—why kill the large *ramatzka* when a little fish would have done as well?—there is a flood which separates brother from brother. We have already commented on the first of these two factors; but taken together one might relate both elements to the peace, serenity, and easy moral relationships associated with the domestic house-hold which is the smallest and most permanent co-operative

171

group in Tangu, as compared with the actual or potential rivalrous or hostile relations to be found outside this circle. In isolation the second element has further significance. Mostly, white men are identified with younger brother, *Tuman*, who did not kill the *ramatzka*; or, as in the fourth version, in spite of the fact that it is *Tuman* who has the initiative, with *Ambwerk* who also was not responsible for killing the *ramatzka*. Whether or not there is a 'felt' kin relationship between the successful brother and white men, there is an obvious association with the abilities white men have. And these abilities appear to be directly related to some kind of innocence, for it was black men or their symbol which killed the *ramatzka*.

THE PRIMAL MYTH: CONCLUSION

Of the many truths parcelled together in the myth one may select as most relevant the final explanation of the present situation. Indeed, it is clear from the way the stories were introduced, as well as from the way each version was put together, that for Tangu the most important truth is the last. Discrepancies of cultural detail are matched by congruence of ends.

The chief protagonists are two brothers who, in everyday life, ought to be in a moral relationship with each other. One of them, representing black men, Kanakas, commits a 'sin' and appears to be doomed to a life of servitude in consequence. He is not endowed with *nous,* or understanding; he can copy but he cannot invent; he is unable to write, and he cultivates yams. The other brother, innocent, has the ideal attributes of a European. Gifted, he follows through the ideal sibling relationship by caring for his more unfortunate brother, and by bringing to him the fruits of his fortune. That is, the myth not only accounts for a present in terms of the past but leaps forward to suggest how the moral relationship of brotherhood can be worked out in terms of the existing circumstances. Primarily, the benefits of *nous*—cargo—should be shared. Another suggestion, founded on the analogy of the way in which real life brothers tend to behave, is that white men and black men should live independently of each other. And finally there is the implication that men so differently endowed cannot live together within terms of the same cultural conventions. For, although white men and black men are brothers the casual disobedience of the one has, literally, put an ocean between them.

Killing the *ramatzka* was no ordinary 'wrong' or 'sin': any man in Tangu will kill a *ramatzka* for eating if and when he sees one. It was not a malicious act, nor was it directed against anyone. It was, on the contrary, the everyday act of an average being who sees the chance of gaining just a little more than he had bargained for: a simple token of humanity well reflected in the way Tangu behaved towards the first recruiters.[1] Yet, the flood followed directly on the act; the 'punishment' was, as it were, an automatic reflex of the action precedent. Nor is there any opportunity for a forgiveness. Who has been wronged? From whom may forgiveness be sought? May a fish forgive? No character who appears in the story is in a position to forgive. The 'wrongdoing' emerges as an absolute.

In implication, however, the situation is further developed. Those who commit a wrong have to bear the burden of guilt in relation to those who have not. The brother who killed the fish may be said to have wronged himself, to have committed a sin against his own being, an act which caused havoc for himself and his descendants. Interpreted, Kanakas have only themselves to blame for their present circumstances.

May such an idea be contained in tranquillity, is there a way out of the impasse?

The myth itself suggests a solution. As a total activity killing the *ramatzka* involved more than one person. In particular, it involved the other brother, white men. Though the killing was done by one brother, black men, it might just as easily have been done by the other, by white men. The fourth version makes the point explicit, and the second has Dwongi spearing the fish without being aware of any instruction not

[1] *Supra* p. 125.

173

to do so. The act of killing the *ramatzka* was, therefore, something that might have been done by anyone. The implication is that black men are in reality no 'worse' than white men; and in spite of, or because of, the wrong done by black men white men ought not to treat them as though they were inferior creatures but as men like themselves, brothers, beings morally responsible for each other in spite of backslidings. The kin relationship between the two brothers is of the nature of a prior moral imperative, and the consequences flowing from the wrongdoing, the guilt, can then be seen as the result of an unfortunate accident of which white men should not take advantage. And at present the onus is on white men to act as though they were the brothers of black men. White men have no reason to boast or be arrogant: their power derives merely from the weakness of others. After all, it might so easily have been the other way about. The toss of a coin and white men might have been as black men are. . . .

'Ah well!' say Tangu when questioned on the matter. 'If he had not killed the *ramatzka* all would have been well.'

If it had been the other way around, then, what would Tangu have done? Standing in the role of injured party Tangu say, of course, they would act as a brother should. But then the fact remains, and no one may gainsay it. What happened happened the way that it did. And it is up to white men to do something about it because they are in a position to do so and because they are the brothers of black men.

No Kanaka may gainsay the fact of sorcery. Sorcery exists. Yet no Kanaka passively accepts the activities of sorcerers. There are means of dealing with them. But when Tangu are confronted with the acts of white men the consequences of their killing the *ramatzka* are thrown right back at them. White men appear to Tangu to contemn Kanakas—as though there never was the remotest chance that they themselves might have committed the unforgivable wrong. Or, from another viewpoint, and not the way Tangu would put it, the arrogance and vanity of white men in relation to Kanakas may be explained through an act that might have given white men a claim to be arrogant and vain.

The points at issue should be distinguished. First, there is the plain expression of guilt; and expectably, guilt can explain why all is not as it should be. Second, having participated in the total activity through which guilt was laid on black men, and because the guilt might have been put on the shoulders of white men, white men themselves are morally responsible, as brothers, for lightening the load. In practical terms white men ought to be sharing the benefits of innocence, cargo, with black men. Third, however, experience shows that white men are not doing what the myth says they ought to do. Why not? Why is it that white men will not co-operate? The dogma that truth is in the myth appears to be at variance with concrete experience. Yet, in translating the meaning of the myths into terms of a political programme there seem to be four alternatives. First, Tangu may work out their guilt and atonement, their problem, by themselves in spite of the physical presence of white men (second and third versions). Second, they may attempt to force white men into the position implied in the first version—co-operation. Third, they may simply accept the present situation (fourth version). Fourth, neglecting the myth altogether, or interpreting them in a single wilful sweep—without regard to their detail—as reflecting the insuperable difficulties involved in living with white men, they may try to rid themselves of Europeans and start afresh.

A Cargo movement asks for repentance and holds out the promise of forgiveness, expiation, and atonement; it offers a share in the cargo; it assures participants of a new life, a new dispensation which will take the place of the old. The alternative means provide a dilemma. Consistently, as we shall see in the chapters that follow, on the level of the myth-dream—where truth is—the idea that white men should be persuaded into co-operation persists. At the political or organizational level, however, charismatic figures find it extremely difficult and even precarious to select this, the second alternative as their guide. In interpreting and articulating the myth-dream they have to excite passions and provide relatively simple, concrete objectives. The youth from Pariakenam took the first of the alternatives; Mambu and Yali, in different ways, took the fourth; Irakau, working slowly and relatively unspectacularly within the implications of the basic triangle, seems to be keeping within the terms of the second alternative. What a charismatic figure cannot do is select the third alternative, let things ride in passive acceptance of the *status quo*; even the quietist solution, steering his protest into the placid back-waters away from the troubled stream, seems barred to him. In making his protest he should meet and transcend the dilemmas before him, not ignore or disdain them. Through the provision of positive political expressions— which imply a new moral order—a new man is revealed in the making, atonement is being signalled, and a new dispensation is being made manifest. But, as the myth makes clear, 'white brother' is not simply a rival, or an inimical oppressor. Nor is he a stranger. He is a brother—one who will help, or who could be constrained to help, because as a brother he ought to help.

CHAPTER VI
The Myth-dream
[ii]

W hat has been called the Primal Myth appears to contain the first, and perhaps basic, expressions of the Cargo myth-dream. From the time when these feelings first gained consent and became lodged in a myth, until 1951 when Tangu participated in Cargo cult activities, the corpus of a variety of experiences with white men was gradually building up. It may be assumed, at least for the time being, that each separate experience was interpreted in the light of the Primal Myth, the hinge of truth in this context. If there were dissentient voices, or contradictory experiences, they were neither vivid enough, nor sufficiently compelling, to refute the principles which, enshrined in the myth, were hardening into dogma. That is, the principles accepted by general consent could have been modified only by those experiences which could command a more powerful consent. In fact, as we have already seen[1] and shall see again in more detail,[2] once principles are established, and have become axiomatic, subsequent experiences tend to reinforce, or are pulled into conformity with, those truths that already exist.

The first tentative explanations regarding the nature of white men were probably being hazarded by Tangu story-tellers towards the end of the first decade of the century. By the end of the next decade, certainly by 1930, but perhaps even before the administration and mission had established themselves in Tangu, the latter half of the Primal Myth had probably assumed its present shape. And then, some years later as 1937 turned to 1938, Mambu came to Tangu.

As far as Tangu are concerned Mambu is the first man we

[1] *Supra* p. 130.   [2] *Infra* p. 211.

know about who tried, on a quasi-intellectual level, to relate the conclusions of his own experiences with white men to his Kanaka tradition. The second was Yali.

In talking to Tangu of their Cargo activities the names of these two men were mentioned over and over again. Both were charismatic figures, leaders of Cargo movements in the Bogia region. They brought together, clarified, and made explicit some of the themes and ideas which were hidden in the myth-dream. Hidden, in the sense that while they remained in the myth-dream they were symbolic representations whose meanings were capable of being apprehended but not comprehended; principles which remained, as it were, internalized—not tied to, or implying to the participants in the myth-dream, a defined course of action.

The particulars of the history of Tangu, their simple technology, and the peculiarities of their cultural values and distributive and political systems, should not obscure the fact that Mambu and Yali acted out political roles in an aura which is, perhaps, a universal. For, when time began men dreamed. They dreamed of themselves, their people, the morrow, and the past: of riches and power; of heroes, stirring times, change, and revolution; of God, the nature of salvation, and the world to come. Always, even when suffused with despair, the dream had a kernel of faith in the future. The stuff of what we call history grew in a dream, was remembered, took shape in the intellect, and was born in action. Everywhere and at all times there have been men and women who were able to see through the worlds into which they were born to new kinds of order. Some themselves gave their dreams form and wrought a change in the way their fellows regarded each other and the world about them. Others gave their dreams as weapons for disciples to wield. Many dreamed their live dreams and though remaining true to themselves, failed to convince others —failed to interpret and carry the fever in their minds. But the dreams, or parts of them, often lived on as rumours or myths which, told and retold, lost what was superfluous and gained point in effect until the dream and its environs were set for the spark. Rebellious to the established order, and

178

loosed from the explicit conventions and logic of the times, the peculiar gift of these dreamers was that they could express and resolve the longings, dilemmas, and anxieties of those among whom they lived. They dreamed a collective dream, and saw a new man. Either by the force of their own personalities, or through the influence of those with whom they communed, or as a result of significant alterations in the dream, even the veriest doubters could be persuaded into calling the dream their own. But, for it to be effective, the dream, or the teaching, had to paint the hopes of the populace and find a place in the popular myth-dream. Either had to be alive in itself, pliable, receptive, and recreative at the same time. Either must be ready to meet as well as to mould community expectancy.

We shall see in the course of this chapter that while Mambu and Yali were men who acted in terms of such universals, they also donned the straight-jacket of their cultural milieu and its organizational difficulties. They had some advantages, many more disadvantages. In particular, they could always command a hearing, and subsequent action by resorting to the imperatives which Tangu and other Kanakas of the region consider to be contained in a dream.

DREAMS

For Tangu dreams are not simple fantasies woven from sleep. They are a normal technique for solving a problem or finding a way out of a dilemma. The great majority of dreams concern food: success in the hunt, or a large harvest followed by a feast. Other dreams conjure dead ancestors who give advice to the living, and many reflect relationships with living kin and acquaintances. Some dreams appear to be merely amusing, and others—concerned with sorcerers or sorcery—are more ominous. When Tangu dream of pigs they go hunting, optimistic for a kill. When a man digs a deep hole and covers it with leaves and branches, or if he builds a more complicated trap above ground, a dream will tell him if either stratagem has been successful and it will provide the directive to go and look. If a man is hesitating over giving a feast he will wait for a dream to indicate to him whether it would be a good idea or not; and usually this advice will come through a dead kinsman, father or brother. When Tangu dream of sorcerers they waken and take precautions because the dream has come as a warning. If a man, or a woman, steals or otherwise transgresses, the guilt is expressed in a dream which is made public. When Tangu fall sick they search their consciences, for most sicknesses are evidence of another's anger, and therefore of their own malfeasance. After an examination of conscience a dream will reveal the nature of the wrong. If a man dreams that a kinsman, his brother, is going to return from a spell of contract labour the dream is considered to be advance information of the brother's imminent return. Finally, Tangu use the imperative contained within a dream as a reinforcement when they attempt to persuade others to a particular line of action or point of view.

One day when an administrative patrol was expected in the village, a queue formed up to see the writer. Each man had been dreaming during the night, and each one had dreamed very much the same dream. They related that, in dream, they (the villagers) had walked round the village and had found everything clean, tidy, and hygienic. When the patrol officer came he treated them kindly, and complimented them on the state of the village. No one in the village was manhandled by the police, nobody was arrested.[1] All was joy. When, in fact, the patrol came to the village the hopes and predictions contained in the dreams were borne out. The villagers were complimented, nobody was roughly treated, no man was arrested.

Whether or not any of those who claimed to have dreamed the dream actually dreamt it in sleep is unimportant. What is significant is that the chosen vehicle for expressing the desires and hopes of these men was a dream. Further, when expressed through a dream hope merges into positive expectancy. Any man may wish or hope for something at any time. But, when in association with a dream the hope comes near to realization. Dreams tend to pull a future into current, sensible

[1] Note the expectations contained herein.

reality; they give definity to hope, adding faith, thereby putting the dreamer in touch with a verity shortly to be manifest.[1]

Normally, dreams are private communications to the individual. This does not mean that dreams may not be communicated to others, but it does mean that it is to the peculiar advantage of the recipient to take note of his own dreams. Dreams have a pragmatic value for Tangu. It is for the dreamer to judge, unless otherwise instructed in his dream, whether or not to divulge his experience. A man is responsible to himself for ordering his life within certain forms and values, and with the aid of available techniques. Some men in Tangu said that they would not consider wasting their time building a pig-trap until they had dreamed of catching a pig. Having dreamed the dream the pig will be caught: unless otherwise detailed in the dream it is up to the individual to decide how the pig may be trapped. The fact that sometimes a dream is misleading and, for example, no pig is caught, does not detract from the general efficacy of dreams as guides to the future, and future activities. Such particular exceptions are of small importance when ranged against the dogma of a general truth. When a dream is not realized, it is considered to have been a trick: '*Bengemamakake!*' say Tangu. 'It was a trick. We were deceived.'

The information and direction bequeathed through a dream may be deceptive or misunderstood, but this confirms rather than denies that dreams can inform and direct. Tangu have sufficient evidence of the efficacy of dreams to support them in their contention that dreams are not experienced for nothing. They are telling experiences, and even when reflective or explanatory dreams are prophetic. They entail movement into the future. If a man dreams, simply, of a pig, he is forced to correlate the dream with other kinds of experience. If he has already built a trap he will visit it, expecting to find a pig there. If he has not built a trap the dream is advice to do so as soon as may be. If he is expecting a pig in an exchange the dream is advance information that the pig will be coming

[1] *Supra* p. 179—the woman who found her child through a dream.

to him soon. The pig in the dream has meaning in relation to the circumstances in which the dreamer himself is placed.

A dream is useful: it predicates a future. But no dream is simply a 'do it yourself' attempt at foretelling a fortune. It comes to the recipient from 'outside'—from the spirits, from the dead. A man may settle himself on his sleeping board with the hope of having a dream that will show him how to hurdle a particular predicament. But this does not mean that he will, in fact, have a dream. Dreaming is not an experience a man can order to his behest and liking. Dreams come, and they come more often to some than to others. Men who are good at dreaming are consulted and employed on a variety of matters.[1] On the other hand, all men may dream, and when a man does dream it is up to him to take action on the favour conferred— he may not have another such advantage for some time to come. And when he acts it is not like an automaton, but as a thinking being with ambitions, motives, and interests; as a man with a knowledge and experience of the world that he lives in, and with an intelligent understanding of those with whom he has personal and social relationships.

MAMBU

The part played by dreams in the lives of Tangu, together with the circumstances of the triangle, the Primal Myth, and the values set upon myths, form a context essential to evaluating the activities of men such as Mambu and Yali. Outside this context the meaning they had is stripped of any real significance.

First Mambu. He was, it will be remembered, a Catholic from Apingam, near Bogia. An able man—he had been marked down as suitable for training as a catechist—he was also sensitive, resolute, and finally, as a bachelor of mature age he was something of an oddity—participating in the peculiar. For the record of what he did and said in 1937-8 we are indebted to the Reverend Father Georg Höltker.[2]

[1] e.g. in identifying a sorcerer. *Supra.* p. 65.

[2] The Rev. Georg Höltker, S.V.D., Die Mambu-Bewegung in Neuguinea Ein Beitrag Zum Prophetentum in Melanesien, *Annali Lateranensi*, Tom V, 1941, pp. 181–219.

One Sunday towards the end of 1937, about a year after he had returned from a spell of contract labour in Rabaul, New Britain, Mambu came to the mission church at Bogia. He was much earlier than usual. He entered the church, removed the dust covers from the altar and tables near by, and proceeded to lay out the prayer books for Mass. Some minutes later the missionary sister, whose duty it was so to prepare the church, came in. She saw, with some surprise, that Mambu had done her work for her. She was puzzled, but she made no fuss. Mambu, meanwhile, remained quietly in the church until Mass commenced. Then he went out.

After Mass the missionary priest, who had heard of the morning's doings from the sister, sent for Mambu, and tried to get him to talk about what he had done, and why he had done it. But Mambu would say nothing.

Then the Angelus bell sounded.

Normally, a Catholic will stand with bowed head, repeating the Angelus prayer. Mambu fell straight to his knees and prayed with passionate fervour.

As the prayer ended Mambu rose, took his leave of the priest, and departed.

A few days afterwards there was another strange event in the mission. One of the missionary sisters woke up during the night, startled to find a Kanaka bending over her in the darkness. Very frightened as he started to clutch at her hands, she was about to call for help when the intruder, whatever his intention had been, slipped off into the night.

The intruder was never positively identified. Those most closely concerned, the resident missionaries, could not but associate the third occurrence with the previous two, and, since there was no one else to suspect, they thought the man might have been Mambu. At a minimum reckoning, even if the incident was no more than a sister's imaginative impulse, it is clear that Mambu had attracted no little notice.

Almost immediately after the nocturnal visitation Mambu started his activities in Apingam, his native village. But his own people would have none of him. There was a little trouble, and Mambu left Apingam for the settlements of Tangu.

There, speaking in Pidgin, he seems to have found a few followers. The resident missionary was away at the time, and Mambu succeeded in collecting a sum of money—the 'head tax'—which he said should be given to him and not to the administration.

When the missionary returned to Tangu he got wind of what Mambu was doing and took immediate action. He recovered the money which Mambu had extracted from Tangu, returned it to the donors, and ordered Mambu to leave Tangu forthwith. It was as a result of his explusion from Tangu, says Father Höltker, that Mambu developed an implacable hatred for the mission.

From Tangu, Mambu went to the Banara hinterland, beyond Pariakenam. Here he found a welcome from the villagers, and here, comparatively isolated from both mission and administration, Mambu settled to his task.

According to Höltker the gist of Mambu's teaching was as follows:

At the present time, Mambu said, Kanakas were being exploited by white men. But a new order, a new way of life was at hand which was dependent on no longer submitting to white men whether they were missionaries, administrative officers, planters, or traders. The ancestors had the welfare of their offspring very much at heart. Even now some were in the interior of the volcano of Manam island, manufacturing all kinds of goods for their descendants. Other ancestors, adopting the guise and appearance of white men, were hard at work in the lands where white men lived. Indeed, said Mambu, the ancestors had already despatched much cargo to Kanakas. Cloth for *laplaps*, axes, khaki shorts, bush-knives, torches, red pigment, and ready-made houses had been on their way for some time. But white men, who had been entrusted with the transport, were removing the labels and substituting their own. In this way, Mambu said, Kanakas were being robbed of their inheritance. Therefore, Kanakas were entitled to get back the cargo from white men by the use of force. The time was coming, however, when all such thievery and exploitation would cease. The ancestors would come with cargo for all. A huge harbour would be created in front of his (Mambu's) house in Suaru, and there the ships of the ancestors—laden with cargo—would make fast. When this time came, all work in the gardens should cease. Pigs, gardens—everything—should be destroyed. Otherwise, the ancestors—who were going to bring plenty for all—would be angry and withhold the cargo.

In the meanwhile, said Mambu, until a sign was vouchsafed them, certain things should be done. The administration had no right to demand a tax: instead, this tax should be handed to Mambu himself. If the administration asked for it the people should say that they had already given it to Mambu, 'The Black King'. Nor should Kanakas clean up the roads or do any carrying: the administration should do it for themselves. Since, also, the missionaries had made common cause with the administration to exploit the Kanakas, natives should not attend mission schools, or go to their churches or stations. Those who disobeyed this injunction would not have a share in the glories of the new age. They would be completely outcast. Any Kanakas who happened to be in a mission church or school when the ancestors came would be burnt up and consumed in a holocaust.

Mambu used to pray by the graves of the deceased, and he demanded payment for doing so. He introduced a form of baptism which, he said, would give full dispensation in the rights of the new days to come. Men and women in couples— two men or two women, but not a man and a woman—would stand before Mambu, cast off their breech-clouts or grass skirts, and have their genitals sprinkled with water.[1] Mambu said, too, that it was not fitting that Kanakas should wear native apparel. Instead, they should wear European clothes, throw away their breech-clouts and grass skirts and bury them. By doing these things the ancestors would be pleased. And seeing the cast-off breech-clouts and grass skirts, they would say, 'Ha! Our children are truly doing well.'

Although it does not seem to be clear whether 'baptism' and

[1] It is not clear from the text whether payment was required for this service.

185

the burial of clothing were carried out at the same time,[1] where the burial of native clothing was actually carried out Mambu participated as Master of Ceremonies. He used a crucifix, holding it in his hands in front of his face and making the Sign of the Cross as the clothing was consigned to the pit which had been made ready. He also made an additional and peculiar gesture with the crucifix whose meaning, if it had any, is not known.

In some villages Mambu caused to be erected small buildings—which Höltker, with apologies, calls temples—some four metres square with corner posts about two and a half metres high. Nothing is known of the purpose of these buildings, but it is perhaps relevant that from the top of the conical roof of palm thatch there emerged a small pole to which were affixed a cross and red flag. Mambu said of himself that he could not be wounded, he was immune. He liked to call himself 'King long ol Kanaka, the King of all Kanakas', and chose the title 'Black King'. On a parting his closest associates used the formula 'Goodbye King!' Mambu also said that marriage was not for him, and although at the peak of his power he might have taken any woman he fancied there does not seem to be any evidence that he actually did so. Like a priest, he remained celibate. Finally, it is recorded by Höltker that Mambu once distributed rice and fish as from the ancestors as an earnest of their good intentions.

Mambu caused trouble. Attendance at schools and churches dropped off alarmingly and administrative officers found their task increasingly difficult. So, action was taken. Mambu was imprisoned in Bogia, and later taken in chains to Madang.

At first, Mambu's followers said that he had only permitted himself to be taken in order to spread his teaching. But, as time passed and Mambu remained in prison, people began to forget about him and the missions recovered their parishioners. In two or three months, says Höltker, the movement had entirely collapsed. By June of 1938 things had returned to normal.

Nobody seems to know what eventually became of Mambu.

[1] But compare Worsley, op. cit., p. 106.

The official records which, no doubt, would have given dates of entry and release from gaol were lost in the Japanese invasion. Perhaps he lingered in gaol and died under the Japanese; or it may be that he escaped and still lives, quietly, *incognito*, somewhere in the hills.

In Höltker's estimation Mambu was a coward who lacked the courage of a real revolutionary. Yet the forces ranged against him were not inconsiderable. He was imprisoned, and for all he knew a rope might have been ready. Had he had access to arms—would he have shown courage, or rash stupidity, by fighting against overwhelming odds? On the facts he was sincere in what he wanted to do, and he was not carried away by popularity. He held to his precepts. He was certainly after power, and the way he extracted cash shows that he had one foot firmly planted in earth. Traditionally, in Apingam as in Tangu, power rests upon wealth. There, too, it is dependent upon marriage, the household, and exchanges. We do not know, precisely, what happened in Apingam. Was it something to do with a marriage? We do not know. Certainly, however, Mambu made a virtue of celibacy and sought political power through cash. There are one or two confirmed bachelors in Tangu, but they are not celibates. Celibacy is a European notion. The money Mambu collected was also European. Both his teaching and his actions were shot through with Europeanisms.

What exactly had Mambu in mind? Even if he lacked the courage of a real revolutionary he had the spirit to exploit a revolutionary situation. He had the mettle to leave his own village, go out among other Kanakas—who might be expected to seek his destruction by sorcery—and preach a new way of life to them. He sought a novel and dangerous course.

We can see, now, with the advantage of perspective, that Mambu simply could not have led an active rebellion. The time was not ripe. And he lacked arms. On the other hand he used the means available to him and he fully succeeded in rousing the population to an awareness of their problems. It is probable, too, that Mambu knew he could go no further than he had done. Having sown his seed, and being powerless to prevent his imprisonment, he accepted his fate. As a Christian he had excellent precedent for doing so. On the whole, Mambu's worth as a revolutionary rests not so much on what he accomplished himself—though this was significant in itself—as on the consequences his actions had for others.

THE MAMBU MYTH

Höltker's is a sober, European version of what Mambu did. By June 1938 'things had returned to normal'. Mambu might have been a flight of midsummer madness.

Mambu did not stay in Tangu very long, yet his visit there and what he did afterwards came to mean much to Tangu. The myth-dream had been refertilized. Mambu himself disappeared into obscurity, the Japanese came, and missionaries, planters, traders, and administrative officers left the Bogia region. The war bore its fruit in famine, forced labour, an increase in sorcery, and the roar of guns and aircraft over the mission station in Tangu. The Japanese went away from New Guinea and in their places came white and negro troops who were generous, who had plenty of goods, and money to spend. In due course the triangle was reformed and a new normality came to Bogia. But none of the stirring events of the decade could eradicate Mambu. As a man he might have been dead. As the image of a man he was still full of life in 1952.

Mambu, say Tangu today, was a Kanaka of the Bogia region who had been working in Rabaul. When he finished his contract he stowed away in a steamer bound for Australia. He was, however, discovered and hauled before the captain of the ship. The captain was very angry with Mambu for stowing away.

He was about to have Mambu thrown overboard lest by going to Australia he should chance upon the secret of the white man when Mambu's former employer, his 'master', who was on the same ship, intervened and saved him. The same man, an Australian, saw Mambu safely to an Australian port.

Arrived in Australia, Mambu was clothed and fed. His

master showed him the sights, gave him rice, spare clothing, beads, knives, canned goods, razor blades—heaps of good things. All this cargo was packed into cases and sent to the quayside for loading. The master's sister wrote a letter, stuck it into Mambu's hair, and told him to go down to the quay where he would find all his cargo marked with such-and-such a sign. Mambu was to board a certain ship together with his cargo and return to New Guinea. If there was any trouble, or if anyone questioned him, Mambu was to produce the letter.

Mambu boarded his ship. He survived several attempts by the captain to have him thrown overboard, but eventually he reached Bogia. If it had not been for the letter probably he would have been killed.

In Bogia, Mambu claimed that he knew the secret of white men, and that they, being jealous, were preventing Kanakas from obtaining it. Kanakas, said Mambu, should not submit to this. They should be strong and throw the white men out of New Guinea into the sea. And to make themselves strong Kanakas needed money. To this end Mambu travelled around the countryside collecting pennies and shillings. But for doing so Mambu was reported to the administration by a missionary and then gaoled. He was dangerous to white men and might destroy their over-lordship.

When the policemen came to arrest him, Mambu said to them: 'You can hit me—never mind! You can maltreat me—never mind! Later, you will understand!'

The policemen were awed, but took him to gaol. That night, though supposedly behind bars, Mambu was seen chewing betel in a nearby village. In some mystical way he had slipped out of his chains. The policemen—who knew of this escape—were too frightened to report the nocturnal excursion —and some informants say that there were several such forays—lest they be accused of neglect of duty. Nevertheless, Mambu could not escape his fate, and he was taken away to Madang. Before he left, however, he prophesied the coming war.

Mambu also performed another kind of 'miracle'. He

produced for an informant, who had gone to '*try*'[1] him, a
banker's packet or 'stick' of money out of thin air—money,
moreover, that was actually used to buy an axe and some
beads. He said to my astounded informant: 'You do not
understand. You are like a child who has yet to learn much.
You do not understand the things that I know.' Mambu then
went on to claim that he was able to get more (money)
whenever he wanted to.[2]

When Tangu tell the story of Mambu their faces are serious.
Bystanders do not interrupt, giggle, or explode into hoots of
laughter as they are wont to do when other stories are told.
The story of Mambu ends silently. Afterwards there may be
embellishments: the number of times the captain of the ship
tried to do away with their hero, the captain's ruthlessness,
the detailed cunning of the way Mambu escaped him, and
the number of times Mambu escaped from gaol to talk and
chew betel with his friends. Unlike their traditional myths—
which Tangu relate with gusto, handing the tale to another
when memory runs short, singing and beating the melodies
and rhythms of the dances sanctioned by the stories and
incidents in them—the Mambu story is humourless, earnest,
part of their own recent past. Like the great sickness, the
fighting that followed, the advent of the mission, the administration, and the Japanese war, Mambu is. He happened.
And he happened the way Tangu say that he happened. He
does not belong to the faraway days when a penis slept
between sisters, when a hawk gave suck, and when men
climbed to the moon on a betel nut palm. His is the myth in
creation, a part of their living eyes' evidence.

THE MAMBU MYTH EXAMINED

In discussing the Mambu myth as Tangu relate it two points
should be kept firmly in mind. Firstly, it contains and expresses most of the elements of the myth-dream; secondly
without the framework provided by Mambu it is questionable

[1] *Try, tri,* or *trai,* Pidgin word meaning 'test', 'try out'.

[2] Published in Cargo Cult Activity in Tangu, *Oceania,* Vol. XXIV,
No. 4, June 1954.

whether Yali would have been effective in quite the same way that he was.

The myth, then, may be reduced to a series of propositions. First, Europeans have a secret which they keep to themselves and which they deny to the Kanakas of New Guinea. Second, the secret is the key to dominance by white men, and it is to be found in Australia. Third, in spite of pitiless opposition—from the sea captain—Mambu succeeds in reaching Australia. There he acquires cargo, and from thence he returns to New Guinea. Fourth, Mambu owed his safe arrival home—and indeed, his arrival in Australia—to the protection and help of his European employer, the latter's sister, and in virtue of possessing a letter or *pas*. Fifth, although the evidence is scant, Mambu appears as essentially Christian—even Christ-like. He is gentle, his replies to those who question him and arrest him might be taken from the New Testament, and he performs a miracle. Sixth, Mambu is not taken for granted. He is tested or '*tried*'. Seventh, Mambu produced not cargo, but money.

The first proposition is common to most if not all Cargo movements. On the other hand it will be noticed that what Mambu actually found out about the secret is not made explicit. Nor, if the myth is to remain effective and forceful, may the secret be otherwise than vague. For, by being obscure the myth remains fertile. There is room for development, for containing successive discoveries as to the nature of the secret. None the less, there are hints. What Mambu eventually produced from thin air by mystical means was money, not cargo. The letter, or *pas*, solved most of the hero's difficulties. Without the patronage of his former European employer and his sister, Mambu would hardly have survived. Lastly, and explicitly, there is still an unknown which Kanakas will come to understand in time.

First, about money. When Tangu talk about leaving for the coast on contract labour they remark that '*moni noken kamap nating long peles*', a Pidgin rendering which may be translated as 'money does not grow on trees in the village'. Tangu know what money is. They know that to get money they have

191

to leave their homeland and work in the European settled areas; and they know that when they have money in their hands they may go to the trade stores and buy European manufactured goods. There is no mystery about it. And in the myth Mambu produced money, not an axe, nor a packet of razor blades, nor a piece of cloth. Even if the incident in the myth is based on an actual occurrence—after all it is simpler to execute a sleight-of-hand trick with money than with an axe—it is significant that nowhere in the story about him does Mambu produce cargo. Instead, he produces money.

It is curious and significant that Höltker's version should have Mambu produce food, and especially fish, as an earnest of cargo, and that the myth, which might have gone the whole hog and given Mambu credit for feeding five thousand, should restrict itself to a small sum of money.[1] Money is rarely mentioned as part of cargo: only when the direct question is asked is the answer in the affirmative. In everyday life, however, the distinction between money and goods is made as a matter of course. That is, when forced into the context of a cult, the distinction between goods and money becomes unreal, in the cult situation money is as difficult as cargo and is identified with it. On the other hand, the myth echoes a simple truth: one way of obtaining European goods is to have possession of money. But how get the money? There is only one known method—taking service with Europeans. And it is also well known that this means can only bring in sufficient to buy an axe and a few oddments.

Mambu himself gets the money mysteriously, indicating at the same time that there is another method besides working for Europeans, but that they, Kanakas, will have to wait for a while before they can come to know of it. In short, though the problem of cargo can be solved by money, until the problem of money can be solved cargo and money present the same problem in relation to the cult. Nevertheless, the truth enshrined in the myth is clear. The key to cargo is money.

Although the story does not make it plain whether or not

[1] I do not think there is any connexion here, directly, with the *ramatzka* fish of the Primal Myth.

Mambu actually landed the cargo he had been given in Australia, it is clear that his own safe arrival in New Guinea was due to the *pas* he had been given. The mere fact of possession is associated with the safe arrival. Perhaps the *pas*, or letter, stands for or indicates the necessity for being able to write, or education in general. At the same time, in everyday life Tangu associate the acquisition of European goods with a *pas*. Those who have served under Europeans have often been sent to the trade store with a *pas*. And on presentation of the *pas* goods are handed over the counter. Administrative officers, missionaries, and planters or traders who require replenishment of stores send letters and in due course the cargo arrives. No money is seen to change hands, no apparent exchange seems to take place, no goods are returned to the store: the cargo comes, is distributed, consumed, and more comes. Those who have worked in the larger townships see the cargo arrive on the quay after having been discharged from the ships. From the quay it goes into large warehouses; from there into shops and stores; and from shops and stores into homes where it is consumed. Each transaction is accompanied by a letter. Letters set the whole process in motion.

Tangu associate a *pas* with action, with trouble, with the triggering of a fresh series of events. When a *pas* is sent, or arrives, it makes guilty consciences uneasy. It may herald the arrival of a policeman; perhaps the administration wishes to see someone—and if so, why? No *pas* is sent for nothing. It starts something. The recipient of a *pas* is always goaded into some kind of activity, a positive not a negative reaction. Now, as far as Tangu are concerned, although the proportion of those who can read and write is becoming larger every day, and though all know that what is written on a *pas* is normally merely a substitute for an oral communication, there is also a feeling that a *pas* has an efficacy, *sui generis*, which words do not have. Several youths tried sending a *pas* to the writer, and were disappointed when nothing came of it. Others related how they had sent '*passes*'—scribbled scraps of paper neatly folded—to traders and missionaries without any

193

results. Why? Europeans sent letters but Kanakas who were poorer had to have money. It is clear that whatever kind of origin cargo might have the *pas* is part of a cluster of techniques required to obtain it. The next question is, What quality or attribute of the *pas* makes it effective? What is self-evident is that a *pas* does things. How does it do them? Yams are not wholly a result of men's skill, and to grow them Tangu require mystical as well as pragmatic techniques— which Tangu themselves do not always distinguish in the same way as would a European. Given that, in the same way there are mystical and pragmatic techniques for obtaining cargo—What part is played by the *pas*? Why is it effective for one man and not for another?

Most Tangu have come to accept Europeans as their teachers, and although they would deny, hotly, that a European was any more than morally equal to them, they recognize that Europeans can dispose certain talents which place them in the position of bosses, analogous to their own relationship of father and young son. The intervention by the employer with the captain on Mambu's behalf seems to reveal an ideal relationship between European and Kanaka employee. The incident indicates there ought to be some kind of moral relationship between them: a moral obligation to reward faithful service with effective meaningful help in addition to payment for services rendered. A man is more than his labour. And since it was through the moral relationship that existed between Mambu and his employer that the former succeeded in arriving in Australia, obtaining his cargo, and returning to New Guinea, the implication is, surely, that if there were this moral relationship between Europeans and Kanakas the tension between them, symbolized in the secret which Europeans are supposed to be withholding from Kanakas, might disappear. To Tangu, in real life, it is just this element of moral reciprocity that is lacking in their relationships with Europeans. Generally, Europeans will not eat with Tangu in their homes. If a European wishes to 'share' his food with a Kanaka the cook-boy is called to deliver a tin of bully beef. The Kanaka is not invited to the European table. Food may be thrown to him as Kanakas themselves throw food to their dogs. Since, for Tangu, moral behaviour is chiefly reflected in behaviour over food it cannot but seem to them that Europeans are presuming on certain skills and abilities to hold Kanakas in contumely. Nor can Tangu do anything to even the score. They have to accept it.

The Mambu of myth obtained his *pas* from his employer's sister—How much did Tangu know of Mambu's association with the European missionary sister? Although there may be a connexion here between one kind of European sister and another there is certainly nothing strange or untoward in Mambu obtaining help from the sister of an associate. In Tangu it is a daily occurrence. Sisters always help their brothers or friends of their brothers. If a man receives help from a woman, or desires to set up an exchange or trading relationship, the woman (in the first case), or the wife or sister of the husband (in the second case), becomes, or is thought of as, a sister. That is, though the Mambu of history may have been trying to create a particular relationship between himself and the priest through the missionary sister, the latter has no necessary connexion with the sister in the myth. If the employer helped Mambu it would be only natural for his sister—and a man must have sisters—to help him too.

The informant chiefly responsible for relating the Mambu story said that he went to *try* him. Tangu, as others elsewhere, frequently indulge in tall stories, or make claims to an ability which they lack. But Tangu are no more gullible than others, and claims to non-traditional skills invite a greater scepticism. When boasting about traditional skills Tangu tend to carry exaggeration step by step out of the possible into the improbable. At each enlargement of his feat the boaster will stop, waiting for the '*jakwap!* true!' from his audience. When the tone of *jakwap* becomes frankly incredulous it is time to stop. And he who would carry the burden of his boast beyond this point will have to be prepared to make his claim good— or take the consequences.

When a man that I knew claimed that he could speak English, and that he knew how to use a shot-gun, both non-traditional skills, but neither of them beyond the bounds of possibility, he was suffered as a wit.

But he pushed it too hard.

One day he was dragged before me by his friends and urged to speak out, in English.

'Naineenananfo!' he blurted out.

'Does he speak true?' they asked me.

'I understand what he says.'

There was a pause, and then: 'He should show us how he can shoot with the gun,' they said. 'Will you let him have your gun—to *try* him?'

The shot-gun was brought out (unloaded), and handed to the boaster. Gingerly, he took it by the barrel, looking for a target.

Just then, opportunely, a pigeon settled on a branch not far away. The boaster caressed the stock of the gun, presenting the piece from the knee. Softly, he murmured a spell. '*Kisim!*' he commanded out loud in Pidgin. 'Get him!'

Not for two months did the boaster show his face in a major settlement. He hid in his hunting lodge. And when he came back he had no peace. Cries of derision greeted him everywhere.

But when Mambu was '*tried*', put to the test, he produced the money. He substantiated his claim. It is true that the apparently impossible can never be a barrier to faith. Indeed, the more impossible the claim the greater is the faith required—and found. Small claims, on the fringes of understanding, can be over-leaped in the imagination and put to the test within a few moments. Large claims which baffle experience and imagination alike have a magnetic appeal. Nevertheless, somehow Mambu did what he said he could do and provided Tangu with evidence that someone could do it. 'Here,' said my informant, 'is the axe-head which I bought with the money Mambu gave me when I went to *try* him.'

YALI

Like Mambu, Yali was a stranger to Tangu though he was well known to them during 1947–8. From the Rai coast south of Madang it is improbable that Yali knew anything about the activities of Mambu. Yet, he revived and re-echoed the Mambu myth; and it was largely because of the myth, one feels, that what Yali said, or was reputed to have said, were regarded in most places in the Bogia region as orders to be obeyed. It was because Yali advised it that Tangu left their scattered settlements and began to concentrate in larger groups: not because the administration and mission had for years exhorted them to do the same. Personal experience of Yali, combined with what had, by 1951, become the Yali myth, lay immediately behind the Cargo cult activities in Tangu. Always, however, behind Yali loomed Mambu.

Yali, the reader will recall, had had experience as a Tultul, a Police Serjeant, and also as a serjeant-major serving with Australian fighting troops. In 1946, after he had been demobilized, Yali started his work in the Bogia region. He went round the villages with the full cognizance of the administration, accompanied by a band of followers or disciples.

In the beginning Yali tried to work within terms of part of the triangle. In each of the villages he visited he appointed boss-boys and 'clerks' whom he ordered to assist the Luluais and Tultuls in their work. Everybody, Yali said, was to obey the administration and its officers. Triumphal archways were to be built at the entrances to villages, and the villagers themselves should collect flowers and put them in vases because in that way work would seem easier. A special house, like the administrative officers' rest house, was to be built in each village for the use of Yali or his delegates, and whenever Yali or a delegate came round to see the villages all the people were to line up and shake hands with them.[1] At the same time as Yali was saying these things, however, one of his assistants, a renegade catechist, was appointing 'Dream men' and giving them boxes filled with soil from 'ancestral ground'. Overlaid with flowers at night these boxes were to be placed beside the Dream men when they slept, thus enabling them to see

[1] Shaking hands is a European custom. When visiting villages on patrol administrative officers make a practice of shaking hands with the senior men of the village.

snakes, rain, clouds, sea, houses, and would-be sorcerers, poisoners, or thieves.

The administration was far from comfortable at the appointment of boss-boys and clerks, and when Yali was accused of assault and illegally collecting taxes, there was no alternative but to place him under arrest. Nevertheless, Yali was too good a man to waste. His extraordinary ability, his influence in the villages, and his own expressed wish to aid the administration in executing its policies resulted in him being sent to Port Moresby. It was thought that if he were properly instructed he might become an invaluable asset to the administration as well as being a useful 'pilot' experiment in recruiting Kanakas to the administrative service. In Moresby, therefore, Yali was given a short course in administrative techniques and requirements. It was, supposedly, made clear to him, too, that manufactured goods could never become available in the form or quantities popularly imagined: they had to be made with the hands, worked for in sweat, and eventually paid for.

Perhaps Yali did both apprehend and comprehend what administrative officers tried to tell him about manufactured goods. But it is difficult to feel any confidence on the matter. In trying to explain to Tangu, at their request, something of the meaning of, and means of access to, manufactured goods in the European environment, it quickly became apparent that the task was not only virtually impossible, but probably confirmed rather than contradicted Tangu beliefs about cargo and Cargo. Pidgin English, with its linguistic adjustments to the European environment went further than the vernacular, but not far enough. And speaking in Tangu entailed the use of ideas and concepts which could not exclude a mystical value. To describe a city such as Sydney in terms of Tangu huts, villages, and jungle paths; to indicate the area over which Sydney is spread in terms of Tangu notions of space; to communicate the idea of several millions gathered together in one city when to Tangu a community of one hundred is large, and Madang is a gigantic metropolis bordering on fairyland—such attempts could only invite sheer disbelief, or the presumption of an ability and command over resources so far removed from what Tangu consider to be normal that it must have implied access to a Divinity, the possession of means to such access, or some inherently superior attribute. In short, the 'secret' of the myth-dream.

Tangu are as logical as any. Their beliefs about cargo and Cargo are contained within Pidgin and within their own language, and the words of these languages derive their meaning from what happens in New Guinea, and, more particularly, from what happens and exists in Tangu. Further, for Tangu, most matters of process, especially of transformation from one state to another, have mystical connotations. Traditionally, a tree trunk was not simply made into a slit-gong: the instrument only became a slit-gong after mystical treatment. Tubers do not sprout roots and vines, babes are not made in the womb, boys do not become men, nor girls women, without mystical treatment. The use of Tangu words to describe the manufacture of European goods implies a mystical element. When a European attempts to explain to a Kanaka the 'truth about cargo' he is merely explaining to himself how he thinks European goods are made; and the Kanaka is satisfied that the European has a special technique whereby he gains access to cargo.

It is at least possible, therefore, that failing the complete transference from one symbolic system to another, the more administrative officers tried to explain to Yali the 'truth about cargo' the more he would feel that his own followers were more right about cargo than he was himself; that Yali, after his course of instruction, was more convinced than otherwise, that white men had a 'secret' which they were holding back from Kanakas.

In addition, however, a European in Moresby told Yali that Christianity was nonsense; that it was only a hoax used by the missionaries, and that what white men really believed in was not Christianity, but Evolution.

Yali was shown a book on Evolution. And one may wonder what he thought of it. Had he understood about manufactured goods he would not have taken Evolution in the way that he did. For the great deception worried him, and he brooded on it. Why had the missionaries brought the Bible to Kanakas when they knew all along that Evolution was the secret?

What grounds might Yali or any other Kanaka have for believing one rather than the other?

We are left with the fact that although Yali appeared to have benefited from his time in Moresby and was keen on supporting administrative policies without additions of his own, from this time forward he seems to have become putty in the hands of his disciples and friends. Supposedly encouraging the villagers to plant cash crops, build better houses, keep the roads clean, use the medicine hut, and report to the medical officer when sick, the actual results of the activities of Yali and his men were large scale secessions from the missions and rapidly falling attendances at schools. Planters reported trouble in the labour lines, and one may read into Patrol Reports an air of truculent defiance among Kanakas. Even if Yali himself was sticking to his brief it seems clear that his assistants, interpreting him, were saying quite different things and going along classical Cargo lines. They were moulding their hero, calling him 'Black King' and encouraging others to do so too. They were building the 'Yali myth'.

One wonders whether Yali properly understood what was going on. The pressures upon him were compelling.[1] He was riding a tiger and could not dismount. One thinks of Mambu being grateful in his heart to the administration for providing him with the opportunity for retiring from the scene, gracefully, making a last too pregnant point. Yali had to go on. No celibate, whether from a sense of confident power, or in order to drown his misgivings, or simply because he was a man who liked to enjoy himself, Yali sported with women. Further, since all women were only too willing he is said to have charged five shillings a head for intercourse.

The end was inevitable. In 1950 Yali was accused and found guilty of rape. He was sentenced to a term of imprisonment.

However, Yali's followers had done their work well. The myth-dream swallowed him whole. Yali would come again.

[1] *Vide supra* p. 8.

If the administration executed him, Kanakas said, he would rise again on the third day to deliver his people. In the Bogia region it was said that when he should come it would be in glory, in a ship full of cargo, after an event such as an earthquake. So forceful was this particular belief that after a small earthquake towards the end of 1952, a plantation labourer, seeing a ship round a headland immediately after the tremor, thought that the Day had come.

Leaping to his feet the labourer snatched a steel grass slasher and, whirling it aloft in a frenzy, rushed for the plantation bungalow, shouting wildly.

Hearing the noise the planter came out to investigate. Too late to escape himself, he barely had time to lock the door to his sister's bedroom before the Kanaka was upon him.

The struggle was brief, but anxious while it lasted. Other labourers sped to the rescue, grappled with the madman, disarmed him, and bound him hand and foot.

After two years in prison, therefore, stories about Yali could still command action. In his heyday he travelled much. He lived in a vortex of rumours which, willingly or in spite of himself, he thrived on. Hard, substantiated facts about Yali are difficult to find. It is completely in character that Yali, who could have had any woman he wanted and be paid for the pleasure, should have been committed to prison for rape. For missionaries Yali was always the arch-enemy, the anti-Christ tearing to pieces in weeks and months what had slowly and painfully been built up over the last half-century and more. They were well aware that Yali was being used by his assistants, and that he was becoming a symbol holding together several disparate Cargo beliefs. Nor did it make the pill any sweeter to know that their own pupils, whom they had trained through many years, were now being most active in aiding Yali and creating the myth about him. Finally, understandably, they were shocked and not a little bitter at what seemed to them to be administrative tolerance of what was going on. For Yali and his men were making it virtually impossible for missionaries to carry on their work.

Other Europeans were also aggrieved. The growling

discontent in the labour lines caught the imagination of planters and traders: they called Yali 'a communist tool' and 'anti-white'. For their part administrative officers were not only loath to call their experiment a failure, they found it difficult to find the kind of evidence admissible in the courts without decreeing an Emergency. Few Kanakas would testify against Yali. He was energizing a myth-dream, and to turn informer would have required great courage and disregard of such consequences as, at the least, isolation from one's own. Europeans might fulminate, but again, they could only place an inference between their troubles and Yali himself. And had Yali worked on, sensibly, within the limits imposed by the triangle, nurturing instead of antagonizing (particularly) the missions, it is difficult to see how he might have been stopped without special legislation or a major resort to force. Had a prison medical officer been forced to pronounce Yali's life extinct, there is no doubt that Yali, or rather, what Yali meant and symbolized to his fellow Kanakas, would have risen again in very truth. As it was it became clear that if administrative and mission programmes were to continue Yali's career would have to be interrupted: and, unlikely though it may appear, the charge brought against him, rape, stuck. Even so, as has been shown, though Yali might be put behind bars, his word and his meaning were still free to carry on their work— divorced from Yali the man.

In later years Yali the man became suspect. He had been committed for rape. Many Tangu condemned him for such folly though there were some who tried either to excuse it or brush it aside as of little importance. But the final proof of the divorce between Yali and what he meant lies in the fact that Tangu cannot criticize what he said—that pertains almost to the scared—but they can and will discuss him as a man as they would any other.[1]

[1] Apart from what I learned about Yali in the field, my information comes from Dr Peter Lawrence, to whom I am most grateful for personal communications. Otherwise see Peter Lawrence, The Madang District Cargo Cult, *South Pacific*, Vol. 8, No. 1, January 1955, pp. 7–13; Cargo Cult and Religious Beliefs Among the Garia, *International Archives of Ethnography*, Vol. XLVII, No. 1, 1954, pp. 15–20.

MAMBU, YALI, AND THE NEW MAN

In Tangu all men are of equal moral stature; and social life depends upon proving this assumption. Social life also requires the exercise of a variety of skills and abilities—particularly those relevant to the politico-economic process. And in this sense Tangu managers emerge as ideal personalities. Young boys would like to be managers when they grow up; it is taken for granted that women prefer their husbands to be managers; and the more renowned managers are always pointed out to the visitor. Managers solve best and most fruitfully the issues of self-will and moral responsibility; they are also faced with solving these dilemmas in their most acute forms. They are the men who can exploit to the utmost certain selected capacities without overstepping moral equality.

Though Höltker shows some sympathy for Mambu's abilities the overall picture that emerges is that of a common agitator. And we must remember that Höltker was a missionary, caught in the triangle. And though Mambu's character remains arguable, certain features of what Mambu is reported to have done, and was, remain incontrovertible. He was a Kanaka, who, unmarried, showing no evidence of traditional productive achievement, not wanted in his own community, and presumably no mean orator, wandered outside the confines of a traditional ideal. The way of his wandering is instructive.

In going round the villages collecting the 'head tax' Mambu was entering the role of an administrative officer. In his preaching, his use of a crucifix, and in inaugurating a form of 'baptism' he was assuming the role of a missionary. He said that some of the ancestors were 'disguised' as white men, making cargo; he wanted his followers to abjure traditional dress and don European clothes; he used a cross and a flag as symbols; he built 'churches'; he said that the cargo, European manufactured goods, would come in ships. And by remaining celibate in spite of temptations it would seem that for Mambu the role of missionary slightly outweighed that of an administrative officer.

At the same time, however, Mambu inveighed against white men in general, and against administrative officers and missionaries in particular.

The Mambu of the myth shows few of the qualities required of a manager in Tangu. He suffers the ignorant with patience, is gentle, performs miracles, and has the gift of prophecy. That he has influence goes without saying. But his influence is derived not from the capacities traditionally required of a manager, but from a new, European model.

Both Mambus preached revolt against European domination, and both accounted for the existing situation in terms of a secret which was discoverable, and a trick which could be laid and made ineffective. In action, however, the historical Mambu made use of European ideas and symbols; and the mythical Mambu, himself a pale reflection of the Christ-image, a European ideal, succeeded in reaching Australia, obtaining cargo, and returning to New Guinea through the good offices of Europeans—not a missionary or administrative officer, but a planter and his sister—with whom he had established a moral relationship. The sea captain in the story is evidently the European as 'enemy', who tried to prevent Mambu from reaching his goal. But, in spite of his efforts, Mambu succeeds. That is, to interpret, though, in general, relations with Europeans may be said to be typically characterized by resentment and hostility, though Europeans are trying to prevent Kanakas from acquiring cargo, Kanakas will eventually win through with the help of European ideas and certain kinds of European—true brother, moral European.

Though, therefore, the Mambu of history may be seen to have selected as a political strategem the fourth alternative in the Primal Myth, ousting white men, the mythical Mambu is made to select the second alternative, co-operation with white men in a moral relationship. At the same time both Mambus assume the roles and attributes of Europeans. On both levels the new man emerges as an amalgam of Kanaka and European ideal.

Using pragmatic means the Mambu of history went round the villages collecting money. The Mambu of myth produced money by mystical means. We know little of the rites recommended by the historical Mambu, but we do know that in some way or other he substantiated at least a part of his claims. Where did he obtain the rice and fish which he distributed as from the ancestors? We do not know. Was he trying to feed the five thousand? Again, we do not know. Nor do we know if, at the time, his provision of rice and fish was regarded as a miracle in the same way as the mythical Mambu's production of the 'stick' of money. At all events it would seem that, at the time, the historical Mambu was deemed to have made good some of his claims at least. He was, too, using politico-economic techniques for consistent ends. He attempted to channel wealth unto himself; he tried to persuade villagers not to pay money to the administration, not to work for them, not to go to school, not to go to church. He made use of political symbols such as 'King'. Yet he, like his mythical counterpart, was imprisoned. As a set of physical activities the movement he started collapsed within a few months of his deportation. Nevertheless, he had struck a spark, and despite his apparent failure he entered the myth-dream. Subtly transformed, he became the new man, a model, an individual Kanaka who had passed through the impasse—a man who was both Kanaka and as European.

When Yali came the new man as represented by Mambu, shadowy, was stiffened with substance and shape.

Yali had fought in a European war with distinction. As a soldier not a labourer. And he had been decorated. After the war the administration thrust him forward as an example, putting real responsibility into his hands. Administrative officers, missionaries, and others talked about him as a friend or colleague, or as an enemy worthy to combat. Yali, in short, had succeeded in becoming recognizably a man in the eyes of those very Europeans who were not thought to accord such status to Kanakas in general. Mambu the Kanaka was borne into the myth-dream clothed as the man recommended by missionaries. When Yali was imprisoned he entered the myth-dream as the man acknowledged as such by all Europeans, particularly administrative officers. Together, as they may be found in the myth-dream, Mambu and Yali project an image of he who is to come: the new man.

This new man, then, will command the respect of Kanakas and Europeans alike. His purpose is to remove white men from the amoral dominance they have currently assumed. His means are European ideals, techniques, and ideas together with the help of certain peculiarly, morally, qualified Europeans. Since the mythical Mambu went to prison when he encountered the superior physical forces of the administration, but succeeded in producing money—a symbol of access to cargo— through purely mystical means in a Kanaka environment, and since as historical figures both Mambu and Yali were imprisoned when they used pragmatic means to gain their ends —the implication is that moral weapons will succeed where resorts to force will inevitably fail; and that in the Kanaka environment mystical techniques seem to be necessary.

As a historical figure who may be seen to have selected the fourth alternative in the Primal Myth, and who failed to achieve his explicit primary and concrete objectives, Mambu hardly exists for Tangu. On the other hand, as the basis on which to build the image of the new man, as the mythical Mambu, he is very much alive in their minds. That is, Mambu meant what he did in the light of the myth-dream. Later, his meaning became divorced from himself, qualified and added to the total content of the myth-dream, and then derived fresh meaning in the light of the amplified myth-dream. Yali compromised. He started by ignoring missionaries and by regarding administrative officers as co-operative moral Europeans. Later, he excluded missionaries. But he could not afford to ignore men as influential and significant within the basic relationship structure as missionaries are, and eventually his followers forced him into a position similar to Mambu's— ousting all white men. As in the case of Mambu, Yali's success was his failure, and where he appeared to be failing he eventually succeeded. In a strictly historical context what Yali did as a man, especially his treatment of women, stand out to Tangu with cautioning clarity. His meaning, on the other hand, abstracted from the man himself and derived from the myth-dream, added to the content of the myth-dream and took on a new gloss within the framework of the myth-dream thus augmented.

When the context is set by the notion of Cargo, on the level of the myth-dream—where Yali is dressed as he ought to be dressed—there are only a few in Tangu who do not articulate his name with reverence. Through the myth-dream the political authority he had was regarded as divinely inspired.

As mythical figures, therefore, as symbols which focus the ideas in Cargo, both Mambu and Yali exist as seminal forces. Their failures in the historical context, their failures to translate the totality of the myth-dream into principles of concrete political activity, were simple pragmatic failures. But in their meaning, in their roles as charismatic figures feeding the myth-dream, they succeeded and will not be forgotten. For, albeit unknowing, so far as they exercised political authority in accord with the myth-dream, they were as divine kings. As such, exerting divinely sanctioned moral power, their relevance was, and is, lasting. But as political leaders who lost sight of, or who ignored crucial elements of the myth-dream, their significance is, and was, transient. Guilt, divine forgiveness, and moral European are all the more 'true' or 'real' because they exist in the myth-dream without necessarily being tied to historical events. The Mambu of history had no Australian adventure. In the mythical Mambu's employer, who is moral European, that element of true brotherhood—in the Primal Myth an unresolved tension between what is and what ought to be—takes on a definite and separate, personified shape.

CHAPTER VII

The Myth-dream

[iii]

By the time Mambu started his movement Tangu and the peoples living between them and the coast had become familiar with things European. They saw administrative officers from time to time and, more often, the less formal missionary. Many from Tangu had been to coastal plantations and had had experience with traders, planters, and ship-masters. They had seen, or knew something about, the variety of material goods that Europeans were bringing to New Guinea. They knew what a steamship was, and perhaps one or two had seen an aircraft. But such things could not be accepted, simply. It is evident from what Tangu say, and also from what is going on in the hinterland today, that Europeans and what they had brought with them were favourite topics of gossip and rumour. When conversation about the crops, or the feast in a few days' time, or so-and-so's marital entanglement lapsed, it was easily brought round to Europeans and their goods.

What sort of people were these *waitsikin*, white men? They scoffed at sorcerers, but were mortally afraid of invisible things called germs; they preached brotherhood and ate in splendour alone, despising Kanaka food; instead of dispensing their wealth in a feast, they hoarded it; they were strong men and fierce, quick to anger; they expected obedience and enforced it when necessary; they had access to all kinds of material goods which came to them in ships in a constant stream. To be sure, after days of hard work, they, the Kanakas, were given some money to buy goods from the trade store. But Europeans merely sat in their chairs. They perspired as they sat, without working. They wrote letters, kept goldfish in bowls, cultivated flowers, cooed at pet parrots, played cards, drank rum, slept late, washed frequently, shouted, gave orders, ate magnificently—and still there seemed no end to the goods that came to them. Even the dullards who shied from thinking about so large a problem could not be other than interested. Information about white men and what they did was important not only to avoid imprisonment, to order personal and social relationships, but also to gain freer access to material goods. But between information and the ends it might win lies understanding.

THE CONFINES OF CARGO

However far Mambu might have been able to see beyond the circumstances of his time, he could only gain a hearing from his audiences by speaking to them in terms which they could understand. If he had produced a quite original programme he would have been unintelligible. Two alternatives remained. Either to have explained himself in terms of notions that were current, affirming them, crystallizing them; or, within the same set of ideas, to have denied their validity. Faced with such a choice, and himself a part of his own environment, it was almost inevitable—and certainly politically necessary— that he should first have echoed the expectations of those who listened to him, and then attempted to push them forward. He was bound by the myth-dream, by the notion of Cargo.

By evoking the latent hostilities of Kanakas towards white men in general Mambu chose, in effect, the last alternative posed in the Primal Myth. Quite clearly, too, the Mambu myth recognizes this as Mambu's mistake and goes on to recommend the second alternative, co-operation, as the best answer.

Yali was also bound by the notion of Cargo, by the myth-dream. What Yali himself actually knew about the Primal Myth, Mambu, or the Mambu myth is irrelevant. In fact he started obeying the injunction in the Mambu myth, the choice of the second alternative in the Primal Myth. He co-operated. He chose as moral European the administration. But by doing so he upset the balance of the triangle. 'Moral European' need not coincide exclusively with some other category. In addition, despite himself, Yali's assistants took the same course as Mambu. They tried to solve the triangle by abolishing it. And if, in doing so, they were concentrating on one aspect of Kanaka feeling they were wholly neglecting the myth-dream which reflects a deeper and more important part of the total relationship Kanakas have with white men. As such, the movements started by Mambu and Yali were failures. But only partially so. Both movements energized and clarified the myth-dream. Through them the myth-dream developed; through feelings and community rapport the original ideas were refined. The triangle is the problem.

Today, as a matter of course, someone from Tangu, or with connexions in Tangu, will normally be found squatting on his haunches in the environs of sub-District headquarters in Bogia. He is a spy, picking up news, who cannot speak English. He is one of the main channels guiding the relationship between white men and Kanakas. He watches the comings and goings of administrative officers, picking up the tag-ends of conversation, looking out for signs of anger. If he sees anger the fact will get back to Tangu. 'The administration is angry.' Almost immediately Luluais, Tultuls, and Doctor boys will set about tidying their villages and exhorting a recalcitrant people to cut the grass verges and dig more latrines. Because the message has got back to them Tangu cannot do otherwise than suppose that it was meant for them. Because administrative officers are usually angry about matters of hygiene it follows that the administration is angry because, in some way, it knows that Tangu have neglected their latrines. And of course it is so. Digging latrines is an irksome task conveniently put off until tomorrow. But, since anger and hygiene are easily connected, an administrative officer's sore tooth or thick head is turned into neat verges and freshly dug pits.

As a matter of prestige the spy likes it to be thought that he can speak and understand English, and the stories he makes up about what he has heard usually tend to reinforce Tangu

predilections about Europeans. How could it be otherwise?
If he is to be thought any use as a spy he must either confirm
or gainsay particular instances of a general expectation.
If he reported something quite outside the range of expectations he would be laughed at. He may report an administrative officer as being angry or not angry because consequences
of import, of a foreseeable kind, are likely to flow from the
anger. He cannot report an officer as having shaved or not
shaved: it is irrelevant unless it can be linked to something
else, an expectation. His job is to confirm or deny particular
and pertinent anticipations. Every intelligence officer, or
agent, must have had an encounter which, because it lies
outside the range of possibilities foreseen by his employers or
superiors, is either immediately dismissed as of no account or
thought of as bluff. Only in the last resort, if ever, will an
experience running counter to, or outside, expectations be
accepted. For Tangu, acting within a very narrow range of
expectations, the reports they receive must have a response.
Because the information is so likely they cannot afford to
neglect it as spurious.

During fieldwork, for a period of six weeks all local arrangements were held in suspension. The spy in Bogia had sent
word that a patrol would shortly be on its way. It was to be a
special patrol. If things were not precisely in order there
would be more beatings than usual, more sentences of imprisonment. Kanaka officials donned their caps. The villagers
grumbled: they preferred to wait for the slit-gongs.

But the officials were adamant. Whatever trouble was
coming it would fall most heavily on them.

Eventually, a patrol arrived. As far as Tangu were concerned the original information had been justified. It happened that there were no beatings, no imprisonments. 'But,'
said Tangu to me when the patrol had gone, 'that was because you were here.'

Days before I arrived in Tangu the news had come through
to Tangu that a white man was journeying to the Ramu, that
he had cargo, and that he would make distributions in Tangu.
Some weeks after I had settled in my first village it was being

211

bruited round Tangu that I had come to sow seed in the maidens, to raise up a new race of men.

Through their spies in Bogia, from returned labourers, Tangu learn much about the world outside. A district officer's lavatory habits, a medical officer's birthday party, or a planter's peccadillo—all are grist to the mill. More often than not the plain facts are accurate. But the interpretations put on them, and the inferences made from them, are not only as often widely amiss, but, as the anecdotes illustrate, they are twisted to conform to current expectations. On the ground, when speaking to Tangu, it becomes evident that what they know and can repeat about white men consists mainly of the kind of misinformation we have been discussing. Acceptance is apparently uncritical. Yet this it is not: criticism follows as an emotional or intuitive process, the resultant finding expression on the level of myth, in the myth-dream. When the myth is retailed, however, the concrete facts and activities rather than the meanings involved tend to guide the mind to an acceptance of further similarly distorted misinformation. For if the message of the myth-dream stands out quite clearly to an investigator, Tangu themselves are not fully aware of it. The situation confines them too closely.

'See this now,' said a friend pointing to an old kerosene tin. 'It seems like a horse which the mission had in the old days. But it is a horse with wings. Why do you not bring those horses to New Guinea for us to see?'

'There are no horses with wings. What you see is only a picture.'

'I know it is a picture. It is a picture of a horse with wings. Who would draw a horse with wings if there were no horses with wings?'

'It comes from an old story—a story like your stories.'

'Ah! So once upon a time there were horses with wings in your country. What happened to them?'

At this point the best response is a deprecatory laugh. One remembers another conversation. Besides, myths are truth.

'How is it you white people know how to make iron?'

'It is in the earth. After many years we learned to dig in this earth and put it in a big fire and burn it.'

'True. . . . You learned that.'

'And then, when you make the fire very hot, the iron runs out like water.'

'Very true. . . . Why do you not burn the earth hereabouts and teach us to make our own iron?'

'Because there is no iron in this earth here.'

'True. . . . Why is there no iron here—in this earth?'

'Because some earth has iron in it and some has no iron.'

'Oh true!'

Tangu exchange significant glances. Why was there no iron in *their* earth? For them the answer could only lie in the adventures of the two brothers in the Primal Myth. For the myth not only explains why Tangu cannot make goods from iron or steel, but it also explains why there is no iron ore in Tangu. Black brother should not have killed the *ramatzka*.

Perhaps the most difficult operation in a Cargo movement is that of reducing the myth-dream to a series of concrete proposals which are capable of commanding action. The crucial part is solving the problem posed by the relationship with Europeans, particularly those problems which arise from the triangular relationship between administrative officers, missionaries, and Kanakas. As a matter of practical politics the dilemma, for the charismatic figure, is how to remain consistent with the myth-dream and yet bring people to the pitch of action—without tickling their hatreds. Mambu himself said that the cargo would not come because Europeans were intercepting it, changing the labels; the myth about Mambu says that the cargo will not come because certain amoral Europeans are stopping it, and that it will come with the aid of moral Europeans. In the myth lies truth. Every piece and facet of the Cargo has a European in it. The ends contained in the Cargo become impossible if Europeans are rejected; they only become possible by accepting the content of the myth-dream. Yet, how may this be done? It is probable that if Europeans had been in the habit of distributing cargo liberally

Mambu would have had to have said, 'More cargo will not come because Europeans are stopping it.' The exhortation in the myth-dream reflects a very real and deep emotional and moral discord between Tangu and Europeans in general. It comes out in the Primal Myth, the Mambu story, and in the fact that despite latter day experiences Tangu prefer, or at any rate persist in, regarding Europeans—especially administrative officers—with deep suspicion.

One day in Tangu a man remarked that a European planter, for whom he had been working, had punched him in the face and kicked him in the belly.

'Why?'

'Because,' said the man frankly, 'I was lazing and not doing my work.'

'Well?'

'It is the fashion of the white man. There is no more to be said.'

The man went on to speak of the planter with no little respect. He was a strong, hard, man who showed his appreciation of work well done as forcefully as he expressed his disapproval. He was a man difficult to hoodwink.

The Kanaka took the pipe from his mouth, pursed his lips, and huffed a shimmering smoke ring. There were no personal hard feelings regarding the blows: only the bitterness of simple acceptance.

In Tangu there are no 'rights' backed by the force of a judiciary and executive. A man's claims on persons and property go so far as counter claims and mystical retaliation will allow: behind every claim is a vulnerable human being who exerts it and who may be forced not to exert it. In the eyes of Tangu the planter had made good his claim to strike by doing so, and it was up to the Kanaka to qualify the claim by counter-attacking. This he failed to do. And in failing he gave the planter more security for exerting his claim in the future. The Kanaka failed in his moment of trial because there was no way of coming back at the planter, and because, indeed, he was afraid of the planter and knew him to be more than his equal. The Kanaka might have done something, just something. He might have spat, or turned the other cheek. In fact he did nothing. Resorting to the administration in such circumstances and attempting to make good a claim not to be struck smacks almost of spite: the sort of thing a sorcerer would do. Normally, in his own native Tangu, a man would instantly retaliate. Tangu live by equivalence. To acknowledge in the act what will never be orally admitted goes deep into the fibre of being. Tangu are men. They have their own conventions for proving their manhood, for establishing their integrity as men. But, faced with a white man, the moment passes them by. They feel themselves children of sin.

When Tangu encounter Europeans, or get into trouble with administrative officers, they would want, instinctively, to be able to 'quarrel it through'. But this they cannot do. Instead, they are punished, warned, or forgiven—each a unilateral act which erases all meaning from equivalence. Nor can the situation be explained away simply in terms of different cultural conventions. The fact is that when Tangu face a European, eye to blazing eye, within arm's length, the sap runs dry. Tangu submit. And they know that they do so. But they would like it to be otherwise. 'Are we dogs?' they cry in impassioned fury. 'Are we not men as they are?'

There are those among Tangu who refuse to go to work on coastal plantations because they cannot bear to face the realization in action that they might not be men. In their own villages and among their own kind Tangu are able to be men; and they wear their manhood with dignity. In a European environment they cannot but feel themselves to be something rather less: their own relatively simple notions are challenged by a very complex structure of mixed authoritarian and egalitarian values. Among themselves, as we have noted, Tangu have no way of expressing an order without using Pidgin. The nearest they can reach is a forcible suggestion from adult to child which is really more of a scold. By the time a boy is ten he is deliberately flouting any suggestion from his elders that smacks of authority. To Tangu giving orders is arrogating to the self something which should not, and until recently did not, exist. Accepting an order is a denial of manhood, submission to a breach of equivalence. When Tangu go to the coast to work on plantations they come under the orders of foremen who themselves take orders from Europeans: the system depends upon orders being given and obeyed. Only a few Tangu are able to stomach it for long. On returning home Tangu are partly relieved that they will no longer have to submit to orders, and partly afraid to re-enter a system which places so much initiative in the hands of an individual and insists on him using it. Native officials in Tangu have to give orders: it is part of their role. Always Pidgin is used. Such a usage conjures the European environment and relieves men of the necessity for retaliating to an attempted order. At the same time, however, the orders are being given to Tangu in Tangu, and Tangu themselves make it quite plain through careful disobediences that they are only obeying the official in his capacity as such; they are obeying the policemen and Europeans behind him, not the man himself. In their own environment Tangu are true to themselves. Part of their problem is how to be as true in another environment.

The Mambu myth draws the image of a man who must submit patiently until understanding comes, the image of the man recommended by missionaries, and the antithetical image of the European of experience. Yali the man who had been a Kanaka official, a policeman, a soldier whose valour in battle had been recognized by King George himself—Yali the pet of administrative officers merged with the image of Mambu and reflected a second side of the triangular relationship between Kanakas, missionaries, and administrative officers. Behind both images, however, lie the frustration of misunderstanding and the practical experience of moral disharmony in the relationship between black men and white.

Misunderstanding may be partially a result of the moral disharmony: it is also, perhaps, inevitable. Until Kanakas can find a way out of their own systems of symbols and make the transference into the European it is hard to see how they can think otherwise than in the way that they do. Everything

Kenapai—a manager

An old man of Mangigumitzir   An old man of Wanitzir

An old man of Manam

individual members of the community experience can either
be made intelligible to others in the community or remain
explicitly outside the confines of understanding. Is the latter
advisable, or even practicable? In their actions Tangu think
not. They try to understand their total experience and can
only do so in terms of their history—in terms of categories
they know. Mere observation is neither intelligible nor
memorable unless immediately related to categories of understanding. Expectations—selection of particular categories—
play a major part. So Tangu make their observations, render
them intelligible, and line them up with expectations. Quite
a normal procedure. Only those whose categories and expectations are wider or different may perceive the end result in
such a way as to call it mistaken. On the mythical level, however, in spite of categories of misunderstanding, truths are
appreciated. Particularly and explicitly that understanding is
not yet (the Mambu myth), and that responsibility is on
Europeans to create the moral relationship on which mutual
understanding depends (the Mambu myth and the Primal
Myth).

THE TANGU ACTIVITIES CONSIDERED[1]

Besides reflecting the themes of the myth-dream, a mental
activity, the rites and ceremonies of a Cargo movement, a
physical activity, may be regarded as attempts to bridge the
gap between one symbolic system and another. Taken separately, each rite emerges as a technique to make the new man
and the new society.

Mambu and Yali, the heroes who were going to make the
new man, used a number of pragmatic techniques and both
ended in prison. As organizers they had either chosen, or had
been forced into, the fourth alternative contained in the
Primal Myth—ousting the white man. And in each case the
attempt had failed. Yali's assistants, on the other hand, were
free. And they, by recommending mystical techniques, had,
in fact, opted for the first alternative in the Primal Myth. In

[1] *Supra* pp. 1–3.

Tangu the tensions implied by the triangle combined with the anxieties inherent in Cargo seem to have come to the point when they had to be released in physical activity.

It was time for dreams to come true. It was time for Tangu to make their own new man.

The signal to do so came, it will be remembered, from the youth of Pariakenam, a village in the area most strongly associated with Mambu. He dreamed a dream entirely mystical in content. And he, or his dream, or he in his dream, selected the first alternative in the Primal Myth.

We have seen something of the pragmatic nature of dreams in Tangu, and there is no evidence to show that the dream that triggers a Cargo cult should be thought to be of more, or less, pragmatic value. A Cargo dream takes place within a context set by the notions regarding dreams in general. Unlike everyday dreams, however, a Cargo dream is not a private communication. It concerns the community, it is made public, and it finishes by being effective for all. It is effective, one may hazard, because it echoes the myth-dream. Its force seems to derive from the fact that it is a dream which anyone might have dreamed; or, when acquainted with the dream, the dream appears as a dream which anyone might have wished to dream. The dreamer is, in fact, the vehicle of a collective dream—a communication for the direction and benefit of all and not for the individual alone. It comes and is acted upon because the community concerned wants it to come and wants to act upon it.

Tangu know, however, that a deception is possible. But if the directives fail in gaining the end the directives are at fault, not the method of knowing what they are. The problem is how to decide, *ante hoc*, whether the directives are a deception or not. Normally, it is always worthwhile visiting a trap because failure to capture a pig means only a walk home and the prospect of better luck on the morrow. That is, in everyday life the consequences of a deception are hardly sufficient to weaken the imperative contained in the next dream; the dream as the vehicle of a directive still emerges as axiomatic even though a particular dream may be a deception. If the informant in a dream, say a brother, was a trickster in life he will continue his pranks after death; but though dreams including him will be regarded with some suspicion they will, none the less, be acted upon. The mandate is a strong one. To ignore it would be stupid.

If anything, in virtue of its relation to the myth-dream, the cult dream contains an even stronger imperative. It says, in effect, 'Do these things now and your fondest hopes will be realized.' After their cult activities Tangu said of the youth of Pariakenam, 'He deceived us.' Nevertheless, if the particular directives in the dream were at fault, the ends were still valid, and the dream as a vehicle of truth was left unimpaired. With the experience of their own private dreams behind them Tangu can make rough estimations of probability: they get to know how reliable their own dream informants are. But they do not care not to act on them. For, who can tell at what particular time what may be a general statistical validity is to be proved? 'Usually he deceives, but today perhaps he will not.' The cult dream comes maybe once, twice, even three times. When the administration reacts by punishing the participants in a cult it punishes not the ends of the dream, not the validity of dreams, but the particular directives which the people concerned may already have rejected as a deception. And, since the dream comes from 'outside', from the dead, from a deity, from ancestors, to punish the dreamer is to punish a mouthpiece. So long as the ends remain valid, so long as the myth-dream exists, other mouthpieces will be found. Even if Tangu are forced to experience large numbers of deceptive cult dreams, and even though they might be able, by that time, to estimate degrees of probability, it is doubtful whether they would, or could, reject the imperative so long as the ends in the myth-dream remain valid. The effective administrative riposte may be found in the myth-dream itself: co-operation towards attaining the ends of the myth-dream.

In Tangu dreams are not considered to be weak reflections of truth. On the contrary, truth springs out of a dream. To be sure, some truths may be apprehended during waking life, but ultimate truth can only be grasped through a dream. And if dreams do not always succeed in revealing a truth the fault does not lie with the method. For Tangu dreams remain a sound basis for arriving at truth even though truth is sometimes elusive.

The word Tangu used to refer to the rituals described in the *Prologue* is *'uap*. As a noun the word ordinarily refers to a garden plot; as a verb, unless otherwise qualified, it refers to labour in the garden. It means 'work', and is translated into the Pidgin as *wok*. Other kinds of activity are denoted by other words. The idea that the rituals might be associated with dances, fun, and excitement is untenable. Tangu were quite definite when they pointed out that the word used for 'dance' was in no way applicable to the Cargo rituals. Nor was the word for 'sing' or 'singing' applicable to the chanting described in the first series. Each of the rituals was a 'work', a *'uap*, not an entertainment, food exchange, feast, or dance. Like the garden plot, and the activities associated with it, both rituals were 'works' designed to produce the means of life or a parallel end.

Taken as a whole the first ritual seems to represent a death and rebirth. One man, the individual, was encouraged into a coma or symbolic death by the joint activities of the others. When he had 'died' the others, society, brought him back to life: to a new kind of life in which he said things which could not be understood by Kanakas as they are. Turn by turn each participant, each individual, attempted his death and rebirth into a new environment. In no dance native to Tangu is an individual picked out for a solo part. 'You do not understand,' Mambu had said. 'You are like a child who has yet to learn much.' If Yali was killed he was to rise again from the dead and come with the cargo.

Very much the same themes of the individual, his relation to society, and the meaning of manhood are apparent in the second series of rites. Mixing male and female sexual secretions after a *coitus interruptus* used to be, and in some isolated parts of Tangu still is, a central pivot of fertility ritual. In days gone by no marriage was consummated between bride and

220

groom until the latter had first drunk a potion of coconut milk and the mixed secretions of his own maternal uncle and the bride, both of whom had previously engaged in *coitus interruptus*. Without this rite, Tangu believed, the marriage would be barren. With the rite it became possible to make man. For it is quite clear to Tangu that between sexual intercourse and conception a further, mystical element intrudes. Again, it is still widely believed in Tangu that no soil will produce quantities of foodstuffs unless husband and wife first copulate in the new garden, *coitus interruptus*, mix their secretions together with a distillation of herbs, and either scatter, or bury, parts of the compound over or in various portions of the garden. That is, taken directly from traditional belief, the rite that made man and the rite that ensured the fertility of the crops were brought together into a new 'work' to make a new man and to produce a new means of life, or wealth—European goods.

Although the two rituals had the same ends and purpose there are clear and relevant distinctions. One was an innovation, the other looked back to what had been efficacious in the past; the one balanced individual against group, and the other put the accent almost wholly on the latter; the communal meal in the first seems to stress the need to have done with community sectionalisms, whilst in the second the fact that Tangu engaged the activities outside their own territory seems to accent their accord with their largest loyalty: '*Nai Kanakatzir!*' There are Europeanisms in both rituals, but in each the particular selection is remarkably consistent with the general trend. The command to '*Otim!*' as well as the plea '*Yu-ker-ap*' may be derived from a wireless recording or even from American Negro troops: either way they are as strange and incongruous to normal Tangu cultural forms as an individual performing alone, trance, a communal meal, and unintelligible utterances. Withal, they form a harmonious whole: an adventure into the novel. In the second ritual the use of heated water for washing—cleansing or purifying—and the substitution of water for coconut milk in making the 'medicine' are both Europeanisms with closely related significances. Kanakas are constantly exhorted to keep themselves clean by washing. By so doing, they are told, they will not contract the skin diseases to which Kanakas are prone, and they will be less vulnerable to sickness. *Sant water*, holy or blessed water to be found in all Catholic churches, is, for Tangu, not only a purifying agent but an aid to fertility. Missionaries bless garden sites, crops, and harvest by sprinkling holy water on the land and its fruits. Tangu youths, pagans and Christians alike, sometimes steal holy water from churches in order to make aphrodisiacs. One cannot be certain that the water used in the promiscuous ritual was *sant water* but that it was meant to serve a similar purpose seems certain. The Europeanisms correspond with traditional practice.

Both sets of rites were, explicitly, techniques to acquire cargo. At the same time it requires no great effort of the imagination to see other relevances of Cargo also peeping out of the rites. Tangu tried to keep the rituals a secret from the missionary; they told the writer nothing—until a moral relationship had been surely established. Then it came easily. The making of a new man, compounded of Kanaka and European, seems to be clearly expressed. European techniques and ideas are there. Finally, there is an approach to new unities. A communal meal without sectional rivalries is a feature which an administration might have tried for years in vain to achieve; and to cross into Jumpitzir to engage in a cult shows, surely, an acute awareness of being a Kanaka, one of many like beings in much the same boat.[1]

MEANS AND ENDS

The ends of the rites practised by Tangu are hardly in doubt: the new man, the new society, the same kind of access to cargo as Europeans have. The means are the problem.

As purely ritual expressions the rites themselves appear to compose fully interconsistent means and ends. They created

[1] Part of this interpretation has already appeared in Cargo Cult Activity in Tangu, *Oceania*, Vol. XXIV, No. 4, June 1954.

the new man, a new society, a new environment. What is crucial is that cargo was expected to arrive, and it was expected to arrive as the result of the use of what a European can only call mystical means. What has to be explained is why Tangu used mystical means to gain a pragmatic end.

That there was a connexion between the failure of the largely pragmatic techniques recommended by Mambu and Yali and the eventual resort to purely mystical means—which had been advised by Yali's assistants as well as in the dream of the youth of Pariakenam—may be safely assumed. Of the connexion itself one might argue that since adequate means were not available a retreat into fantasy was expectable.[1] Yet, such an argument would have to rest on the assumption that what was fantasy for a European was equally fantasy to Tangu; and since cargo was expected it is difficult to see how fantasy, as we normally understand the word, can be involved. Rather is the connexion to be traced to the pragmatic nature, for Tangu, of dreams, and to the character, for Tangu, of myth. Once we allow—as we have to allow—that both myths and dreams contain truth, then the acting of the myth, the action of truth, becomes intelligible and reasonable. If the truth is in myth, and dreams contain both truth and an imperative, the cult activity seems a logical consequence.

In their ordinary daily lives Tangu habitually use both mystical and pragmatic techniques, and they regard both as essential for gaining an end. Copulation in the garden will not make up for a badly chosen site, but it will go most of the way towards ensuring that a carefully selected piece of hill-side will produce plenty of fat tubers. Tangu gardeners regard themselves as technically proficient. They know a good soil when they crumble it in their fingers. They know which hillside is too wet, too dry, too exposed, or over protected. Between clearing a site and gathering the harvest they do, they reckon, all that any man can. So that if something goes wrong that is not obviously traceable to some 'natural' cause the fault is laid in a mystical context—in the rite, or in the

[1] cf. Raymond Firth, The Theory of 'Cargo' Cults: A Note on Tikopia, *Man*, 1955, LV, 142, p. 141, where this is implied.

way a man has thought or behaved in relation to others.
The bulk of the older men in Tangu sincerely believe that
gardens today are not as large, the soil not as fertile, and the
harvested crops not as plentiful as they were when they were
boys. They say that this supposed overall drop in production
is because the Christian ritual is not as effective as the pagan.
Younger men argue the point. The problem becomes, 'What
ritual *will* be effective?'

The search for adequate means and techniques goes on day
by day; but it takes place within an atmosphere determined
and unified by the notion of Cargo and its chief sensible
component, cargo. There is little separation of particular
contexts of relevance, of particular means to particular ends.
Ritual copulation is good for the crops, and it is good for
children. Why should it not also be good for cargo? Since cargo
is European, European techniques ought to suffice. So Tangu
send '*passes*'. Nothing happens. Why do European techniques
fail for Kanakas? Given that all techniques have necessary and
interdependent pragmatic and mystical constituents—what
particular balance of choice from a large number of alternatives
will suffice for gaining the end? What European techniques
are mere 'padding', and which of them contain the seed of
efficacy? Tangu cannot do otherwise than attempt to translate
the techniques of Europeans into their own idiom; and while
a European observer can see that until Tangu make the
transference into the European idiom cargo will elude them,
Tangu themselves are not placed to appreciate the point.
Their understanding of Europeans, and things European, is
limited by the way in which they understand themselves and
the world about them.

Again we are forced to return to the reality of myth and the
pragmatic nature of dreams. Cargo is the problem of the
European environment. The myth-dream distinguishes particular problems, and suggests solutions to them. The cult-
dream provides an imperative to action. And because Cargo
is the problem of the European environment, European
problems are related to the myth-dream, to cargo, and to the
cult activities—not only on the level of techniques towards

cargo but on the plane of the new man, the new individual and the new society. Thus, organizational problems are also being worked out at the ritual, or mythical level: where truth is.

In the first of the rituals described rice was specifically cited as part of the cargo. And rice is not a traditional crop. Rice is associated with Europeans, and it is the staple diet offered to Kanakas on contract labour on plantations. Today, Tangu grow rice for themselves. The seed was given them by the administration with the idea of providing a cash crop. Tangu were shown what kind of ground was suitable for the crop, how it should be planted, weeded, and harvested. Responsibility for working the rice field, it will be remembered, is placed on Luluais and Tultuls who are supposed to recruit, organize, and supervise the necessary labour. Since, however, rice cultivation is not a household responsibility, and because it plays no part in food exchanges, few have any personal attachment to, or interest in, the undertaking. Some native officials, it is true, feel that because the task is a productive activity a good rice field might add to their prestige. Nevertheless, not only are they reluctant to forgo the time from their own gardens, but they have no effective means of forcing the community to make the same sacrifice. Consequently, the work tends to be rather haphazard, and gives rise to numerous grievances.

When, eventually, the meagre crop is harvested further problems present themselves. On what basis is the crop to be distributed? Who is to carry it down to the market at Bogia? How may the profit in cash be shared out? As we have seen, the traditional methods of allocating tasks and distributing wealth depend upon kin relationships, sectionalisms, and oppositions within the community; upon households as productive units in exchange or co-operative relationships. Rice cultivation, an activity entailing the co-operation of the whole community, organized by the administration through its own nominees, does not fit into the existing distributive structure and provides Tangu themselves with a serious organizational dilemma. Other non-traditional crops, such as maize, introduced by the mission and given to household units to grow as they wished, raise no problems. They make important additions to the household diet though they are not generally used in formal exchanges. And these crops, unlike rice, though equally associated with Europeans, are never part of the cargo.

The requirement, from the administration, that in order to cultivate rice the community should be organized as a whole, devoid of sectionalisms, is clearly reflected in the arrangements for the cult rituals. Like cargo, rice pertains to the entire united community and not merely to parts of it. Yet, perhaps because it presents a single set of problems with no ready and obvious means of solution, it has been absorbed into the total meaning of Cargo. Rice contains a European joined to a problem: since other crops present no problem to Tangu the European in them is irrelevant.

When cargo means simply Europeans' goods the notion that there will be more than enough for everybody conveniently erases the distributive problem. And to ask questions about it places Tangu right in front of the whole set of problems contained in the meaning of Cargo. That is why Tangu regard such questions as silly. If all the single problems contained in the Cargo could be separated out, together with adequate solutions, the notion of Cargo would hardly arise. As it is, all the problems are indissolubly connected together in the idea of Cargo—and it follows that while the idea persists the single problems cannot be distinguished and adequately and methodically tackled as such. As experts in producing the material wealth of the community, and as leaders, Tangu managers were more concerned with the cargo than others. There were several dilemmas. If there was going to be plenty for all they would be released from the treadmill of working, plotting, and manœuvring—was this desirable? Characteristically, the problem was pushed to the background. The first thing was to get the goods. And as someone had to do the organizing to obtain them it seems to have been clear to the managers that if they were to retain their positions, and if the techniques contained in the rumours, teachings, and dreams were good, then they would have to take the lead in mastering them best. In addition, they had to place themselves in the van of public opinion. It will come as no surprise, therefore, to learn that before the cult rituals took place managers began to have dreams favouring some kind of mystical activity. Nor, since managers can only exert influence within terms of the community sectionalisms, is it more than remarkable that though they could excite desires and emotions they could not push them to the point of action until the dream from outside nullified sectional rivalries, left no single manager with the credit or blame, and relieved the community of having to bestow either on one single Tangu.

Tangu destroyed nothing, made no sacrifices before engaging their Cargo activities. They added to their full store of knowledge and resources a complex of new techniques which were well worth a try in relation to the ends they were said to be going to achieve. They had also managed to articulate to themselves—through the rites—what is suggested in the myth-dream. The failure of the rituals to achieve their ends brought no retributive measures on the managers by the community. For Tangu what had been proved wrong were the particular techniques used; and since these had received public approval all were equally to blame for selecting what turned out to be ineffective. Had the community turned on its managers it would have been an admission of being led, and, therefore, both a betrayal of equivalence in general and of each individual's moral responsibility and equivalence with others. Commenting on the youth from Pariakenam, as we have noted, participants in the activities were contemptuous. '*Bengemamakake!*' they said. 'He was deceiving us.' Regarding the administrative action they were only a little more thoughtful, and it seemed at the time that the experience had taught Tangu only to be circumspect, more secretive in their activities. It had not taught them that Cargo cults were futile.

The older managers who had had a hand in the rituals were more than disappointed at the failure. Just as they are coming near to the retired list and are finding it difficult to resolve the problem of productive work and social contacts in the face of younger and more energetic rivals, so are the problems of Cargo rather beyond them. For them the most advantageous solution is a mystical one. If they can find it they will be able to create wealth without the purely physical strength required of them. These are the men, too, who know least about Europeans, who have suffered the full shock of fifty years of continuous change, and who are least able to appreciate the significances of the different kinds of techniques required to produce a variety of goods. Therefore, in conversation with them, one is returned continually to the question of what kinds of rite would be effective. Having spent their lives in the grip of a double series of events—one of which they could handle and forecast, and the other an unpredictable quantity—only a successful ritual stands between these old men and a miserable retirement.

Meanwhile, for the young men, other kinds of solution are beginning to emerge. They are still caught on the horns of the pragmatic and mystical but a variety of further experiences are beginning to flow into, and qualify, the notion of Cargo. As symbols with meaning Mambu and Yali still walk in their thoughts. But there is also the analogy of the hard work, foresight, cunning, and sober manipulation of persons contained in the managerial ideal. The young men of Tangu see and talk to Manam islanders quite often—either on the coast or when they come to Tangu on trading journeys. They have come to know about Irakau, how he has succeeded in becoming quite wealthy by competing with Europeans on their own terms by planting coconuts and selling copra, and how he has worked within the implications of the triangle—manipulating administrative officers and missionaries—to gain his own ends.

Finally, largely as a result of mission educations, the young men are beginning to make the necessary transference out of their own understanding into the technical idiom of Europeans. If the right means can be found they will have access to manufactured goods and they will gain access to cargo.

THE MANAM ACTIVITIES CONSIDERED[1]

The scene in Manam is set by the triangular relationship between Kanakas, administrative officers and missionaries. The atmosphere is a mixture of fear, fantasy, and a child's Christmas Eve. Irakau, our fourth charismatic figure, is the central character, though he himself never comes on stage. Manam islanders themselves are gripped by the notion of Cargo. They are concerned for themselves and their children, not with loyalty to a particular administration or mission. The Europeans, on the other hand, are vitally concerned with Manam islanders. They want them to be just 'so'! Inevitably, all are drawn into the vortex of problems that make up the Cargo. The questions being asked by Manam islanders are, What is truth? What things are true? What does the new man look like? Administrative officers and missionaries are saying, each in their own fashion, 'Listen. Do as I say. I will tell you exactly.'

Manam islanders, who are in any case dubious, can only reply by looking yet deeper into what most concerns them— Cargo.

Since before the first World War the S.V.D. mission in Manam, sited near Baliau village, had forged ahead steadily with its work. By 1940 very few Manam islanders had not been baptized. The resident priest knew the Manam language, the customs of the people, and he had had upwards of twenty years' experience on the island. After the second World War, however, and coinciding with Yali's rise to fame, things became very difficult in Manam. Attendance at the mission church and schools dropped steeply, and the resident missionary sisters had to be withdrawn after being stoned by rebellious parishioners.

During 1952 the (new) resident priest, much younger than his predecessor, was subjected to a series of insults and attacks. Islanders would gather round his house, stare unblinkingly at his every movement, and jeer. During the day at

---

[1] *Supra*, pp. 3–13.

irregular intervals, and sometimes during the night as well, youths would lob stones on to the corrugated iron roof of his house. When he journeyed through the village the priest was met with cold stares, insolence, and laughter. Nobody would carry his baggage for him. Mission stores were pilfered. And to cap the sum of his troubles the Seventh Day Adventist mission had seen fit to introduce a Kanaka teacher into a village not far from the S.V.D. station itself. Nevertheless, with great moral and physical courage the priest had per-severed. His task as a missionary was to bring a knowledge of God to those who did not know Him, to make Christians of pagans, and, having baptized them, to educate them in Christianity. And this he was willing to attempt whether the opposition was militant, passive, or as refinedly tormenting as it was.

These things I came to know only after my arrival in Manam. It is doubtful whether any administrative officer was fully aware of the missionary's plight or his problems at the time. He was unable to say much. If he was to ask for admin-istrative help he would be severing the last remaining thread holding Manam islanders to the mission. For the islanders knew that they could rely on the mission to help them against the administration if the latter were threatening. And this confidence the missionary was unwilling to sacrifice. Provid-ing there remained some basis for mutual trust and co-opera-tion there was always hope for the future.

On the coast, before going to Manam, traders and planters were describing Manam islanders as 'big-headed', 'insolent', and addicted to thieving. Skippers of small ships were reluctant to visit Manam if it could be helped, for even though Manam islanders are good sailors and keen traders they were said to cause trouble as crew and had earned a reputation for fast practice. Administrative officers were well aware of a generally unsatisfactory situation, but rather than do anything positive—which might aggravate things—pre-ferred to wait and allow it to 'sort itself out'. They were interested in, and pleased with, Irakau. The solution, they thought, lay with him.

Irakau had achieved some success and notoriety as a Kanaka businessman. He had established a coconut plantation near his village, Baliau, and he had organized most of his co-villagers into working teams based on the European model so far as the ends of their labour were concerned. His overhead expenses were far less than those of a European planter and he was putting his copra on the open market at very competitive prices. European planters and traders, appreciating Irakau's command over cheap labour through kinship bonds and traditional values, forced to work hard for their own profits, and seeing in Irakau and his organization a threat to the conventions within which they themselves competed, respected the man's initiative and drive without being favourably inclined towards him. Moreover, Irakau was not being forced to comply with the many labour laws and scales of rations they themselves were finding such a burden. They were content, therefore, that Irakau was finding it a problem to market his produce because ships were reluctant to call at Manam.

Generally, in their own eyes if not in the view of Kanakas, administrative officers had put themselves in a position of support for Irakau. They felt that he was honest, hardworking, competent, and, on the whole, an asset to his community. He might succeed where Yali had failed. He was a starting point. Believing, too, that Manam society was divided into two rigid castes, *Tanepoa* and commoners, administrative officers were pleased that Irakau, reputedly not a *Tanepoa*, had achieved fame and made his mark through his own commercial ability. Democracy and Progress, it was thought, were on the march. The mission, on the other hand, in rather closer contact, considered that if Irakau did not actively participate himself in certain mystical and anti-Christian activities and rites, he certainly did not discourage them and was probably the genius behind them. Finally, though all would agree that the island was 'unsettled' missionaries, being closely involved, may have tended to overrate the total situation, and administrative officers, not suffering stones on their roofs, may have underrated it.

On arrival in Manam I found that within terms of their role and situation missionaries had good reasons for their suspicions. Because no other vessels would call at Manam, Irakau had had to rely entirely on mission ships to take his copra to Madang for marketing. Because no other European body or individual would lend Irakau the necessary capital for his ventures he had had recourse to the mission—which had not failed him. The mission claimed, however, that Irakau was long overdue in repayments; and while not wholly absolving Irakau himself the mission were inclined to attribute most of the blame to his secretaries who, the mission maintained, were bleeding him and falsifying the books. Again, employees of Irakau had been discovered marking unlabelled bags of mission copra with Irakau's cypher.

Other things apart, therefore, on a crude economic level the mission saw its enlightened support of Kanaka enterprise being repaid by cheating and thievery.

Religious life on the island was decaying. Though nearly the whole population had been baptized and instructed, not a single married woman was a regular church-goer, and indeed, very few married women came to Mass at all. Among the unmarried maidens there was a respectable number of regular communicants. The men on the island were almost wholly recalcitrant. Of three hundred Catholic male adults in Baliau and environs some thirty were considered worth reminding of their Easter duties, nine came to confession on the Saturday, one came to Mass on the Sunday and he did not communicate.

The only way the mission can deal with religious laxity is to exhort, to admonish, or finally, to excommunicate. And though overhasty recourse to excommunication might have raised the percentage of church attendances it might also have done more to undo the work of the last thirty years than any other single action. For, excommunication translates into the Pidgin idiom as '*Pater rousim mipela*, the missionary has thrown us out'. And it is the usage and associations of the word *rous*[1] which make excommunication not simply a religious, internal mission, matter, but an avenue to Cargo

[1] From the German *heraus*.

Planting yams: preparing the earth

Tangu maid—going to draw water

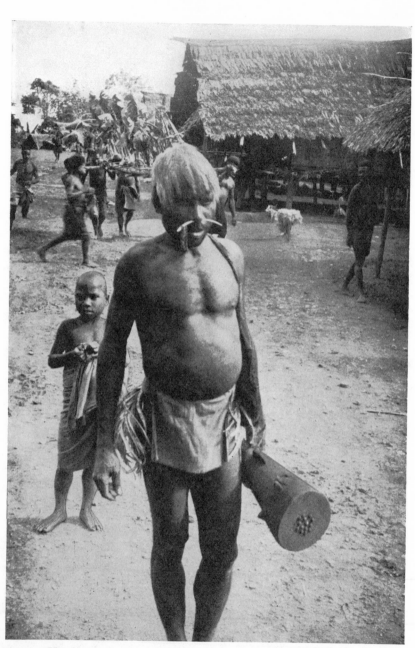

Kwaling going to a dance (head-dress of cassowary plumes)

and anti-European attitudes. Commonly used by Europeans as a peremptory order—especially when Kanakas gather round to watch the white man at work, play, eating, or drinking—*rous* ordinarily carries overtones of anger and latent if not overt hostility. When used of things the word means 'put out', 'take away', 'get rid of', 'eliminate'; when used of persons it means 'go away', 'get out'. In both contexts it carries the implication, 'You (it) are (is) not wanted any more'. That is, whatever Europeans may say they intend by the word, Kanakas take the common implication as said. Accordingly, they feel a deep resentment. One's sympathy goes out to both parties in equal measure. Europeans value their privacy: Kanakas think it indecent and immoral—for in their mode of thought only sorcerers and evil men do not want company.

It may be taken that satisfactory human relationships demand some kind of predictability in regard to mutual obligations as well as subservience to a common moral norm. For Kanakas *rous* flouts both these requirements. Perhaps it is just because no other word is available that Kanakas have seized on *rous*, insisted on its implications, and used it as a lever or symbol to express their opposition to Europeans. Nor may the implications of *rous* be avoided by saying it nicely, with sympathy. Kanakas would only think the European was afraid, trying to curry favour in a particularly despicable way.

In Manam several islanders had been excommunicated. Having established a community acknowledging God by free consent the only last sanction is withdrawal of community privileges. And yet, perhaps excommunication was the result of a series of mistaken inferences. Missionaries, for example, necessarily earthbound, are generally inclined to lay the blame for laxity in religious matters more on positive attitudes on the parts of Kanakas and less to interaction with themselves as Europeans and individuals. Thus, for the mission in Manam it was Irakau's influence, Yali's influence, the Anti-Christ, and the machinations of Seventh Day Adventists which were held responsible for the current slump. Yet, conversations with excommunicates in Manam revealed no enthusiasm for the rival sect, Seventh Day Adventist, even though the latter was represented in Manam by a Kanaka teacher. And despite the fact that Adventist teaching is not uncomplimentary to Cargo expectations—in particular, at the time, in regard to the second coming of Yali—the regimen is usually far too strict for Kanakas. Tobacco, betel nut, feasting, dancing, pork—all must be eschewed. Life becomes, quite literally, one long wait with nothing to do in the meanwhile except talk quietly, meditate, and eat vegetables. In Manam most of the Adventist converts were such simply out of spite. They knew full well how much it irritated the resident Catholic priest. They felt he would rather they were honest pagans than Adventists. And they wanted to turn the knife in the wound. They were bitter about being excommunicate.

And yet, as the *Prologue* makes clear,[1] there was no fundamental opposition to Christianity in Manam, no denial of God—or even in intention of Catholicism. They said their prayers as they had been taught but they wanted to say them together as black men, by themselves, separately from the body politic represented by Europeans. An old problem in the Christian experience.

Irakau himself was a fairly regular church-goer. But missionaries believed this to be a 'front' because his co-villagers were the most lax. Missionaries were also convinced that Irakau made mystical bamboo flutes secretly in the bush for some un-Christian, esoteric purpose; that when villagers of Baliau made the Sign of the Cross they added to the names of the Trinity '*Irakau na Yali Amen*'; that when youths of Baliau stoned the nuns of the mission Irakau might have, but did not, check them. It may seem uncharitable of the mission to doubt Irakau's sincerity, but one does not have to be a cynic to recall that he depended on the mission for more than religious comfort. Indeed, it was just this kind of 'hypocrisy' that was keeping the mission in Manam linked to Kanakas and preventing either from rushing headlong to points of no contact whatever.

There was also, of course, the administration. For though

---

[1] *Supra* p. 7.

Manam islanders appeared as generally hostile to the mission they rely on mission vessels for bulk trading, and they also use it as a shield against possible administrative action. Whilst I was there an islander returned from the mainland with the story that an administrative officer had gone to Karkar island and extracted twenty-five shillings from each adult male, twenty shillings from each married female, ten shillings each from youths and maidens, and five shillings from widows or others. As soon as the story was bruited in Manam frightened islanders came to the mission laden with pigs and other goods. They wanted the missionary to take their livestock and goods into safe-keeping so that the administration would not be able to sequestrate them, and they asked the missionary for loans of money with which to pay what they interpreted as a tax. To the missionary the event was a godsend. He knew nothing about a proposed tax impost, nor had he any money to lend. But he did promise to see fair play and press the islanders' cause.

Just such renewals of relationships do much to clear the way for the ultimate success of the mission effort.

In fact, as it turned out, the activities in Karkar had been wrongly reported and interpreted. An administrative officer had started, with the full support and consent of the people of Karkar, to organize a co-operative scheme for marketing various kinds of native produce. He was raising the necessary capital.

It is significant that an administrative activity which was directed to the welfare of Kanakas, and which might have been correctly reported, should have been interpreted as one with inimical intentions; that in a situation involving the administration the mission at once became an ally; and that the mission cannot but take advantage of such a situation to further its own ends. When I, a visitor, asked an islander what he thought I had come to Manam to do, he replied at once and frankly that he thought I was an administrative officer 'come to do them no good'.

Readiness to find fault with the administration is not only implied within the triangular relationship between Kanakas, mission, and administration: it derives from the fact that the administration is the most powerful of the three elements, from confusion, and from the idea of the Cargo. Some Kuku-rais (equivalent to Luluai in Manam) told me they had been exhorted by some administrative officers not to be brow-beaten by Irakau but to set up businesses in competition. They explained to me that they were puzzled at this advice. First, if they were to compete against Irakau, who was going to provide the necessary starting capital? Second, they did not feel they were being browbeaten, they did not want to oppose Irakau, and they did not see why they should oppose him. Besides, they added, other officers had proffered what they had understood as contrary advice. If they had done the one, they felt, they would get into trouble for not doing the other.

Again, it has been mentioned that the administration had it that Irakau was not a *Tanepoa*, that business ability had over-come caste restrictions, and that progressive Democracy had commenced to evolve in Manam. Yet, the islanders them-selves regarded Irakau as a *Tanepoa*. It is true that Irakau was never a Luluai or Kukurai, but he lived in a *Tanepoa* house, carried out the traditional role of a *Tanepoa*, and wore the emblems of a *Tanepoa* in Manam. In fact, he is the son of a younger brother of a Kukurai. Irakau's father inherited the office from an elder brother because the latter had no other heirs; and the next in line was Irakau's elder brother who took the office whilst Irakau was away on contract labour. Irakau is a *Tanepoa* because he was begotten by a *Tanepoa*: he is a boss, a traditional organizer. Further, even without the genealogy Irakau would be regarded as a *Tanepoa* because he is a boss and an organizer—just as Jesus Christ, the Queen of England, and all Europeans in a role of authority in Manam are regarded, honorifically, as *Tanepoa*.

Take another confusion. One of Yali's recommendations was that houses should be decorated with flowers. So, when there are flowers in Kanaka houses Europeans feel that a Cargo cult is about to commence, that flowers in houses sym-bolize Yaliism and anti-European feeling. A natural suspicion in the circumstances. When, however, administrative or mission officers seek out such flowers and destroy them—as happened in Manam shortly before I arrived—and even resort to opening cupboards, looking under floorboards, and in the roof thatch to find them—then it is difficult not to see the point of view of Kanakas who, in their own mystical idiom—and given that Europeans have some secret which they are withholding from Kanakas—become even more convinced that there must be 'something in it'. Otherwise why should Europeans go to such lengths to destroy them?

Finally, there is the notion of Cargo. As far as Manam islanders were concerned Irakau had become *the* boss and organizer. He was playing the European game and doing well at it. Like Yali, he had proved himself a man in European eyes. He was the hope against unilateral domination by Europeans. Also, irrespective of what Europeans were doing and saying he was steering Manam into prosperity. Manam islanders are loyal to themselves. They were loyal, too, in 1952, to Irakau, who represents them to the outside world—which is represented to them mainly, and almost exclusively, by the mission and administration. When either the mission or the administration fight Irakau they justify the notion of Cargo. If for some reason Irakau should fail in his endeavours he will have failed because of Europeans—thus vindicating to Manam islanders one aspect of Cargo. If he goes on succeeding through opposition from some Europeans it will be considered a continuing warrant for all that is contained in the Cargo.

If all Europeans were categorized as a single entity—instead of being divided into different kinds with different roles —the resulting one-to-one relationship might easily lead into a series of impasses from which neither party might be able to extricate itself with honour. As it is the 'hypocrises' and 'treacheries' implied by the triangle not only prevent the notion of Cargo gaining too absolute a value, but they provide the opportunity for finding the moral European. And this, as the myth-dream stresses, is an idea which Kanakas must find embodied in a person. An administrative gaffe throws Kanakas

237

into the hands of the mission; a mistake on the part of a missionary brings the willing help of an administrative officer; and administrative officer and missionary may, through discussion, find common ground in their problems with Kanakas.

If the roles put upon administrative officers and missionaries in their relations with Kanakas tend to produce those tensions which nourish the notion of Cargo, it is also true that intellectual comprehension of the fact and (therefore) qualified and frequent renewals of relationships can be capable, slowly, of laying the basis for mutual respect and moral equality.

It has been repeatedly stressed, though perhaps never often enough, that the problem of the triangle is a structural one and does not necessarily imply criticism or otherwise of the individuals actually involved. In just this sense, if the experience in Manam narrated in the *Prologue* is to be explained, it should be pointed out that it quickly became apparent to Manam islanders that as a European—bent not on exhorting, converting, counting heads, adjudicating, trading, or punishing, but on simple conversation—something removed from the normal was expected of me, a visitor outside the conflicts of the triangle. Years before, long before they had started to become thoroughly involved in Cargo, Manam islanders had experienced a social anthropologist. They said of the late Honourable Camilla Wedgwood, that 'she knew how to plant taro. She dug the hole. She cooked the taro just as we do. If a man died she sat in the middle with all the other women and grieved for him. She was not like (other) white people. She was just like us black-skinned folk.'

Before I went to Manam I had been a happy guest at sub-District headquarters at Bogia. On arrival in Manam I made straight for the mission. I had, thus, thoroughly associated myself with missionaries and administrative officers. Accordingly, Manam islanders thought, as they admitted quite frankly, and as we have noted,[1] that I was an administrative officer 'come to do them no good'. This surely accounts for the first reception at Baliau, and, indeed, at other places too. On the other hand, so soon as the villagers realized that I was

[1] *Supra* p. 235.

neither missionary nor administrative officer their responses were quite different. Nor, since they had no knowledge at the time of a connexion between myself and Miss Wedgwood, was their second response an echo of former times. Only the old remembered Miss Wedgwood. Also, I lived in the mission, not in the villages. Yet, I was made welcome. My presence occasioned releases of pent-up feelings. I was asked for a message. I felt, in some small way, the pressures that Yali and Mambu must have felt.

First, I was a stranger. I was not somebody they knew anything about. I was not a missionary, nor an administrative officer, nor a trader, nor a planter. I was the kind of relatively uninvolved European they might have met during the war, and whose behaviour and disinterested generosity they appreciated. Second, since no social anthropologist can properly undertake a piece of research without at least pretending to an assumption of moral equality, a moral relationship with the people he lives among is implied in his work, even if it is lacking in his own personal make-up. When Baron Miklucho-Maclay landed on the shores of Astrolabe Bay in 1871 he was unarmed. The Kanakas, who had never before seen a white man, fled from him. Unimpressed, Miklucho-Maclay walked on until he found a man cowering under a bush. He shook hands with him, and made him a friend. He stayed fifteen months. And despite a variety of troubles he endeared himself to the native of the region.[1] Nevertheless, whatever his personal qualities—and they were fine ones—it must be faced, more grossly, that Miklucho-Maclay was a visitor just as all modern social anthropologists are. And for a visitor without a permanent financial or political stake in the country or its people there is

[1] It cannot be emphasized too much that handshaking is a European and not a Kanaka custom. At the same time it is evidently what is *in* the handshake, its meaning, that counts. The natives Miklucho-Maclay met had never seen a white man—so far as is known. Yet the man he shook hands with seems to have understood the meaning of the handshake almost at once. *Vide:* Frank S. Greenop, *Who Travels Alone*, Sydney 1944, esp. pp. 48–50, 55–60.

Other random accounts of this amazing man may be found in— Alfred Russell Wallace, *My Life*, Volume II, Chapman and Hall, London 1905, pp. 34–6. John C. Galton, *Nature*, Vol. IX, 1874, p. 328.

everything to gain and little to lose by making, or pretending to make, an assumption of moral equality. It is his role.

As we have seen, a role which implies an assumption of moral equality, the moral European, is welcome. He is part of the Cargo: partly an end, and partly a means to the ultimate end.

Once the role of moral European had been established it is intelligible also that Manam islanders should have attempted to take the matter further and cast the visitor in the role of charismatic figure. Cargo is, as has been suggested, a series of urgent dilemmas. Events are experienced and interpreted in the light of the Cargo myth-dream. More especially is this so when the participants concerned are on the upsurge of a wave of emotional fervour. Any passing problem, such as how to deal with a tourist, is apt to be absorbed into the notion of Cargo. More important, perhaps, is the fact that the notion of Cargo contains only a limited number of roles. Since I, the visitor, was not an administrative officer, nor a missionary, nor any other kind of European they had actually met or become familiar with, and since a moral relationship had been established at Baliau, I was qualified to be moral European. Since, too, it could be taken for granted that as a European I was a man in the view of other Europeans, this combined with the moral relationship squared with the image of the new man in the myth-dream. There was, therefore, at least an outside chance that I might be the expected charismatic figure. It was worth trying. In any case, as moral European and qualified to help, some kind of directive or message would be expected of me.

It is possible that the Manam islander who drew the diagram in the sand was testing me in much the same way as Tangu had 'tried' Mambu. In adopting the term 'brother' as his term of address he had accepted the moral relationship and had cast me as moral European. It is probable that had I said something positive about the Unknownland located on the far left of the diagram (Figure 1), I would have passed his test for charismatic figure. However, in the event, it was clear to him that if I knew more about the Unknownland than he did I could not, or would not, articulate it and therefore had no more right to be charismatic figure than he had.

If we examine his diagram, regarding it not as geographer's map or a sailor's chart, but as a representation of Cargo, a 'Cargogram', some significances emerge. The concentric circles may be taken to represent the archetypal Uroboros,[1] the generative principle. The artist himself made this point explicit when he referred to its centre as the place where *bigpela bolong ol gat ap*, where the Creator generated Himself. The triangle to the left, the Unknownland, may be a heaven or paradise. It may contain the essence of Cargo, the new environment with new men living there, where cargo comes from. It might have been identified as Se-wen-de, mentioned by the author of the fourth version of the Primal Myth. But since he would not come out with it, and I dared not put the leading question, the matter remains open. White men, men who make cargo—which includes the Japanese—are placed in the left-hand sector, nearest the Unknownland. Those unable to make cargo, black men, are in the right-hand sector. That is, as in the Primal Myth, the world is divided between those who have access to cargo, and those who do not.

Manam island is located on the right, furthest away from the Unknownland: substantially, there is no access to cargo in Manam. But Rabaul, Moresby, Aitape, and Manus are placed on the borders between those who have access to cargo and those who, generally, do not. Rabaul, Moresby, and Aitape are major administrative bases where large consignments of cargo arrive regularly. Manus is not only an administrative base where cargo arrives, but during the war it formed part of the very large United States naval base situated in the Admiralty islands. There were workshops and a factory for making aerated waters. In these places access to cargo is comparatively simple. In Manam it is not.

To get to the Unknownland the White sea and the Blue sea have to be crossed. Perhaps the White sea stands for white men, and more particularly for moral European. Certainly it is

---

[1] *Vide:* Erich Neumann (trans. by R. F. C. Hull), *The Origins and History of Consciousness*, Routledge and Kegan Paul, London 1954.

feasible because for Manam islanders access to cargo lies through the White sea, through the moral European. The Blue sea is more difficult. As a colour it is comparatively rare in New Guinea. Policemen have blue uniforms, native officials are given blue caps to wear. And blue is also seen in Catholic mission chapels where it is chiefly associated with the moral purity of the Virgin Mary. Green is the dominant colour in New Guinea, and since Englishmen, Germans, Japanese, and Americans have all been involved in New Guinea affairs during the maturation of the Cargo myth-dream, it is fitting that they as well as Kanakas should be immersed in a Green sea.

South America? Perhaps an American negro soldier from the 'Deep South', or an official from the United Nations.

The point being made is not that the diagram in the sand necessarily means these things, but that a graphic representation which might evoke titters of amused interest becomes intelligent and intelligible when the mind that is viewing it is familiar with the Cargo myth-dream. The diagram expresses ideas about Cargo which, because they are in the myth-dream, may be grasped without too great an imaginative effort.[1]

ANTI-EUROPEANISM

When the environment is determined by their traditional values Tangu and Manam islanders succeed in being true to themselves. They can become men. In the Europeanized sectors of their lives, however, they appear to themselves as less than men; and the myth-dream reveals the new man fitted to play the part of a man in the new environment. At the same time Europeans, themselves imprisoned in the same situation, though men in their own native environments, tend to become more than themselves in New Guinea. Without participating in the myth-dream they are part of the atmosphere of Cargo. To them expressions of the myth-dream are inimical and hostile. Without fully comprehending the nature and content of the myth-dream, they feel it is there.

[1] Parts of the exposition above appeared in Racial Tension in Manam, *loc. cit.*

They call it 'Yaliism'. And they fear it. Exerting infinitely more power and influence over others than they would in their own homes, realization of the myth-dream would pull them into moral equality with Kanakas—a perfectly wholesome relationship which is, however, twisted into political and economic antipathies. They do not know about the new man or the moral European: their vision is blocked by the political agitations of Yali and his like. An unusual incident in a village is regarded with suspicion: it may be the first sign of a Cargo cult. So the techniques of suppression are mobilized in the mind if not on the ground. A missionary sees signs in the sky; a planter believes himself to be watched by a Russian submarine; an administrative officer searches for flowers. A Kanaka who stands up for himself tends to be regarded in emotional terms as a 'trouble-maker', or as 'disloyal'—'Who does he think he is—Yali?'

He would like to be.

And yet the problem of anti-Europeanism in Cargo is quite evidently limited to the way in which particular roles are engaged—mainly those of administrative officer and missionary. The notion of Cargo does not hinge on anti-European feeling: it turns on the fact that Kanakas do not see in the roles of administrative officer and missionary as they have experienced them a necessary assumption of moral equality. By and large the roles of other Europeans do not create insoluble problems: they neither persist nor impinge often enough. One cannot but feel that Europeans who see in Cargo cult little more than reaction to white domination are taking themselves more seriously than do Kanakas. For Kanakas the problem is more urgent and more personal than whether they shall be ruled by white men. They want to know where they stand in the world as men. And they know they can only do this with the help of Europeans—moral Europeans.

In Manam, as elsewhere in New Guinea, no common view of the historical process emerges. Some see the past as golden, the present as insufferable, and the future possibly pregnant with hope. Others find a refuge in resignation, or cynicism. Yet, when explicitly faced with their problem Manam islanders

243

grope towards a common view of history both on an actual and on a mythical level. Like Tangu and others in the Bogia region they are distressed because they cannot find the uniformities which will yield a generally satisfactory explanation linking present with past and providing a departure for the future. Some attempt to solve the problem by enlarging the scope of traditional myths; others recruit to their aid Bible stories which, through sin, explain what interests Manam islanders most: privilege, caste, and status differences.

Being a ranking society themselves Manam people understand privilege; what they do not understand is the complete lack of *rapport* between themselves and the administration and the mission. Most, like Tangu, adhere to the belief that a wrongdoing on the part of an ancestor robbed them of the good things in life and the ability to understand why and how white men do the things they do. If the wrongdoing could be identified atonement might be possible. And with atonement would come the good things in life. One man in Manam claimed to have surely identified the wrongdoing. It arose, he said, from the fact that two mythical heroes, brothers, had been quarrelling over a woman. Now, he added, the brothers were beginning to make it up to each other. The quarrel was ending. The evidence that the quarrel was ending, he said, lay in the fact that Manam islanders, under Irakau, were selling their own copra on the open market. Since it was because of the quarrel, he said, that black men had what they had, it must surely be because the two brothers were coming to terms that they in Manam were marketing their produce and so gaining access to cargo. We are back to the Primal Myth.

Finally, there are others in Manam who find a way out through the idea that there is something basically different between white men and black men: '*Natink mipela bilak sikin igat narapela arse bolongen,* I think we black-skinned folk have a different origin [are a different species from] white people.' The Primal Myth again.

Manam islanders understand privilege, but they demand that a certain sort of dignity and responsibility should go with it. They are a proud people. The physical world about them, as for Tangu, is but a reflection of truths contained in myths. Unable to extricate themselves from their roles in relation to the administration and mission they are, none the less, trying to pull the sensible world into conformity with myth by down-to-earth political and economic activities. They are proud of Irakau. He is justifying their own notion of the best kind of manhood in competition with Europeans. Competing against him is almost unthinkable. By his actions he is filling in the past, creating truths; and he is bringing the past into line with the present and foreshadowing the future. His current economic success—sensible, concrete, measurable in sacks of copra and coin, and evident in his home, furnished and equipped in European style—is the partial fulfilment of the myth-dream. Administrative officers and missionaries are being forced into the co-operative role.

In Irakau Manam islanders can see their problems slipping into place and perspective. The two brothers who have been quarrelling over a woman are on the verge of making friends.

The Cargo myth-dream is not necessarily anti-anybody. It contains a positive set of principles and ends whose fulfilment requires the help of Europeans, moral Europeans. But at the point of charismatic articulation, when the myth-dream is being reduced to a political movement, those Europeans occupying roles considered by Kanakas to imply an amoral relationship with them come under attack. The European, and chiefly administrative problem, is to work out how to enter the co-operative role and so short-circuit the need for charismatic articulation. That is, if administrative officers could keep abreast of the myth-dream, themselves reducing the moral principles contained therein into political activities, it would be reasonable to expect Cargo cults to die out.

The myth-dream which spans generations—not the momentary crises, physical expressions in a local cultural idiom, the symptoms—is the significant phenomenon.

CHAPTER VIII

Cargo

To answer the question 'Why do Cargo cults occur?' would entail raising profound metaphysical issues beyond the scope of this book. Hysteria, dream visions, tensions, release of tensions, rites, ceremonies, time, and place are all too easily explained away. They pose the sort of problems one can pretend to be wrestling with by circling warily round them. Nevertheless, certain features seem plain enough. It is clear that if cargo means manufactured goods, Cargo embraces a set of acute moral problems; that Cargo movements are not due simply to a misunderstanding concerning the origin of manufactured goods, but that they are embedded in, and arise from, a complex total situation; that free access to cargo is but one—if the most spectacular—of many problems contained within the notion of Cargo; that even if one regarded Cargo cults as proceeding from a mistaken view of the process of manufacture it would be necessary to explain why the mistake was made—and then persisted in.

The chief element in the Cargo seems definitely to be the myth-dream. Whatever the previous nature of the myth-dream—and there is little doubt that a myth-dream always exists—it would seem to become a Cargo myth-dream upon the first acquaintance or apprehension of white men or their goods. At this point guilt becomes explicit. Guilt explains the differences between white men and black; it accounts for diversity of attributes, and it accounts for the patent disparities in command over material resources. An irreversible act which is a wrongdoing, a disobedience, is considered to be the root cause of inequalities in endowments and resources. Thereafter the Cargo myth-dream grows and develops within a field set by the conflicts of interests within the relationship between Kanakas and white men; in particular within the triangular set of relationships implied by the roles and interests of administrative officers, missionaries, and Kanakas. And what is significant to the growth of the myth-dream, what the myth-dream feeds upon, are the moral conflicts engendered by the triangle. So long as planters and traders remain such neither Tangu nor Manam islanders mind very much. The problems are small and can be resolved. Kanakas understand a commercial or economic relationship; they know there may be sharp practice—they are not as innocent babes; they realize a seller will try to obtain a high price for his goods, and they know how to bargain, how to bring the price down. Finally, within the purely economic context they are well placed to learn from experience. But when traders and planters don the mantle of missionary, or of administrative officer, by assuming moral superiority, they enter the triangle and become as though missionaries or administrative officers. They deny themselves in the commerical or economic relationship and are assumed to be seeking an added, unfair, advantage by relying on their status as white men instead of on their abilities as traders.

Neither missionary nor administrative officer, on the other hand, demands a *quid pro quo* in the economic field. On the contrary, each—personally as well as in a representative capacity—provides Kanakas with cash itself, the opportunity to earn cash, and with material goods. Neither asks for a like return, but each does demand of Kanakas a moral surrender, acquiescence to a highly variegated but unsystematized set of political and religious forms and beliefs. In effect this is playing Mephistopheles—attempting to buy a man's soul. In addition, both missionaries and administrative officers compete for this moral surrender in terms of trust, loyalty, confidence, and obedience. As happened in Manam, however, when a missionary enters the trading or commercial role he is acceptable—as such. As a missionary engaged in overstated positive evangelism he is not.

The most significant theme in the Cargo seems to be moral regeneration: the creation of a new man, the creation of new unities, the creation of a new society. On the whole the accent is equally weighted: the integrity of the new individual is balanced against the form of the new society. And both new man and new society are to be a true amalgam or synthesis, not a mixture of European and Kanaka forms and ideals. The principal route or medium through which these ends are to be attained is the moral European who is acceptable, not simply because he is what the myth-dream would mean by a moral being, but because his role is the fulfilment of the myth-dream; because he will demand of Kanakas what they are prepared to give; because, being moral European, Kanakas will give him what he demands. The alternative to that transcendence of the European and Kanaka environments which envisages a synthesis of both is to attempt to ignore Europeans altogether and revivify only what is thought to be traditional—an alternative clearly expressed in the Primal Myth, attempted on one level by the youth from Pariakenam and more emphatically illustrated in, for example, the Mansren cult of Biak.[1] Nevertheless, the problem is one; the means to its solution varied—though rarely in Melanesia can it be quietist. Whether the moral worlds to be synthesized are as different as the European and Kanaka, or as seemingly close as those relevant to an older and younger generation within the same culture, what is sought are moral unities valid for both. To an older generation 'Beatniks', 'Skiffle groups', and the like are perhaps more puzzling than Cargo cults are to administrative officers and missionaries. Yet in either case 'moral European' is simply a name for the channel through whom—or which—differing sets of moral values may be apprehended as one.

Access to cargo seems to be the primary symbol predicating the ends contained in the Cargo. The means to these ends, the ways in which the ends may actually be realized on the ground, are articulated by the charismatic figure who ought to reflect the new man and at the same time appear as the epitome of conflicts and desires becoming resolved, or even already resolved.

[1] *Vide:* J. V. de Bruijn, loc. cit.

Charismatic articulation attempts to translate the myth-dream into principles or objectives which are capable, not merely of being apprehended, but comprehended by the community. Then the community can act on them. And it is at this point, when the myth-dream is being externalized—pulled out of the being of each individual and out of the community in which each individual participates—that trances, hysteria, fits, and the like occur.

It may be that these psycho-physiological phenomena are simply cathartic—though how far that word is not simply an escape-route in shorthand is difficult to say. What seems to be happening, however, if only for a few minutes, is that men are becoming new men. The Tangu rites could hardly show this to be so more conclusively. What is happening is that men, hitherto bound by themselves, their own lives' experience, their needs, habits, customs, and conventions, are being loosed into the world of their dreams. They are making a passage from the conflicts of two worlds into the bliss of one other. They are doing it rapidly, together. They are translating life into being, division into unity, a mystical experience comparable, at the opposite pole, with the slip into death. Here time and space have no meaning. Awareness of the self, the individual, encompasses awareness of others. Through a shared psychological experience the psyche of each individual comes to know itself socially. Established after years of being nurtured, restrained, and buffeted by the pressures of family and community life psyche and social personalities loose themselves from relationship and fuse into one. They come into contact with truth.

TRUTH, MYTHS, AND DREAMS

Every activity has its particular criteria of validity, a locus in truth. And in relation to a Cargo movement the myth-dream seems to be just such a locus. The rites and activities are true or not true, valid or not valid, effective or not effective, in relation to the myth-dream. In a context of Cargo the myth-dream is truth, and moreover, the several truths contained in

249

the myth-dream emerge as imperatives. Ideally, the task of the charismatic figure can be seen as an attempt to realize these imperatives in action. And only rarely does he completely succeed in doing so.

Myths in general have the attributes of objective truth largely because, perhaps, they are stories having a weight of common consent. This does not mean that storytellers cannot make their own additions to a particular myth; but it does mean that the additions they make have to obtain popular consent if they are to remain parts of the myth. Myths are stories stamped large with social approval.

Once a statement or proposition is given consent it becomes true, a part of truth, assuming an existence which is not necessarily contingent on explicit withdrawal of consent. For, having achieved objectivity or truth in a myth a statement may persist in the myth long after those who retail or who listen to the story say they discount its validity for the present. Then the statement becomes a historical truth. And, so it would seem, the longer a statement is contained in a myth as truth the longer it will persist. New truths, or rather, statements which are becoming truths, and which are expressed in the additions of individual storytellers, are extremely vulnerable to, and dependent upon, consent. But once the first tentative consent begins to harden into solid approval the lodgement becomes more and more secure, more and more independent of explicit consent or inarticulate dissent. Conversely, if at first a truth is entirely a community's babe, entirely dependent on approval, as it becomes independent of the latter so does it tend to mould the thoughts of the community in the way of its implications.

The first additions to the Primal Myth were probably greeted with the same appreciative laughter as other kinds of additions to other old myths are being greeted today. A positive response from the audience encourages repetition and expansion. Conversely, interruptions and corrections force the author or storyteller to give his delivery collective shape, collective authenticity. Without interruptions from myself it would have taken each of the authors of the four versions of the Primal Myth only a few minutes to reach the point when the *ramatzka* is killed. Only the author of the fourth version was interrupted by other Tangu to any extent thus far. Up to this point the truths are not only well established, unassailable, but they are historical. Then come newer truths. And these are embellished. Given his head a storyteller would repeat the exchanges between *Tuman* and *Ambwerk* in relation to every kind of European product known to him. But, as in any art, storytelling has its discipline. The audience is held, and dissents or confers its consent when the story touches intimate feelings.

Rather than assault the imagination too violently Tangu storytellers tend to make a deft selection of significant points. Their raw material consists of incidents which they have witnessed or heard about, which might have occurred yesterday or last month, and which have caught the public imagination; of rumours which can be embellished; of fascinating pieces of misinformation which can be decked out with tact to elicit an appreciative laugh, or score a point. And, like storytellers anywhere, Tangu resort to their dreams and daydreams for material.

As has been shown, dreams are for Tangu a repository of truths which are always relevant for the self. They spring from a total experience: from an experience of society, of other unique individuals, of the physical world, of the mystical world, of both the quick and the dead. They spring, too, from psychological experience; from an awareness of the self in relation to others, from cognizance of being, and from deep in the psyche. To cross over to Tangu and enter with them into dreamland is to venture beyond the confines of civilized man. For here are lodged those truths which white men tend to hide in asylums.

It is one thing to examine the rites in which Tangu engaged and to find in them consistency in relation to the problems that beset them; quite another to be intellectually aware of those problems and then try to work out suitable rites which will express them. Yet we do not find it strange that such ceremonies could emerge from a dream. Nor, indeed, do Tangu.

On the other hand Europeans do tend to think it odd that Tangu should use their dream experiences to order everyday life. However, once having granted that dreams contain truths it is at least logical, if not always advantageous in European terms, to make use of dream experiences in other contexts of life. When a Tangu talks to his father he is undergoing a real experience. When he consults with his dead father in a dream he is undergoing a quite different kind of experience—which may or may not be as clear as either might wish —but which is certainly as real.

When A converses with his elder brother B it is a real experience which happens several times a day, every day, for many years. Then B dies. In Tangu A dreams that B comes to have a chat with him. His visits are frequent during the period immediately following his death, and then they tend to become progressively rarer until A nears the end of his span— when they tend to become more frequent again. Often enough, and certainly if A and B were close confidants in life, A and B continually meet in dream. In life not every conversation that A has with B is thought to be significant: they occur several times a day. After B's death, however, every meeting is telling. For if the dead have many of the characteristics of the living they lack one that is essential: physical life. And in virtue of what they lack the dead possess attributes which the living do not. Normally invisible, in dreams they make themselves manifest. Space does not fetter them, and time does not trip them by the heels. What the dead say has significance precisely because they are dead when they say it. And the dead, because they are dead, can oversee all, and once had physical life, cannot but have a far wider experience and knowledge of the truth however hard the living might try to harness them in convention, and however inadequate the translation of an encounter into the idiom of language.

Statements communicated through dreams are, therefore, more true than the statements of living men and women. Even trickeries and deceptions are more true. They are absolute. If, in life, B tricks A, A can reply by deceiving B.

But if B is dead he can trick A to his soul's content and A cannot trick B.

Myths and dreams are interdependent in the sense, first, that much of the content of dreams tends to become articulate in myth, and myths, or parts of myths, are retold in dreams. Secondly, though myths and dreams are intimately related to truth the relationships are not of the same kind. Myths contain truths, dreams are avenues for perceiving the truths which are later embodied in myths.

A European observer might say that myths are true, or more true, because they are not simply personal views but statements of dogma acknowledged by the community as a whole. Tangu themselves say that myths are true because they are myths. It is axiomatic. If pressed, Tangu will add that myths are true because they belong to the ancestors, because they exist, and because they derive from the truths of the past which are always truths. The validity of dreams is also axiomatic. They are true because they derive from the ancestors, from the dead; because even when no ancestor appears in the dream the dream had been 'sent' anonymously—not made up by the living. Myths are social repositories of truths, and dreams are accepted as windows through which individuals may perceive the truth.

The European contribution has been to throw doubt on the content of myths without invalidating the principles by which truth may be sought or preserved. Tangu still discover their truths through dreams, and still store their truths in myths. But in the current situation, given certain problems, and not being provided with adequate tools with which to tackle them, Tangu have had recourse to the truths in their myths. To their dismay, now that they need them, they have found there a lumber grown over with cobwebs. To be sure, some pieces still shine; but they do not suffice to explain their ever widening environment. White men have not been slow to offer them substitutes, but, with doubt in their minds, Tangu have cause to wonder which is more true, more valid, more useful. What are the criteria of truth? On the whole Tangu have been forced back into traditional hinges of choice: myths, dreams, and emotional responses. Even had they preferred to take operational or organizational criteria of fitness and efficiency the administrative system deprives them of the option. Tangu are not asked, nor allowed to initiate. They must obey. They are considered not to be 'ready'.

Within the ferment of truths which might only be half-truths or nothing at all, the charismatic figure emerges as an articulate vehicle bringing order and intelligibility to a largely inchoate mass of experiences and feelings. For a period he himself becomes a veritable symbol of truth, an individual, enshrined in himself, at one with society, absorbed in the myth-dream. He can never be wholly a failure. Through him —through what he says and does—what appears to be false or useless is set aside and abandoned; and what appears to be true or useful for the future is garnered in the myth-dream and further refined. But if, for a while, the charismatic figure appears as the criterion of truth, truth itself is contained in the myth-dream. He fails as a person when the directives and principles he provides do not completely reflect and validate the myth-dream as it exists when he makes his appearance; and he succeeds in so far as he has meaning and validates a part, or parts, of the myth-dream.

THE NEW MAN

Tangu gossip is like gossip anywhere else in the world. Men and women say things about other men and women; accuracy is beside the point. Rumour-mongering is different. Rumours arise out of social situations containing affective alternatives: the accuracy or truth of the matter is important because the yea or nay will affect future thought and action. Several examples have been given of the way rumours collect round the possibilities of administrative action, of the particular twists they take, and their results; and it has also been shown how ready both Tangu and Manam islanders were to put their own interpretations on the role of the writer. And the mis-interpretations are important because they are affective, and because the basic questions to which the original observations try to give answers may be resolved in—What is the nature of the white man? What is the nature of man?

Tangu are interested in white men in rather the same way that certain journalists are interested in the actions of Russian political figures. There is the same hunt for significance and relevance, the same What next?, the same attempts to project possibilities. Tangu do not, cannot, take it for granted that white men are human in the same way as they are. So, within the limits of their own understanding, Tangu go to some pains to find out about white men. But, as we have seen, these same limits of understanding not only shape the questions they ask, but predicate the answers. Questions arise from the problems in Cargo, and answers spring from the assumptions in Cargo. Nevertheless, the more objective information about white men, information that is freed from conflicts of interest, is lodged where it might be expected to be found: in the myth-dream. And in the myth-dream we find the new man.

Mambu the man does not emerge as an easy character to assess. Whether or not he had courage may remain a debatable point. But he must have had a keener intelligence than most or he would not have been marked down as a possible catechist. His imagination seems to have been balanced by a nice common sense, he was perceptive, and a man without ability could not have organized a movement as he did. In the myth about him, however, Mambu becomes much more influential than he was as an historical figure. Perhaps because he meant so much more than he was. Yali was certainly a capable man, but it seems fairly clear that he owed most of his reputation to his friends and his enemies. It is surely significant that as Yali the man became more and more perplexed within himself, as he degenerated into libertinism, as he began to use power to satisfy personal desires, his social stature expanded and grew large. Real principles and interests involving relatively large numbers of people were at stake. And they met in Yali. If he was the spark, the flames that he kindled were not in his power to control.

As has been shown, both Mambu and Yali made their own

particular contributions to the shape of the new man. As charismatic figures they sufficed, temporarily, to contain the new man. When their days were done what appeared to be significant to the community in their deeds, words, and attributes became a part of the myth-dream. Neither Mambu nor Yali was necessarily the sort of man every one would like to be in fact. But both were certainly the kind of men almost every Kanaka would like to admire and point out as an example to others as an ideal which each one of them should, or ought to, emulate.

Irakau, whose involvement with Tangu and their affairs was minimal, was still in the ascendant in 1952 when the events narrated in the *Prologue* took place. Drawing on their experiences with Yali the mission was not wholly mistaken in thinking that Irakau's friends and followers were attempting to make him more than he was. And it would surely be asking too much of a man to expect him to resist successfully the community pressures which were pushing him into a position from whence he might exert an absolute power. In resisting the pressures to positive action, in maintaining relationships with administration and mission, Irakau was being true to the myth-dream—which is widely disseminated over the Bogia region—but not being nearly spectacular enough. He was demanding of his community the same nerve and capacity for restraint as he himself had. The youth from Pariakenam illustrates the other extreme. In himself he may have been a nonentity. But he was a lad who had a dream, who saw truth, at a crucial moment in time. In other circumstances the same dream might have been laughed at.

The charismatic figure, it would seem, the centre of a Cargo movement, may or may not have abilities of his own. But because of some qualities he may have, or because of what he is doing, or through a mere accident of time and place, he takes the centre of the stage and through the myth-dream other merits are heaped on him. He himself has something. He must have. But on the whole circumstances, the men about him, rumours, and the community which gives the rumours validity, actually create him.

Although ordinary men may see in the charismatic figure the projection of a new social ideal it is only for a brief period of time. For most of their lives they are faced by themselves as individuals. Each may feel himself to be a man, but only a few may be able to recognize him as such. And not many who feel themselves to be men can have the confidence of knowing it without the signal approbation of their friends and comrades. When Tangu are among their own kind they know they have to keep proving to themselves and to others that they are men. The methods of doing so are known and accepted, the proof of their manhood is clear.

Outside Tangu these same men are lost. The criteria of manhood are many and diffuse. A proud bearing, good in Tangu among Tangu, can be 'bigheaded' in front of a European or a Kanaka foreman. And 'bigheaded' is not only a term of opprobrium, it means no work, no cash. The instant riposte, enjoined in Tangu—and habitual in Australia itself—is punished by Europeans in New Guinea. Containing one's pride with dignity may be regarded as sulking.

What makes a man? How can others recognize a man and treat him as such when they see him?

Charismatic figures have the quality of manhood, and they derive it from the ambience of the myth-dream. Ordinary men, on the other hand, are forced to deal with the realities of day-to-day life. They have to gain self-respect—which is a product both of a critical assessment of the self by the self, and of a knowledge of standing in the community. They need a clear image of what a man should be and do.

Tangu carry the image of a manager. They are also aware of other images which tend to obscure the definite outlines of the managerial ideal. A late reveller's vision, one part of the European model has money, material goods, power over others, confidence, and omnipotence: items of day-to-day experience and observation. Another part, largely the result of missionary teaching, contains the Christ-image, flat and un-rounded, gentle and self-sacrificing. Yali revivified the tra-ditional warrior, portraying the warrior of tomorrow. Irakau illustrates the shrewd entrepreneur. Where is the new man—

257

the moral entity which can be shrewd, gentle, self-sacrificing, and capable withal?

Tangu would like to be men amongst men, not merely men among Tangu. Even if in themselves they feel themselves to be men, among Europeans they cannot know that they are men. Some, it is true, may wear a policeman's uniform; and others may rejoice in the title of boss-boy or boatswain. But, for the most part, in the European environment, Tangu are labourers or domestic servants doing women's work. Europeans sport their manhood, their social worth, in fine houses, equipment, and access to cargo. Like Tangu managers they have behind them a solid achievement, something to show, something which accounts for their influence and power. But in the European environment Tangu have nothing, nothing material to show they are men, nothing by which they may demonstrate that as the divine creator stands to his creation so men stand to their own material goods.

In Tangu gardens and harvests are the basis on which a man's reputation is built, and the means through which a mutual equivalence can be proved. Without cargo Tangu cannot prove an equivalence with white men. And since an assumption of moral equality is lacking there is no way of maintaining any kind of equivalence with white men. Only with the moral European do the possibilities of manhood become realizable.

Without a past and a future, it would seem, a Kanaka can hardly be secure as a man. 'I am me' does not suffice. 'I am the son of a bush-Kanaka' is no matter for pride at the present time. Inevitably, the question becomes, 'What can I be in the eyes of my fellows, my children, and my ancestors?' If the past can justify the ancestors it gives the living a foothold in the present, especially in relation to Europeans. And it provides a departure for the future. European teaching, however, and experiences with Europeans, have all tended to make the ancestors seem small. They got the myths wrong; they handed on deception, not truth; their memories were bad; they sinned; they were unable to write; they invented and practised distasteful customs; they had no understanding. Through them the right to cargo was forfeit.

But apart from the ancestors there can be no past. Ancestors contain the past just as the past contains ancestors. In a Cargo movement the ancestors emerge as heroes once more. They are all right; they become respectable; they can make cargo; they have not forgotten their descendants. Even now they are sending cargo to their offspring—but white men are intercepting it, changing the labels, stealing it. . . .

If Tangu were more worthy of the ancestors, if they were in some way more men than they are, inimical and amoral white men would be thwarted. Then the cargo would come. Through Mambu the myth-dream counsels a period of waiting and learning. But who, caught in the toils of the present, may wait on the future? Tangu want to be men now, while they live, not in fifty years' time when they are dead. If they must be rehabilitated ancestors they would still like to put their children on the path towards manhood. Access to cargo has become the symbol of manhood.

THE NEW SOCIETY

The new man emerges from the myth-dream with some definity. There are the Tangu manager, *Tuman, Ambwerk*, Mambu, the mythical Mambu, Yali, the youth from Pariakenam, and a number of other individuals from whom he can be made. But the new society is necessarily vague. If Tangu were able to comprehend their own society as well as one other they might have a comparative yardstick with which to make a new one. As it is, however, though Tangu apprehend their own society they cannot truly be said to comprehend it on an intellectual level. Nor do they comprehend the massive European society of which they are beginning to be a part. And the forms of a society require comprehension not simply apprehension. The implication is that the new society will take shape round the new man; that having created the new man societal forms will mould themselves to his nature. Otherwise, the only clues the myth-dream provides is that the new society will be one with wider unities than at present, and one in which the new man will be able to develop his potentialities.

Nevertheless, because a European observer can comprehend Tangu society to a certain extent, and though he cannot outline the kind of social organization Tangu would like to have, he can point out some of the organizational difficulties that have played a large part in begetting the problems of Cargo. For, though the idea of manhood requires consent to the image of a man, and particularized and acknowledged capacities by which the community may recognize him, without a clear notion of what kinds of activities a man should engage in, and for what purposes he does them, there is, for the individual, none but an experimental point of departure from the self. A man becomes a man within terms of activities that are organized.

Consider, first, rice. Growing rice in Tangu could be an important, even an essential activity. Left to themselves there is little doubt that Tangu would grow rice in units of households. Combinations of households would co-operate together on a single plot for one year. And it might be that having co-operated on a single plot for one year they would do so for a second and a third. There is at least the possibility that because rice, like clearing a garden site, requires a co-operative effort, it might, because it requires such an effort over a long period—unlike clearing a garden site which is a temporary affair—stabilize co-operative groups. It might be that the harvested rice would be used in exchanges. But, because rice commands a cash price as yams do not, it might be sold for cash to buy tools, equipment, clothing, and other kinds of cargo. In turn, possession of such goods would come to indicate social worth, prestige, and substance. And the managerial values could be expected to expand so as to contain the profits from the new crop.

However, the administration insists that growing rice should be a community venture under the supervision of Kanaka officials. If, along with the seed and the orders to grow the rice the administration had provided some organizational procedure through which the villagers could be regularly recruited to the task; if there were some means by which the crop or its profit could be satisfactorily distributed; if there were some means of transporting the rice to the point where it can command a cash sale; if the native officials responsible for organizing rice cultivation were enabled to reap something other than thick heads and anxieties for their labours—then rice growing in Tangu might be a useful and popular activity. As it is, categorically debarred from organizing themselves, Tangu have been presented with no alternative but to pursue an unfamiliar task in a virtually impossible way.

Tangu realize that the offices, roles, and duties of Kanaka officials are important. And they also realize that much of the future depends on accepting authoritarian values in some form. Yet, may an office be recognized as really important if it carries responsibilities without stipend, without rewards, without prestige—if inefficiency is punished and efficiency goes unrecognized? Those Tangu who are capable men tend to regard Kanaka administrative officials as 'suckers'. Others regard them as 'stooges'. It is true that, were it not for sorcery, both Luluai and Tultul could hold the potential of tyranny.[1] But unless an official is also a manager he cannot command the respect of his fellow villagers. He is truly a puppet.

A manager does not relish appointment to an administrative office because he begins to lose the merits of either role. When wearing his cap his orders must be obeyed. When he takes it off he is bound by equivalence. He has to do things with his cap on which he would never dream of doing without it. If it is possible for anyone to be a good Kanaka administrative official, a manager—the 'natural leader' in his own community—certainly cannot be. That is, the situation does not permit the best men to take the most responsible roles; valuable economic activities and political roles are divorced from those ideas and other activities which should give them meaning.

If it be said that there must be some way of marrying

[1] cf. H. Ian Hogbin, 1951, esp. pp. 151–63.

political offices to a structure that traditionally precludes them, and some way of carrying on an economic activity which, on the merits of production, will yield political influence, then, substantially if only temporarily, this is precisely what the charismatic figure does. He organizes a political body, and presents a programme which, through himself and the combined efforts of the participants, will realize their political and economic aims. And, as we have seen, on the level of ritual, of the myth-dream in action, Tangu did so reorganize themselves.

If circumstances were altered there might be no need for a charismatic figure. If, for example, Tangu were possessed of an institution—such as a representative council of managers or elders—they might be able to decide explicitly and for themselves what forms of organization might best suit them. But Tangu do not have such a device. *Br'ngun'guni* depends on what is implicit; on established notions of what is moral or amoral; on the consent and rapport of a whole community gathered together. The whole essence of *br'ngun'guni* is that responsibility is not delegated to an authoritative body empowered to act for the whole community. Tangu are aware that their dispersal as well as the fighting consequent on the great sickness could have been halted had they had an authoritative mechanism, commanding consent, which might have, for example, altered the rules about vengeance. For, unless there is a political mechanism which can take note of changing circumstances, and which can make explicit decisions regarding reorganization, the individuals concerned can only collide with their own outdated community values.

The Mambu myth reveals a willingness to make changes in the managerial values. How may this change be brought about without the aid of a device for doing so—otherwise than by allowing the conflicts of value to express themselves as emotional frustrations made manifest in myths and resolved in rites? Community values have a momentum of their own, and while, through historical events, they may change in small ways over a period of time, gradually evolving, drastic and sudden changes surely require a political mechanism to meet them and deal with the consequent problems of reorganization.

Maize, an introduced crop, has caused Tangu no trouble because, being allowed to grow it as they wished, the activity was quite simply absorbed into the existing distributional system. Nor is maize any part of the Cargo. Its introduction predicated no problems. Rice is part of the Cargo, and its introduction has involved Tangu in an acute organizational problem.

Without fully comprehending its significance Tangu see the organizational defects of their society as a fault in themselves —a factor closely related to their expressions of guilt. Since the system they possess was bequeathed them by the ancestors Tangu are behaving intelligibly in blaming the ancestors—in the Primal Myth—for leaving them with an organization which makes access to manufactured goods very difficult if not impossible. At the same time, however, they feel it cannot always have been thus. When the mission first came to Tangu it was made welcome—it meant peace, it was repairing the damage done by the great sickness. But since that time, since the advent of Europeans, in relation to their widening horizon and progressive appreciation of Europeans, their abilities, and their goods, the traditional structure has seemed to shrink in significance and ability to cope. Even if Tangu had been well organized at the time when Europeans came there, their increasing comprehension of things European would have eaten into their native ethnocentricism so as to make them less and less proud of themselves and their creations in relation to Europeans and European culture generally. Therefore, runs the implication, the ancestors, living Tangu, and Europeans—who have made Tangu seem small— are jointly responsible for the present state of affairs. If the crime could be expiated and atonement made Tangu could join their ancestors in a timeless continuum; if, also, Europeans could be persuaded into co-operation then the organizational defects could be made good and the cargo would come through. As indeed it would.

In Cargo movements the first step, rehabilitation of the

ancestors, is achieved. They are making the cargo—making access to cargo possible. The second step is more crucial. The myth-dream puts the onus, the initiative, on the brother with *nous*, on Europeans. And surely it is right to do so. Only Europeans, moral Europeans, have the knowledge, the will, and the power to make the necessary changes in organization. In particular, the administration which has the power is placed to become moral European.

In fact, because Europeans, particularly the administration, are obdurate and will not co-operate, the charismatic figure is forced into one of the two remaining alternatives. Irakau has been able to hold out because, being himself personally of some commercial consequence, he has been able to force both mission and administration into at least partial co-operation.

All Kanakas are faced to a greater or lesser degree with much the same problems of internal reorganization. And because neither the mission nor the administration seems to be willing to take the initiative, here and there Kanakas have had to take it for themselves. None the less, they are caught on the triangle. Mambu tried to extricate himself by making both administration and mission into one single 'enemy'—white men. The only alternative the mission and administration offered him was to ignore them completely. In fact, however, the triangle is inescapable. The missions have saddled Kanakas with their most valuable burden—the image of a man. And the missions co-operate with Kanakas when the latter have trouble with the administration. On the other hand, since missionaries are Europeans they cannot but identify themselves with much of the content of the administrative effort—including its apparent intransigence. Administrative officers themselves have the welfare of Kanakas sincerely at heart, and, so far as their roles will allow them, they attempt to realize their objects with dignity. If many see a major part of this 'welfare' as 'releasing Kanakas from the grip of the missions' it is but one aspect of their struggle for the loyalty and gratitude of Kanakas, of their attempt to extend over Kanakas a greater proportion of influence, of an inner desire to enforce a moral surrender to themselves or their secular 'gods'. How often one has heard missionaries exclaim with impatience at the actions of administrative officers! And how often have the latter cursed the 'interference' of the former! Kanakas say, '*Mipela stap long namer tasol,* We are in the middle. That's all.'

Ultimately Kanakas have the whip-hand because they have the power to grant or withhold what both European elements seek from them. Presently, both administration and mission force Kanakas to be opportunists in their own interests, and they can accept the advances of either the better to thwart the other. In doing so, in accepting the pushes and pulls of the triangle, Kanakas are obeying the behest of their myth-dream. If Europeans will not co-operate voluntarily they will have to be forced to co-operate. In the process of playing one off against the other each is beginning to learn something of the other's problems. And in the learning lies the possibility of co-operation.

Kanakas realize without being fully intellectually aware of it that New Guinea cannot for long remain a multiplicity of small groups isolated from each other by differences of culture and language. They are keen to learn Pidgin not only because it is a language which can deal with the European environment as they find it today, but because Pidgin makes them *wan tok*, one tongue, one people. '*Nai Kanakatzir!*' Tangu say. They are beginning to feel themselves Kanakas together. They have begun to share heroes, they share the desire for access to cargo, and they participate together in Cargo movements. The seeds of what must, one day, be a State, or Confederation of States, have been sown.

The crucial question which remains is whether an anti-European charismatic figure is necessary or not; whether the emergence of men like Mambu and Yali is related only to an amoral leadership at the top. The implication of this analysis is that moral European and charismatic figure can be one; that if missions and administration could follow out the proposals of the myth-dream they would themselves fulfil the role of the charismatic figure. If, on the other hand, they do not follow out the myth-dream it seems fairly clear that one day a charismatic figure will emerge who will either force them into co-operation—or force them out of New Guinea.

MORAL EUROPEAN AND
THE CHARISMATIC FIGURE

Looking at Tangu alone one might be justified in saying that their circumstances before the advent of Europeans made the search for a new man inevitable. Indeed, it had already started. But we cannot say the same of Manam islanders. They seem to have composed a stable and well organized society. They were a proud and independent people with a sure faith in themselves. The feeling—and it can be no more than that— is that their ideas of the new man began to take shape when they saw what white men had to offer, and grew as it became more and more apparent that the European world was not only much larger, more complex, and more powerful than theirs was, but that the longer they looked at them the more able and ingenious the men who belonged to this world became. There is a limit, perhaps, beyond which the acceptance of differences in status, capacities, and command over resources can no longer be borne.

In 1952, at any rate, both Tangu and Manam islanders were enveloped in the notion of Cargo—a complex of moral problems set in a field of organizational conflicts largely if not wholly created by what has been called the triangle. Within this field events, when they occurred, seem to have been received and interpreted, used or discarded, by Kanakas in relation to particular constants to be found in the myth-dream. Antagonist and protagonist seem to have found in events levers to further interests which themselves seem to have been largely determined by their roles in the circumstances. And so far as it concerns Kanakas, both interests and roles are to be seen in the myth-dream. Further, as we have seen, these interests are not merely reflected in the myth-dream, they derive from it. The myth-dream is the locus of truth.

Once it is appreciated that the myth-dream is not simply a

mirror to life, but, so far as Kanakas are concerned, is the truth which life should reflect, then the basic expression of guilt in the myth-dream becomes of crucial significance.

The knowledge of the existence of these expressions of guilt lies behind the suggestion that if Europeans had been in the habit of freely distributing manufactured goods Mambu would have said that more cargo would not come because Europeans were stopping it. That is, access to cargo is not simply access to European goods, but access to European goods within a particular moral relationship. A relationship characterized by Europeans admitting that they, or their symbol, were simply lucky in not having killed the *ramatzka*—lucky but not virtuous. From that point—the admission of moral equality —co-operation becomes possible. Unfortunately, the longer this particular guilt is allowed to establish itself as a truth the more difficult it becomes to dislodge it. The notion of this guilt had, moreover, entered the minds of Tangu long before they came into established and regular relationships with white men. It is intimately linked to the idea of the new man. It is also linked to the fact that because they have access to manu-factured goods Europeans must be in some way more deserving, more manly, than Kanakas are. If the possibility of a Cargo movement was born when Tangu realized that white men, or other beings, were on the whole vastly more capable than they were, that possibility turned into a probability when the relationships characteristic of the triangle were formed.

The implications are clear. Unless Europeans admit their 'luck' in being as they are, and dispose of themselves, their goods, and their ideas on a basis of moral equality—and thus admit to the possibility that they themselves might have been equally guilty—the situation can only call forth more and more charismatic figures who will be forced into fostering acute xenophobia.

In the meanwhile, failing the necessary help from Euro-peans, charismatic figures continue to appear, trying to solve the central dilemma of Cargo—How to intellectualize, formu-late, and so put into effect the demands of the myth-dream when men themselves are imprisoned in a particular structure of ideas, relationships, and interests; how to think in terms of 'B' when all current thought and action, ideas, and values are characterized by 'A'. With each appearance adequate intellectualization of the myth-dream comes a step nearer. And when a charismatic figure does intellectualize the myth-dream he will be in a position to capture it. At present, however, he is but a child of the myth-dream itself, and Europeans, not a Kanaka, are best placed to make the myth-dream their own. At present, though certain cultural values are swiftly becoming widely diffused, the autonomy of the many and particular cultural groups is still strong enough to resist particular kinds of amalgamation or leadership. Tangu have not been able to produce a charismatic figure of their own: and the structure of leadership and socio-political relations goes a long way to show why not. On the other hand, an outsider in the charismatic role does seem to be acceptable. Mambu, Yali, and the youth from Pariakenam were all outsiders. So also was the missionary whom Tangu accepted in the early days when their troubles, so far as Tangu could appreciate them, were wholly due to themselves. Much more ethnocentric than Tangu, and equipped with a quite different social structure, Manam islanders never had much to do with Mambu. He was a bush-Kanaka. They scorned the youth from Pariakenam, and though they were much influenced by Yali, they accepted for themselves Irakau, a *Tanepoa*.

Yali's influence over both Tangu and Manam islanders is instructive. For, not only did he fill the charismatic role awaited by both Tangu and Manam islanders, but he was, in himself, so very much a creation of the Europeans caught in the triangle. He not only appeared to Tangu and to Manam islanders to be setting out to resolve problems common to them both in relation to Europeans, but he was himself recognized by Europeans as a man of some consequence—as a man. Add to this the fact that the writer, a European visitor, was expected to have a charismatic message for Manam islanders after he had established a moral relationship, and the convergence of charismatic and moral European roles becomes even plainer.

What has emerged from the preceding pages is that the charismatic role is that of feeding the myth-dream. As political figures Mambu, Yali, and the youth from Pariakenam ended as failures. As food for the myth-dream, on the other hand, they could hardly have been more successful. Irakau, however, could be interpreted on his actions as trying hard not to be the kind of charismatic figure that Mambu, Yali, and the youth from Pariakenam were. One may see in his behaviour the attempt to be a success in concrete politico-economic terms rather than only feeding the myth-dream. And were it not for the fact that Irakau is being pressed by his associates to assume a more dramatic part, one may see him slowly developing in himself a combination of the roles of planter or trader, missionary, and administrative officer.

So far as Irakau is significantly bound by his own Kanaka values he fulfils the role of moral European by being in a moral relationship with his fellow Kanakas, and being the agency through which access to cargo is being realized. And once it is accepted that the charismatic role is that of energizing the myth-dream, then, for Europeans, the role of moral European becomes of crucial importance. Particularly is this so at the practical level of being a missionary, or of being an officer entrusted with the administration of the Territory. For although Europeans are caught up in the atmosphere of Cargo antithetically, if they were aware of the myth-dream, if they could divest themselves of their antagonisms to the themes of Cargo and assume the role of moral European, they would satisfy the demands of the myth-dream. There would then be no need for charismatic figures to nourish the myth-dream. But there would emerge Kanaka businessmen and politicians who, because the Europeans concerned were moral Europeans, would be able to work co-operatively within the circumstances obtaining and play their part in the overall development of New Guinea.

Finally, once it is accepted that the charismatic role is to sustain the myth-dream, not completely fulfil it, much light is shed on the fact that it is so often *after* a charismatic figure has failed in his political or organizational role that he becomes of real significance. Of course, because the charismatic figure nourishes the myth-dream it does not necessarily follow that he must fail at the organizational level. Often, however, the best organizers are not charismatic figures. The youth from Pariakenam did not organize the rites in which Tangu participated. He dreamed them. What he dreamed stimulated the myth-dream. And other men, competent organizers, arranged for the rites to take place.

RITES AND TECHNIQUES

The rites and ceremonies of a Cargo movement are normally the best advertised, and it will be useful to consider, in the light of some events that took place in Malaya in 1954, the link between myth-dream, rites, and cargo.

One evening, not far from a small village in southern Malaya in the region of Batu Pahat, a semi-lunatic Chinese woman, who used to spend her days sitting in the shade of a tree by a stream, had a dream. Perhaps it was a vision. She saw a god who, appearing before her, announced his name and told the woman that if a temple dedicated to himself were built by the stream he would cure the skin diseases of those who came to worship there.

In a short while most of the Chinese folk in the area came to hear of the dream.

The Chinese pharmacists of the region, and other investors, started to collect the capital necessary to build a temple. In a few months the temple was built, costly relics and decorations were bought, and on its completion the building was sanctified and dedicated by an exclusive order of monks. A travelling circus, a repertory company, and famous opera stars were engaged to celebrate the occasion. The opening ceremony drew a large crowd. A local barber and two of his friends who had urged the project forward took their stints as mediums in the temple. The old lady herself sat by the door of the temple rocking gently back and forth, crooning to herself, and occasionally going into transports of ecstasy. Sometimes she had to be forcibly restrained from doing damage to herself and to others.

270

The enterprise was an immediate success. Sufferers from a variety of skin diseases, who for years had been treated by European or European trained doctors without any visible results, were cured, or reported to have been cured, within the week. They worshipped, paid a temple toll, gave money to the poor, and paid the mediums who translated messages from the god into prescriptions which were then made up by the local Chinese pharmacists. The fame of the temple spread. Every week-end busloads of pilgrims came for the cure. The tourist traffic brought a thriving trade to scores of small shop-keepers, hawkers, and vendors of knick-knacks, relics, and foods. The pharmacists prospered, donations to the temple multiplied, and the old lady was showered with gifts.

The therapeutic process by which the sufferers were cured, or believed to have been cured, is here irrelevant. What is significant is that some were cured, or generally believed to have been cured. The end was attained, or believed to have been attained. And irrespective of this end many benefits were distributed. Not only may the end be said to have justified the means, but the means themselves were self-justifying. As an economic enterprise the temple was a great success. Consequently, it will come as no surprise to learn that such cults are a regular feature of Chinese life in Malaya. They are institutionalized. They work. And they work on two distinct but connected planes. At the mystical level the cure is not guaranteed. The therapy lies in the hands of the god, and only he may decide whether the case is deserving or not. Failures to cure, therefore, account for themselves in mystical terms. The god is unwilling, or the case not sufficiently deserving.

At the economic level payment is made to the mediating machinery, not to the god. What need has a god of money? The monks, mediums, and temple attendants do their jobs. They can do no more. Obligation is not on the god to cure, but on the mediums to gain a prescription—which they do. The god may be cajoled, tempted, persuaded, railed at, or even disavowed: but he remains where he is, sublime, completely self-willed. The connective between the economics of the affair and its mystique, is a therapy which, however, is entirely contained in the logic of the mystical belief. Particular failures to cure are accounted for in terms of the decision of the god, completely short-circuiting the old lady, her vision, the temple, the pharmacists, the mediums, and the prescriptions—though one must always allow for the conceited and self-deceiving who, feeling themselves entirely worthy and deserving of a cure, will consider themselves cheated of their money if the god refuses to cure.

A general failure to maintain a minimum record of cures does not, therefore, invalidate the means. The god, who obeys his own laws at his own choice, has become unwilling. At the same time, the success of the cult as an economic enterprise is dependent on the pragmatic cure, or what is believed to be a pragmatic cure, which itself is achieved through the divinity. Within terms of a particular organizational apparatus men do their best to open a channel to the god, but they cannot constrain him to cure.

The rites and ceremonies of a Cargo cult cannot be separated from the myth-dream: the one is an attempt to express the other. The Malayan cult preserves and re-emphasizes existing roles and relationships. The end is a therapy already contained in a single moral system: the hurdle is in the 'worthiness' of the individual. Where, in a particular case, there is no therapy there is no obligation to make the leap between an intelligible economic enterprise and a mystical belief contained in a logic of its own. The connective, the therapy, is an empirical requirement—which is none the less effective if the cures are faked so long as they are believed to have been effected—not necessarily linked to either processes in their logics, but vital to the maintenance of the activity as a whole. The ends of a Cargo movement are the new man, a change in his present nature, an alteration of the roles and relationships on which his nature currently depends, the fusion of two moral systems. The explicit and concrete symbol of the ends is cargo, access to material goods. A failure in the rites reacts on the whole *corpus* of Cargo. But because the rites and ceremonies are a particular kind of expression of the myth-dream itself they may be regarded as means which are self-justifying in themselves. They feed the myth-dream. The apparent failure, as a European might see it, is in fact a success because by feeding the myth-dream the rites provide a new departure from which fresh means may be sought.

The Malayan cult is repetitive because it works. Cargo movements repeat themselves because the myth-dream requires nourishment, because they fail and must work. If the Malayan cult were to fail in gaining a therapy, or some cures, precisely the same techniques would be used in relation to another god, or to the same god in another place. The techniques themselves are not in doubt because they are known, or firmly believed, to have worked in the past. They are institutionalized, parts of a regular way of life. And this is precisely what Cargo movements are not. The techniques of a Cargo movement must keep changing until success is achieved, until there is a synthesis of moral environments, until the whole individual is realized, until access to cargo satisfies the demands of the new man in the myth-dream.

CONCLUSION

The choice between relating the circumstances of what might be a unique series of events and relationships, an historical recreation, or containing the same events and relationships within broad categories, a sociological inquiry, is a difficult one. The story of the Tangu myth-dream might be peculiar to Tangu. How far is it not? In the last century what has been written down here might have been called 'an evolutionary process', but today, in spite of some attempts at rehabilitation,[1] and because of its ambiguities and historical associations, there is some reluctance to employ so perfidious a servant as evolution. It has too many faces. There are, also, certain difficulties in attempting to relate Cargo movements to the general conditions in which they occur.[2] It requires, first,

[1] cf. S. F. Nadel, *The Foundations of Social Anthropology*, Cohen and West, London 1951, pp. 104–6.

[2] cf. Cyril Belshaw, 1950b, p. 124, where he says that the 'similarities of Cargo movements must be due to the similarities in local conditions which produce them. . . .'

an adequate distinction between cult and conditions, and further, a thesis which purports to reveal a relationship between cult and general social, economic, and political environment, and which does not account for Cargo movements not taking place when the same conditions obtain, cannot command much confidence. The negative instance is of crucial importance. But the problem is, one feels, a false one—entirely dependent on what is meant by conditions, and on how the conditions are described and made relevant. For Cargo movements represent a growth, an attempt at synthesis, a movement of values springing out of precedent systems of values. They are at one and the same time symptomatic, and actively productive, of change. They are creative of new forms which themselves are derived both from current social environmental influences as well as from the traditions and history of the body social. They are typical millenarian movements acted out in terms of a particular cultural idiom. And the key to the changes, new forms, and syntheses envisaged lies in the myth-dream.

The content of a myth-dream is the more easily definable where a situation of disnomy obtains. In the *Preface* the word 'disnomic' was used to describe the situation in which a Cargo movement had already occurred: it is a shorthand term to indicate a general characteristic of all or certain pertinent social relationships within the total structure of relationships. This characteristic is probably best described as 'incertaintie': in his everyday life, or in certain relevant sectors of it, an individual is faced with selecting one of two or more apparently equally weighted or even, sometimes, contradictory courses of action which are more or less approved by the community he lives in. Further, the double—or treble—scale of values are relevant in the one situation—which is to be distinguished from a general situation in which one scale of values operates in some well defined circumstances and a second in others. Disnomic describes an acceleration in the number of particulars in an environment without a corresponding series of categories within terms of which they might be comprehended and mastered; it describes the situation in Tangu when the numbers of inter-

274

marriages between the peoples of the four neighbourhoods so increased as to give the next generation a choice in the exercise of claims deriving from different kinds of descent system; it describes the situation on the introduction of manu- factured dogs' teeth, and just after the great sickness; it describes the situation in Tangu today in relation to the ever widening horizon of European ideas and goods. The 'more' disnomic a situation is the more scope there will be for the man who 'knows what he wants', who can see the wood despite the trees, who on the one hand may be selfish, self-seeking, ambitious, or ruthless, and who on the other might be able to bring order and certainty into the community by the presentation of well defined principles of action which reflect the aspirations of the community.[1]

For Tangu as well as for Manam islanders the primary element creating the disnomic situation is the complex of activities and organizational dilemmas that derive from the existence of the triangle.

So far, then, we have the myth-dream, disnomy, and a series of organizational dilemmas which create the disnomy, and which, in the particular case, arise from a triadic distribu- tion of authority, interests, and values generally. It remains to isolate five significant factors which appear to enter into the process of realizing the myth-dream. First, there is the locus in truth. On the level of realization this locus is the myth-dream itself. And though an observer must attempt to show why, or in what way, the myth-dream is thought to contain truth, when all is said and done he is still saying that a myth-dream contains truth because it is believed that it does. It is one of those fundamental axioms which is

---

[1] Something similar to disnomic is envisaged, perhaps, by 'anomy'. Yet an anomic society seems to be a contradiction in terms—unless the strict etymology of anomy is neglected and it is agreed that anomic describes not a total absence of laws, but rather a relative absence of well defined laws, or a superabundance of laws of which the individual may select one or more and take the consequences from those of his fellows who would have selected another or others. Alas! Anomy has had a chequered sociological career, and it seems best not to use the word here.

'self-evidently' so and on which all peoples everywhere tend to base their behaviour. Secondly, there is the complex of physical activities—rites, ceremonies, throwing stones, drawing in the sand—which re-express the myth-dream in another form. They act out and externalize the content of the myth-dream, bringing participants into a closer, more intimate relationship with it. They may occur diffusely, as in Manam; or they may take place within a more easily recognizable and definable complex as in Tangu. Third and fourth are guilt and the new man. Guilt is there: it is openly expressed, it tends to be used as an explanatory concept, and, in its connexion with expiation and atonement, lies behind the urge to create a new man and a new society. These in themselves are a reassessment of the individual in relation to his fellows.

Fifth and last there is the containment, the symbol of the myth-dream. As with most meaningful symbols there is no convenient and exclusive one-to-one relationship between symbol and meanings. It embraces the myth-dream, and it includes roles, goals, and objects and persons which stand for it as well as the channel through which it may itself be realized. Part of this symbol is cargo—a concrete goal. Diagrams in the sand, tortoiseshell arm bands, rites, and activities stand for it, express it, and conjure its meanings in their particular ways. The charismatic figure, here closely identified with the role of moral European, personifies the myth-dream, and is the channel through whom the contents of the myth-dream may be realized. He it is who articulates the myth-dream; whose activities nourish and refine the content of the myth-dream; who stands for the new man; through whom guilt and organizational dilemmas will be over-leaped; and through whom access to cargo will be gained. In a certain sense, if only temporarily, the charismatic figure—a single individual—*is* the myth-dream. But he himself is transitory. When he can no longer personify the myth-dream he fades out of the picture. Nevertheless, his meanings survive, adding to, or qualifying the total content of the myth-dream. And his name, evoking the man of flesh and blood, is a channel both to his meanings—his own peculiar synthesis of the self in society—and to the apprehension of the myth-dream as a whole. In him are resolved not only the particular antitheses severally implied by the triangle and different expressions of the myth-dream, but also the primary tension between that in the individual which is divine, or self-willed, and the community which imprisons him in its moralities.

Throughout this book the words 'moral' and 'divine' have been used to distinguish two main categories of power which sometimes appear as oppositional forces. And because a Cargo movement is an essay in the relations of powers we may sum up its meaning directly in terms of these categories. Moral powers, howsoever used, are the powers habitually exercised by men in community. They imply, and are characterised by, the prestation, reciprocity, obligation, and constraint. Divine powers, on the other hand, are those powers which men cannot generally constrain, which have an absolute quality, but to which men in community have opportunities of access. They include self-will, and hierophanies that are also kratophanies. An exchange or prestation is a typical moral transaction. Phenomena such as thunder, lightning, and earthquakes are typical manifestations of divine power: man cannot put them under constraint. Nevertheless, these phenomena influence man's moral behaviour. Because neither Tangu nor Manam islanders can control their dreaming, dreams are a manifestation of the divine, and dreaming is for them a divine experience. But dreams influence their moral behaviour. And when a man acts on his dream—does something because of his dream—he is exercising a moral power which he has derived from the divine. While not being able to put the divine under constraint, there is access to the power contained in what is divine. So also—irrespective of the fact, in parenthesis, that both Tangu and Manam islanders regard the characters in myths not as men, but as unconstrainable divinities—since neither the content nor the form of myths are considered to arise from the conscious, controlled thoughts and reflections of men, but myths nevertheless exist as they are, and were, unconstrainable, unobliged to men, exerting power over men, influencing their moral behaviour, there is

277

the same kind of relation between man and myth, the moral and divine, as between man and dream. Further, by defying current obligations the individual who thus exercises his self-will may be acting immorally or amorally; in his arrogance, exemplifying hubris, he may be regarded as usurping the kind of power considered divine; or it may be that he is acting in accordance with his perception of what a radical reassessment of present moralities ought to be like.

Being *mngwotngwotiki*, truly equivalent, is, in terms of the Tangu structure of ideas, an approximation to or with the divine: it is a transcendence of the obligatory prestation in conformity with the requirements of the moral order. For Tangu, the scorcerer, the over-ambitious manager, the European, and the charismatic figure have much in common. Because each in his way exercises self-will to deny existing obligations, each is touched with what is divine. Being unobliged is the divine prerogative. But whereas sorcerer, ambitious manager, and European are seen as usurping the divine, denying obligation when it suits them, simply from arrogance, contrary to morality, the charismatic figure is regarded as transcending a present morality. For he uses his self-will not merely to seize an advantage of power for himself, but in order to act in accordance with the new moralities that are implied in what is divine, the myth-dream which the community shares with him. Sorcerer, ambitious manager, and European are culpable because they usurp, or arrogate power to themselves without the consent of the community. The moral European, on the other hand, being true brother, abides by the rules, does not deny obligation. And, like the charismatic figure, he has it in him to transcend a present morality without assuming for himself, by himself, the kind of power associated with the divine. Because they do not deny obligation, and so far as their actions reflect the dictates of the myth-dream, charismatic figure and moral European are able to gain the consent of the community.

Trying to pull the material world into conformity with dream, myth, and self-will represents the attempt to translate the possibilities of power inherent in, or revealed by, the divine into moral powers exercisable in the community by the members of the community. The three phases of the myth-dream—formation, physical or concrete expressions, and reformation—reveal first the divine at work in men's minds, then the attempt at concordance, and finally the return to the mental activity. During the first and third phases participants in the myth-dream live on the two distinct levels of reality. Observed and known to them through their five senses—but not necessarily intellectually comprehended by them—is one world. As, if not more acutely experienced, felt, and perceived is another. In the second phase the two levels fuse into one and both worlds are congruent. An access to power regarded as divine becomes moral power, power exerted by men. Whether such acts of translation occur diffusely, as in drawing diagrams, weeping, or throwing stones; or in more concentrated form, as in a series of rites which involve members of the community acting in concert—they are either attempts to sustain in the moral world a vision of synthesis with what is divine, or they are lunatic. Accepting that such acts are not merely lunatic, it is not difficult to see that realizing and mastering this vision—externalizing it into concrete reality—implies the exercise of new moral capacities which, in turn, imply a new moral order. Seen in the light of the myth-dream the diagram in the sand made sense. It was not lunatic. A man was externalizing the myth-dream in graphic representation, and so making it known to himself and to others what kinds of moralities lay dormant in himself and the myth-dream. Through the myth-dream, which is shared by the community, the self-will of the charismatic figure is reflected in the self-will of the individuals who make up the community: through him a current morality is transcended in approximation with what is divine.

The first of the two distinctive kinds of myth which make up the heart of the myth-dream, the Primal Myth, evokes relations of power between peoples in a cultural idiom of brotherhood; refers these relations to an act, an absolute act which excites what is divine—thunder, lightning, storm, and earthquake—which no moral being, man, is in a position to forgive, and which, therefore, can only be nullified by what is divine; and after invoking the kind of relationship that brotherhood ought to imply, it goes on to suggest alternative moral solutions. But the underlying and closely related themes are, first, the casual disobedience which moves the divine, vitiates a particular kind of relationship with the divine, and which, emerging as guilt, entails certain consequences; and second, the necessity for re-establishing that sort of new and different relationship with the divine which, by including atonement, expiation of guilt, will imply an end to the consequences flowing from the disobedience. This central tenet of satisfactory, essentially guiltless relations with the divine is echoed in the second myth, the Mambu myth. Not concerned with those who, considered divine, are, and were before time began, this classical 'hero legend' deals with a person who actually lived, a moral being involved in the moral order who went on a quest for cargo—but who is as though divine. There are the engagement of individuals—not necessarily as symbols of peoples—the interplay of the moral powers they exercise, and, after a series of hazards overcome, eventual access to manufactured goods through the good offices of moral European—who is white brother behaving as a brother should. But not necessarily access to cargo. The goods Mambu brought home with him drop out of the story entirely; and he himself makes it as explicit as he can that if access to manufactured goods depends upon money access to cargo depends upon a particular relationship with the divine. For cargo is that which makes man more than he is; which makes a man a whole man, guiltless; which makes man more than he is because it proceeds from the divine at the will of the divine. Possession of cargo—not simply manufactured goods, but these goods arriving in a particular context— would be the visible and concrete sign of expiation, of atonement achieved, of the new dispensation granted.

It is neither easy nor always advisable to attempt to separate symbol from meaning. Each is of the other. Yet since rice—and not other kinds of crop, introduced or otherwise—is a part of cargo, but Tangu have access to rice, it is clear that as symbol rice cannot stand simply for itself or for access to itself. It can, and does, on the other hand, stand for the organizational problems and redistributions of powers involved in arranging for a regular and satisfactory kind of access—the sort of access Tangu might have enjoyed if the guilty ancestors had not left them with a social system and capacities which cannot deal with the situation as it is. In the same way cargo does not stand merely for access to manufactured goods. It stands for what is understood by the new dispensation. On the one hand there is the bare fact of having possessions, of being able to create and dispose of a variety of goods, of demonstrating that kind of competence which, distinguishing men from the beasts, reveals a particular kind of access to what is divine—the creative principle. On the other hand, the obverse of the same coin, cargo also stands for that redefinition, reallocation and distribution of moral and divine powers which, in relation to the competent new man—who will have possession of goods and access to cargo— would be both the product and evidence of atonement achieved, a new dispensation.

The disnomy—the organizational dilemmas, the triadic distribution of different and uncertain kinds of powers and authorities together with the apprehension of an ever expanding range of particulars which outstrip comprehension— questions the current allocations of materials and powers of disposal, emphasizes the lack of a regular institutional framework within terms of which materials and ideas might be comprehended and categorized, and powers exercised, and, it follows, implies the search for the ability and competence which can distinguish, separate, reallocate, and harmonize particular kinds of authority. Not so much the protest of the oppressed against an oppressor—though these are the terms which a political leader finds most advantageous, and which an investigator could find most appropriate, because familiar, for purposes of analysis—a Cargo movement is a protest against the disnomy. Participants look back—and forward— to times of certainty. They are searching for criteria of definitive consent, for sovereignty, for those institutions relating the moral and divine which are expressive of sovereignty. They do not seek rice; they have it. Nor are they more than ordinarily anxious to possess manufactured goods; they can buy them with cash received as wages or in trade. But they are anxious to realize what these things—regional and culturally determined concrete referents—mean to them: the redefinition of powers both moral and divine, the capacity to redefine for themselves, the reallocation of powers, and the reintegration of the individual in relation to these powers.

This thesis is reinforced by the behaviour and meaning of the charismatic figure. He represents the new man and personifies certainty. He is taken to have communication with the divine, and in the context of Cargo he stands in relation to the community as, or like, a divine king. He is an individual exercising self-will in accord with the myth-dream who is, temporarily, the fount of moral powers, the channel through whom divine powers are exercised, the living instrument through whom moral authority is enlivened and tempered by divinity. By being as though divine, sovereign, and the vehicle of sovereignty, he conveniently resolves the problem of an uneasy and uncertain separation of powers. He also represents the individual whose self-will is reflected in community morality, who is as he would like to be, whose community is as he would wish it to be, and who is himself what the community would want him to be. As the new man he is both Kanaka and moral European. As a living person in a particular historical and cultural context he may, however, fail to live up to what is required of him. He may be steeped in pride, self-regarding, or touched with the fraudulent; his fusion of myth-dream and material world may be more, or less, adequate; he may be unable to sustain his synthesis; outside forces may destroy him. Yet through him—because it is just this harmony of the one and the many, of separable moral powers in accord with the divine, that he attempts to stand for, symbolize, embody, or be—inconsistent sets of moralities, the products of different kinds of powers variously and uncertainly defined, allocated, and exercised, are temporarily transcended.

The difference between Mambu and his meaning, between Mambu the man and Mambu the hero, parallels the difference between manufactured goods and cargo. If Mambu's historical activities, and personality, had meant only what they directly implied, neither would have changed so significantly in the myth about him. A charismatic figure ascends to a position of authority because he is able to articulate the myth-dream, because he can personify the new man. By being thus in accord with the myth-dream he gains the consent by which he is enabled to exert political authority. But in order to become an effective political leader he tends to distort the myth-dream and to represent it as a manageable dichotomy— oppressed against oppressor. In so acting, however, he is ignoring the dictates of the myth-dream. He overlooks what is involved in the new dispensation, forgets about divine for-giveness, and disdains the moral European. In the excitement he has aroused, and in the face of the energies he has unleashed, he may even be forced to disregard the fact that as the new man he also embodies what is meant by moral European. He eschews, in short, those very factors which have lifted him to power. And if at this point, despite what has become in relation to the myth-dream an essential usurpation of power, the charismatic figure can then dispose sufficient forces, it is possible he may continue to exercise political authority. In the Melanesian situation, however, this is difficult. In pre-senting the disnomy as a simple dichotomy a charismatic figure draws against himself forces too powerful for him to contend against. He does not have to struggle to power: the myth-dream gives it to him. Thereafter, when he no longer reflects the myth-dream, he must, like all political leaders, either fight hard to win the consent that will keep him in power, or use those numerous techniques which are available to enforce such a 'consent'.

Appendix A

A full bibliography of Cargo cult material up until 1952 has been compiled by Ida Leeson, Bibliography of Cargo Cults and other Nativistic Movements in the South Pacific, *South Pacific Commission*, Technical Paper No. 30, July 1952, which contains over one hundred and fifty references. And many further articles have been written since 1952. The list below contains a selection which may be of interest to the general reader.

Abel, Charles W. *Savage Life in New Guinea*, London Missionary Society, London, 1902 (pp. 104–28).

Allan, C. H. Marching Rule: a nativistic cult of the British Solomon Islands, *Corona*, Vol. III, No. 3, 1951, p. 93.

Barrow, G. L. The story of Jonfrum, *Corona*, Vol. III, No. 10, October 1951, p. 379.

Belshaw, C. S. Native Politics in the Solomon Islands, *Pacific Affairs*, Vol. XX, No. 2, June 1947, p. 187.
  Island Administration in the South West Pacific, R.I.I.A., London 1950.
  The Significance of Modern Cults in Melanesian Development, *Australian Outlook*, Vol. 4, No. 2, 1950, p. 116.
  Changing Melanesia, Melbourne 1954.

Berndt, R. M. A Cargo Movement in the East Central Highlands of New Guinea, *Oceania*, Vol. XXIII, Nos. 1–3, 1952–3, pp. 40 and 137.
  Reaction to Contact in the Eastern Highlands of New Guinea, *Oceania*, Vol. XXIV, Nos. 3 and 4, 1954, pp. 190 and 255.

Burrows, William. The Background of Marching Rule, *Pacific Islands Monthly*, Vol. XX, No. 11, June 1950.

Bruijn, J. V. The Mansren Cult of Biak, *South Pacific*, Vol. 5, No. 1, 1951, p. 1.

Cato, A. C. A New Religious Cult in Fiji, *Oceania*, Vol. XVIII, No. 2, 1948, p. 146.

Chinnery, E. W. P. and Haddon, A. C. Five New Religious Cults in British New Guinea, *The Hibbert Journal*, Vol. XV, No. 3, 1917, p. 448.

Elkin, A. P. *Social Anthropology in Melanesia*, O.U.P., London 1953.

Firth, Raymond. Social Changes in the Western Pacific, *Journal of the Royal Society of Arts*, Vol. CI, No. 4909, 1953, p. 803.
  The Theory of 'Cargo' cults: A Note on Tikopia, *Man*, LV, 142, 1955, p. 140.

Guiart, Jean. 'Cargo Cults' and Political Evolution in Melanesia, *South Pacific*, Vol. 5, No. 7, 1951, p. 128.
  Forerunners of Melanesian Nationalism, *Oceania*, Vol. XXII, No. 2, 1951, p. 81.
  John Frum Movement in Tanna, *Oceania*, Vol. XXII, 1952, p. 163.
  Report of Native Situation in the North of Ambrym, *South Pacific*, Vol. 5, No. 12, 1952, p. 256.
  Culture Contact and the 'John Frum' Movement on Tanna, New Hebrides, *Southwestern Journal of Anthropology*, Vol. 12, No. 1, 1956, p. 105.

Hogbin, H. Ian. *Experiments in Civilisation*, Routledge, London 1939.
  Transformation Scene, Routledge and Kegan Paul, London 1951.
  Social Change, Watts, London 1958.

Höltker, Georg. How 'Cargo Cult' is Born, *Pacific Islands Monthly*, Vol. XVII, No. 4, 1946, p. 16.

Inglis, Judy. Cargo Cults: The Problem of Explanation, *Oceania*, Vol. XXVII, No. 4, June 1957, p. 249.

Inselmann, Rudolph. 'Cargo Cult' not caused by Missions, *Pacific Islands Monthly*, Vol. XVI, No. 11, 1946, p. 44.

Keesing, Felix M. *The South Seas in the Modern World*, Allen and Unwin, London 1942.

Lawrence, Peter. Cargo Cult and Religious Beliefs among the Garia, *International Archives of Ethnography*, Vol. **XLVII**, No. 1, 1954, p. 1.
The Madang District Cargo Cult, *South Pacific*, Vol. **8**, No. 1, 1955, p. 6.

Lett, Mollie. 'Vailala Madness': wave of religious fanaticism that swept Papua in 1919, *Pacific Islands Monthly*, Vol. **VI**, No. 5, 1935, p. 25.

MacAuley, James. The Distance between the Government and the Governed, *South Pacific*, Vol. **7**, No. 8, 1954, p. 815.

Mair, L. P. *Australia in New Guinea*, Christophers, London 1948.

Mead, Margaret. *New Lives for Old*, William Morrow, New York 1956.

Miller, J. Graham. Naked Cult in Central West Santo, *Journal of the Polynesian Society*, Vol. **LVII**, No. 4, 1948, p. 330.

Paton, W. F. The Native Situation in the North of Ambrym, *South Pacific*, Vol. **16**, No. 5, 1952, p. 392.

Pos, Hugo. The Revolt of Manseren, *American Anthropologist*, Vol. **52**, No. 4, 1950, p. 561.

Quinlivan, P. J. Afek of Telefomin, *Oceania*, Vol. **XXV**, Nos. 1–2, 1955, p. 17.

Read, K. E. Effects of the Pacific War in the Markham Valley, New Guinea, *Oceania*, Vol. **XVIII**, No. 2, 1948, p. 95.
Missionary Activities and Social Change in the Central Highlands of Papua and New Guinea, *South Pacific*, Vol. **5**, No. 11, 1952, p. 229.
A 'Cargo' Situation in the Markham Valley, New Guinea, *Southwestern Journal of Anthropology*, Vol. **14**, No. 3, 1958, p. 273.

Stanner, W. E. H. *The South Seas in Transition*, Australasian Publishing Co., London 1953.
On the Interpretation of Cargo Cults, *Oceania*, Vol. **XXIX**, No. 1, September 1958, p. 1.

Williams, F. E. The Vailala Madness and the Destruction of Native Ceremonies in the Gulf Division, *Papuan Anthropology Reports*, No. 4, 1923.

Orokaiva Magic, Oxford University Press, London 1928.

The Vailala Madness in Retrospect, in *Essays presented to C. G. Seligman*, Kegan Paul, London 1934.

Appendix B

A list of the Religious Missions operating in the Territory of New Guinea in 1952. (Taken from the Report to the General Assembly of the United Nations on the Administration of the Territory of New Guinea, 1952, p. 204.)

Assemblies of God in Australia
Australian Lutheran Mission
Baptist New Guinea Mission
Bismarck Archipelago Mission of Seventh Day Adventists
Catholic Mission of the Divine Word
Catholic Mission of the Holy Ghost
Catholic Mission of the Most Sacred Heart of Jesus
Christian Missions in Many Lands
East and West Indies Bible Mission
Evangelical Lutheran Mission
Franciscan Mission
Lutheran Mission, New Guinea
Marist Mission Society
New Guinea Anglican Mission
Methodist Missionary Society of New Guinea
Methodist Overseas Mission (New Guinea District)
New Guinea Lutheran Mission (Missouri Synod)
New Tribes Mission
North East New Guinea Mission of Seventh Day Adventists
North West New Guinea Mission of Seventh Day Adventists
South Sea Evangelical Mission

Nationalities of 'European' personnel engaged in mission work:

Australian	269	Irish	13
Austrian	13	Italian	7
British	28	Luxembourgese	4
Canadian	2	Polish	5
Czechoslovakian	3	Swiss	2
Dutch	34	United States	139
French	12	Others	19
German	170		

Index

291

MYTHOS:
The Princeton/Bollingen Series in World Mythology

C. G. Jung & Carl Kerényi / ESSAYS ON A SCIENCE OF MYTHOLOGY

Carl Kerényi / ELEUSIS: ARCHETYPAL IMAGE OF MOTHER AND DAUGHTER

Stella Kramrisch / THE PRESENCE OF ŚIVA

Jon D. Levenson / CREATION AND THE PERSISTENCE OF EVIL: THE JEWISH DRAMA OF DIVINE OMNIPOTENCE

Roger S. Loomis / THE GRAIL: FROM CELTIC MYTH TO CHRISTIAN SYMBOL

Bronislaw Malinowski (Ivan Strenski, ed.) / MALINOWSKI AND THE WORK OF MYTH

Louis Massignon (Herbert Mason, ed.) / HALLAJ: MYSTIC AND MARTYR

Erich Neumann / AMOR AND PSYCHE

Erich Neumann / THE GREAT MOTHER

Richard Noll, ed. / MYSTERIA: JUNG AND THE ANCIENT MYSTERIES

Maud Oakes with Joseph Campbell / WHERE THE TWO CAME TO THEIR FATHER

Dora & Erwin Panofsky / PANDORA'S BOX

Paul Radin / THE ROAD OF LIFE AND DEATH

Otto Rank, Lord Raglan, Alan Dundes / IN QUEST OF THE HERO

Gladys Reichard / NAVAHO RELIGION

Géza Róheim (Alan Dundes, ed.) / FIRE IN THE DRAGON

Robert A. Segal, ed. / THE GNOSTIC JUNG

Jean Seznec / SURVIVAL OF THE PAGAN GODS: THE MYTHOLOGICAL TRADITION AND ITS PLACE IN RENAISSANCE HUMANISM AND ART

Philip E. Slater / THE GLORY OF HERA

Daisetz T. Suzuki / ZEN AND JAPANESE CULTURE

Jean-Pierre Vernant (Froma I. Zeitlin, ed.) / MORTALS AND IMMORTALS

Jessie L. Weston / FROM RITUAL TO ROMANCE

Helmut Wilhelm and Richard Wilhelm / UNDERSTAND-
ING THE *I CHING:* THE WILHELM LECTURES ON THE
BOOK OF CHANGES

Heinrich Zimmer (Joseph Campbell, ed.) / THE KING AND
THE CORPSE: TALES OF THE SOUL'S CONQUEST OF
EVIL

Heinrich Zimmer (Joseph Campbell, ed.) / MYTHS AND
SYMBOLS IN INDIAN ART AND CIVILIZATION